HOUSE OF Mr MAUREY

Mr ARMSTRONG

Mr BRAMWELL BO

M^rs ARM RONG

ELIZA ARMS

⊗ARMSTRONG'S HOUSE
32 CHARLES St MARYLEBONE

Inspector Minahan Makes a Stand

Bridget O'Donnell

Inspector Minahan Makes a Stand

OR

THE MISSING GIRLS OF ENGLAND

PICADOR

First published 2012 by Picador
an imprint of Pan Macmillan, a division of Macmillan Publishers Limited
Pan Macmillan, 20 New Wharf Road, London N1 9RR
Basingstoke and Oxford
Associated companies throughout the world
www.panmacmillan.com

ISBN 978-0-330-54464-1

1 3 5 7 9 8 6 4 2

A CIP catalogue record for this book is available from the British Library.

Printed and bound by CPI Group (UK) Ltd, Croydon, CR0 4YY

For Jes, for everything

Author's Note

When I first discovered Inspector Jeremiah Minahan he was standing alone, in the early 1880s, watching a brothel in Chelsea. His presence there raised a query. Why, if he was a policeman, did he appear to be conducting his own private surveillance of a west London madam? Why not instigate a police investigation? It was this question that drove me to pick up Minahan's thread and follow it where it led: through the letters, court transcripts, speeches and pamphlets still to be found in the archives of London, Lewes, Dublin, Cambridge and eventually, Oxford, where I finally understood what drove Minahan down his singular and fateful path. What follows aims to be a factual account of my discoveries, the answer to my question.

In the text all speech is drawn directly from contemporary source material and was quoted in the newspapers, witness accounts and courtrooms of the day. The endnotes mark the progress of my researches, but these are the stitches that make up the tapestry, the bigger picture, which is best enjoyed as it is: as a true and remarkable story.

My devil had been long caged, he came out roaring.

Strange Case of Dr Jekyll and Mr Hyde,
by R. L. Stevenson, 1886

The most desperate of London roughs would think twice before placing himself within MR. MINAHAN'S grasp.

Christian Commonwealth newspaper,
4 June 1885

Contents

Cast of Characters

Bow Street Police Station, Covent Garden

Inspector Jeremiah Minahan (b. 1842), an Irish officer based at Bow Street station until March 1882, where he suddenly discovered a capability for waywardness.

Chief Inspector Wood, Minahan's superior, who did not approve.

DS Charles Berry, a detective sergeant.

DS William Reader, a detective sergeant.

PC Tom Flawn, a young constable.

George Broach, a drunken prisoner.

King's Road Police Station, Chelsea

Inspector Jeremiah Minahan, who arrived in Chelsea from Bow Street in April 1882 and proceeded to graduate from waywardness to outright rebellion.

Superintendent William Fisher (b. 1837), who did not approve.

Inspector Charles Ross, Fisher's loyal henchman, who did not approve.

PC McIlwain, Ross' loyal henchman . . .

PC Hocken, a young constable.

PC Hide, who failed to clean up the dirty station.

Uverdale Road, Chelsea

Barbara Pennant Minahan (b. 1838), Jeremiah's wife, the daughter of a Welsh bishop.

Church Street, Chelsea

Mrs Mary Jeffries (b. 1820), a brothel-keeper, trafficker and infamous queen of the London sex scene.

Maria Watts, Mary Jeffries' former maid, who left in disgust.

George Bellchambers, Mary Jeffries' former coachman, who left in disgust.

Elizabeth Bromwich, Mary Jeffries' more ambivalent former maid, who simply left.

Ann Clark, a cook whose kitchen window lay opposite Mary Jeffries' brothels.

Mr Bailey, Ann Clark's short-tempered master.

Montagu Williams (b. 1835), Mary Jeffries' congenial defence barrister.

Lisson Grove, Marylebone

Charles Street –

Eliza Armstrong (b. 1872), a missing girl, sweet-tempered and loyal.

Mrs Elizabeth Armstrong (b. c. 1848), Eliza's worn-down, hard-drinking mother.

Charles Armstrong (b. c. 1844), Eliza's chimneysweep father.

Nancy Broughton, the Armstrongs' neighbour.

'Bash' Broughton, Nancy's husband.

Rebecca Jarrett (b. 1846–50), Nancy's friend and former workmate, and Eliza's new 'mistress': a troubled woman with a dark past.

William Cooke, the long-suffering local magistrate.

Elsewhere –

Madame Louise Mourey, a shady French midwife.

Henry Smith, a concerned cab driver.

Westminster and Mayfair

The Harcourt family –

Sir William Harcourt (b. 1827), Liberal Home Secretary, a man of oafish physique and intellect: Inspector Minahan's arch adversary.

Loulou Harcourt (b. 1863), Sir William's son and private secretary.

Thérèse Harcourt (b. c. 1835) Sir William's first wife.

Elizabeth Cabot Ives (b. c. 1831), Sir William's second wife.

Frances, Lady Waldegrave (b. 1821), Sir William's ambitious aunt.
George Granville Harcourt, (b. 1785), her old grumpy husband.

Sir William Harcourt's friends –

Richard Monckton Milnes (b. 1809), politician, poet and man of letters: the 'cool of the evening', the black of the night.

Reginald Baliol Brett (b. 1852), Sir William's protégé and Loulou's friend.

George Cavendish-Bentinck (b. 1821), a Tory MP and Sir William Harcourt's Mayfair neighbour.

Fleet Street

William Thomas Stead (b. 1849), editor of the *Pall Mall Gazette*: a lusty puritan.

Mr Jacques, a reporter for the *Pall Mall Gazette*: Stead's shadowy sidekick.

Thomas Catling (b. 1838), editor of *Lloyd's Weekly*.

Henry Hales (b. c. 1829), a tenacious reporter for *Lloyd's Weekly*.

Scotland Yard

Lieutenant-Colonel Douglas Labalmondiere (b.1815), Assistant Commissioner of the Metropolitan Police.

Inspector Edward Borner, a police officer.

The Soho Placeurs (Traffickers)

John Sallecartes (b. c. 1836), a Belgian thug.

Frederick Schultz, Sallecartes' partner: violent, dark and handsome.

Emile Regnier (b. c. 1845), a former French Communard and habitual thief.

Edouard Roger (b. c. 1841), a Brussels brothel-keeper.

The Guileless Girls

Adelene Tanner (b. 1860), a vulnerable girl trafficked by Sallecartes and Roger.

Emily Ellen (b. 1859), a feisty girl trafficked by Sallecartes and Roger.

Lydia King (b. 1860), a trafficked girl.

Reformers and God-fearing radicals

Alfred Dyer (b.1849), a Quaker, publisher and social purity reformer: shy and furious.

Josephine Butler (b. 1828), a relentless campaigner for female rights, and a woman of beauty and intellect.

William Bramwell Booth (b. 1856), Chief of Staff of the Salvation Army: a quiet fanatic who was bullied at school.

Dr Elizabeth Blackwell (b. 1821), America's first female doctor, now residing in Hastings.

Benjamin Scott (b. 1814), Chamberlain of the City of London, a self-made successful financier and social reformer.

Henry Varley (b. 1835), a Notting Hill butcher and evangelical preacher.

Prologue

A Mother Seeking A Lost Child

Marylebone 1885

I fear some harm has happened to her.

Mrs Armstrong, *Lloyd's Weekly*, 12 July 1885[1]

The court reporter arrived at the *Lloyd's Weekly* newspaper office with his morning's dispatch written up in duplicate. It was another stiflingly hot day, a Saturday, 11 July 1885. The article he had sweated through London to deliver told the story of a missing girl, reported by the child's tearful mother at the Marylebone police court that morning. Calling at Fleet Street offices strewn with 'newspapers, letters, wet proof-sheets, files of "copy" and great splashes and dried up pools of ink', the newsman sold his tale of the vanished child to the popular *Lloyd's Weekly*, the liberal *Daily News* and the radical *Reynolds's Weekly*.[2] Only the editor at *Lloyd's* and his special correspondent, Henry Hales, spotted the scoop, a story so big it would help double their circulation to one million, the first Sunday paper ever to achieve such a readership. Henry Hales was sent to find the missing girl's mother – at once.

It had been a challenging week for London's newspaper editors. The last five days had seen all sales woefully outclassed by a rival paper, the *Pall Mall Gazette*, which had sparked outrage and rioting over the publication of its series of reports on juvenile prostitution and the traffic of adolescent British girls overseas. The reports described how young girls disappeared into the labyrinth of vice that lurked beneath London's surface, with accounts from procurers and brothel-keepers, bullies and *placeurs* (traffickers) recorded in 'interview' and described to the public in unprecedented detail. These included the tale of a thirteen-year-old girl named 'Lily', sold into iniquity by her drunken mother for '£5'; and the boast of a foreign *placeur* that two hundred and fifty girls like Lily were traded across the Channel every single year.[3]

This was not new information. In the previous five years there had been repeated official and unofficial evidence of a regular traffic in British girls to France, Holland and Belgium. A House of Lords Select Committee had recently exposed an entire gang of foreign *placeurs*, caught inveigling adolescents into *maisons closes* (discreet brothels in which the prostitutes were not at liberty to leave) in Brussels and Antwerp.[4] The Earl of Dalhousie had told the House of Lords that these traders in virtue believed their work was perfectly legal. In a letter Dalhousie read to the Lords, discovered during a Home Office inquiry into the traffic, he quoted a Dutch *placeur* reassuring his colleague 'they will do nothing to you in London'. The Earl then admitted in the House that this 'was true'.[5]

*

At the Marylebone police court earlier that sweltering morning, Mrs Armstrong, a poor but 'apparently respectable' woman, had asked the magistrate for assistance in finding her thirteen-year-old daughter.[6] Since London's police-court magistrates issued guidance to the lower classes in local disputes and family matters, and with the girl's disappearance complicated by the involvement of a neighbour, it appeared that Mrs Armstrong was seeking the magistrate's advice, rather than going directly to the police.[7] Her missing child was called Eliza. She had been absent from her home in Charles Street, Marylebone, for six weeks.

The police courtroom was filled with the dirty, waiting bodies, the lingering breath of the overnight 'drunk and incapables' and the smell of stale sweat. (A Marylebone magistrate would later liken the same courtroom, 'with its sickly blue tiles running round the walls and its hideous wooden fittings', to a 'lavatory'.)[8] Each day the magistrate would plough through 'fifty criminal cases, thirty summonses [and sign] a hundred or two different documents'.[9] When her moment finally came, Mrs Armstrong stood beneath his gaze. She was around thirty-seven, but looked much older. Her shoulders were hunched and her cheeks drew down about her long nose, as if her facial muscles had never known a smile.[10]

She appealed, she said, 'for his advice in regard to my daughter, who I have not seen or heard of since last May [when a] neighbour asked me if I would like Eliza to go out in service, because she knew of a very nice situation'.[11] Mrs Armstrong identified this neighbour as Nancy Broughton. Eliza's new mistress, the woman who had taken the girl away, she described as a tall woman with a limp. Eliza's new place 'was said to be at Croydon' and the girl had promised to 'write home to her parents once a week', but no letters had arrived.[12]

Mrs Armstrong's neighbour, Nancy Broughton, had since told her that *she* had received a letter from Eliza's new mistress with a sovereign, saying her daughter was quite well. But when Mrs Armstrong wrote to the house – near Manchester – the letter was returned, the address 'Not known'.[13]

'How is it,' asked the magistrate, 'that the girl should be at

Manchester when it was clearly understood she was to live at Croydon?'

'Eliza's master,' explained Mrs Armstrong, 'is a commercial traveller and moves about a good deal.'

At this point, the anxiety over her missing girl appears to have overwhelmed Mrs Armstrong. She broke down and wept bitterly.

The Marylebone magistrate waited. His silent thoughts may have mirrored those of a colleague and contemporary who had recently published a memoir entitled *Metropolitan Police Court Jottings* (1882). In this he allocated an entire chapter to women like Mrs Armstrong, stating that:

> No more difficult duty devolves upon the police magistrate than of deciding a case . . . dependent upon the testimony of the lower orders of females . . . So great is the exaggeration . . . and so extravagant are their assertions . . . that to ascertain the truth amounts to a moral impossibility.[14]

In broken sentences and with a faltering voice, Mrs Armstrong continued: 'My dear girl,' she said, 'is only thirteen years of age and I fear some harm has happened to her.'[15]

The men of the court were certain of one thing. Mrs Armstrong's daughter, at the age of thirteen, had little protection under the law. Having left home with her mother's blessing, she had volunteered for whatever 'service' had befallen her and was past the age of consent.[16] It did not yet appear that she had been kidnapped or abducted or decoyed (tricked and trafficked), though in the wake of that week's *Pall Mall Gazette* revelations, such notions must have been uppermost in the minds of all those who heard poor Mrs Armstrong's woe.

'Do you mean to say,' asked the magistrate, that 'you let the girl go away with strangers without making further inquiry than what you have just explained?'

'Well sir,' said Mrs Armstrong, 'she said I would hear from her every week.'

'Then I consider it a very great negligence on your part,' he replied, and ordered the police to make inquiries.[17]

Across the weekend, the bureaucratic wheels of local law enforcement slowly began to grind, but the *Lloyd's* special correspondent, Henry Hales, worked faster.

This veteran reporter had an instinct for scandal and had secured his reporting career with a similar story sixteen years earlier. This too had focused on a young working-class girl, a twelve-year-old, who to Hales' disgust had been chased through the streets of Soho by a lascivious old gentleman in broad daylight.[18] Originally from Birmingham, 'one of the most radical cities in England', Hales had a keen eye for class inequality and the injustices of metropolitan life.[19]

In 1885 a quarter of Londoners lived in poverty. Just a few years later, Charles Booth's survey thrust this up to a third, numbering the 'poor' and 'very poor' at more than one million. The vast majority of the London working-class earned around a pound a week (twenty shillings) of which they paid out roughly four to five shillings in rent for one room in districts described by Booth as 'poor' at best or 'vicious' at worst. On his 1889 *Map of London Poverty*, he coloured such places blue or deep black. 'Well-to-do Middle-class' streets were red, and the streets of the 'Upper Middle and Upper-classes' were, naturally, painted a yellow gold. Forging through the city heat, Henry Hales rushed past red and gold, red and gold, until he alighted on the wrong side of the Marylebone Road, and everything went black.

Mrs Armstrong lived with her family in a first-floor room in Charles Street, just off Lisson Grove. It was a locale notorious long before Hales pitched up with his notepad and pencil. In 1881, *British Architect* magazine crowned Charles Street the worst slum ever made:

> As regards Nos 1, 2, 3 and 4, in this filthy street . . . there is from 5 to 6 feet of wet, black sewage under the basement floors. The footings of the walls . . . do not reach a solid foundation . . . The damp [rises] from 10 to 12 feet above the basements . . . the houses [are] so dilapidated no structural alteration could render them habitable.[20]

Mrs Armstrong was lucky, then, to live at no. 32.

As Hales turned up the street, he was smacked by the stench of 'cabbage leaves, stale fish and every sort of dirt'.[21] The day's searing temperatures had driven everyone out of doors, standing or sitting on doorsteps; quarrelsome, hot, dirty – the children crawling on hot stones. Observing these same streets in summer, the social reformer Octavia Hill recalled how 'every corner of the place looks alive'.[22]

Mrs Armstrong and her husband Charles, a chimney-sweep, shared their room at no. 32 with Eliza, three young boys aged eleven to four and a new baby girl. The house was divided between six families, twenty-four people in total.[23]

While he stood around waiting for Mrs Armstrong to return, Hales may have heard her neighbours' thoughts on the whereabouts of young Eliza. Some accused the mother of purveying her daughter to a local woman's 'friend' and drinking down the profits.[24] Others later recalled Mrs Armstrong's fondness for singing and dancing while drunk, something her sweet daughter emulated.[25] Mrs Armstrong, however, when she finally arrived, pointed both Hales and the finger of blame in the direction of Nancy Broughton, who lived at no. 37. She told him she thought it was 'very strange' that Eliza's new mistress had given Nancy Broughton a sovereign, and 'the girl an entire new outfit of clothing'.[26] This mistress was, she recalled, a 'rough-looking woman . . . who used to walk lame and go about on crutches'.[27]

When Hales went to interview Nancy Broughton, on the other side of the street, he found a plump, kindly-faced woman with a turned-up nose. Nancy claimed to Hales that she was 'greatly troubled such a stigma as that of decoying a girl should be attached' to her. No one in Charles Street, it seemed, believed Eliza was gone to a respectable position. It was Nancy's husband who told Hales what he really needed to know. 'The name of the mistress who had taken Eliza [away] was Rebecca Jarrett'.[28]

Nancy and Rebecca Jarrett had become friends while working together in the laundry room of Claridge's Hotel in 1883, until Jarrett had fallen ill with a diseased hip and lost her place. 'On the Monday before Derby Day,' Nancy told Hales, 'Mrs. Jarrett came to me and told me she wanted a servant girl, a girl between 13 and 14 years old.' Nancy promised to 'try and get her a girl by the following day' and introduced Jarrett to Mrs Armstrong.[29]

'Are you perfectly willing for your daughter to go,' Jarrett had asked Eliza's mother, 'or I will not take her. Is she over thirteen?'

'Yes,' said Mrs Armstrong, 'I am sure she is over thirteen.'

'Are you willing to go?' she asked, looking now at Eliza. 'Because you must be willing to go or I cannot take you.'

'Yes,' said Eliza, 'I should like to go.' Eliza was an affectionate girl; small and still childlike, she had long brown hair and dark eyes.

'But,' said her mother, 'I think you ought to pay her some wages for the first month.'

'No,' said Jarrett, 'I will buy her new clothes to begin with, and then pay her two shillings a week wages afterwards.'[30]

According to Hales' report, the deal was then struck. Eliza was taken to the local shops, where Jarrett bought expensive new boots, a dress and a hat for her. A long way from the plain habit of a servant girl, the purple dress alone, at 8s 6d, cost the equivalent of Eliza's promised monthly wage; and when Jarrett added a pert red feather to Eliza's new hat, the 'flashy' trimming suggested an altogether different career for a young, pretty girl of her class.[31] To anyone who saw her now, Eliza looked loose or available. In the parlance of the day, she looked unmistakeably 'gay'.

Breaking her promise to see her daughter off, Mrs Armstrong did not bother to say goodbye. Later that night she was 'took off' by the police for 'drunkenness' and forced to make an appearance – involuntary on this occasion – at the Marylebone police court.[32]

With great delicacy, Hales opted not to go into the details of Eliza's new clothing in his *Lloyd's* article, though he did mention the house Jarrett took her to. It was in Albany Street on the east side of Regent's Park, next to Albany Barracks: a street full of brothels.[33] Signing off with a flourish, Hales informed his readers that 'the mystery of [Eliza's] disappearance remains to be unravelled'.[34] On filing his eight hundred words back at Fleet Street, he lit a fuse that would explode into scandal, arrests and imprisonment for those involved. It was the greatest scoop of his career.

Part One

CHELSEA 1882–1884

Chapter One

Serious Charge against the Police

> It is true, that the great majority of the men of the 'force' discharge their duty with efficiency; [but] there are exceptions to the good rule . . . Virtue's perfect armour is not invariably represented by the helmet and the coat of blue.
>
> James Greenwood,
> *The Seven Curses of London*, 1869[1]

Outside the police station in Chelsea, office clerks enjoyed an evening's liberty; King's Road flower merchants stored their sweet-smelling wares and omnibus drivers turned their horses east, preparing to depart the 'World's End' and return to the city. Inside the station, two policemen opposed each other across their cramped and filthy office, spoiling for a fray. One was Inspector Jeremiah Minahan, the other was Charles Ross, an officer of junior rank who had, once again, ignored Jeremiah's command: 'I will not,' Ross had announced to the station sergeant, 'obey Inspector Minahan's orders'.[2]

'I shall report your conduct to the Superintendent,' Jeremiah warned Ross when he returned on duty.

'I will go and see him with you,' Ross retorted loudly, 'the Superintendent knows what you are. No Superintendent would have you in his division.'[3]

Ross' humiliating words, his display of outright contempt, had not always been Jeremiah's experience. Before Chelsea, he had been stationed at Bow Street, E: Division, one of the most prestigious police bureaus in the Metropolitan Force. His nineteen-year career had been exemplary and he was repeatedly rewarded for meritorious conduct and bravery.[4] Now he found himself a pariah in Chelsea, a semi-rural backwater: subject to the affronts of inferior officers and with no hope of further promotion. It was a vertiginous fall that had begun just twelve months earlier, when Inspector Jeremiah Minahan, officer no. 43862, had suddenly stopped doing what he was told.

*

On 25 March 1882, Jeremiah was still based at Bow Street police station in Covent Garden, his shift due to end at 6 a.m. It was a wet, mean Saturday night. Marauding gales and snowstorms beset the entire country, sinking ships, uprooting houses and blowing in plate-glass windows.[5] During the early hours of Sunday, London was blitzed by snow, hail and rain. To lessen the fray inside the station's crowded waiting room, Jeremiah had ordered two constables to keep their newly arrested 'drunk and disorderly', George Broach, standing outside. Pressure of business meant Broach would have to wait in the rain before Inspector Minahan could issue the charge against him. It was an order he would regret.[6]

Jeremiah, at thirty-nine, was in his prime. He had built up a good career in the Metropolitan Police and cut an impressive figure at work, nudging seven feet tall in his blue uniform and custodial helmet.[7] His Minahan tribe was a striking brood: broad dark moustaches emphasized square jaws and prominent cheekbones; intense, slightly hooded eyes countered strong straight noses. Family photographs show the Minahan men in suit jackets, their buttons straining to contain the physical force within. Huge hands jut from their sleeves like pale, sleeping shovels.

The newly opened Bow Street police station had been completed the previous year. It was a purpose-built Italianate block, four storeys tall, and contained two police courts, the station and a secluded yard surrounded by cells. Jeremiah's division stretched across the centre of the metropolis, from 'Charing Cross to Regent's Park and from King's Cross to the Thames next Temple Pier'.[8] As such, Bow Street was an important police station in the city, a symbol of an efficient, modern institution, proudly carved in Portland stone.

This splendid pile resembled the opera house and West End theatres in the neighbourhood, but was in stark contrast to the tight courts and alleyways that festered in its shadow. Bow Street's back streets included the notorious parish of St-Giles-in-the-Fields, which had, by the late 1870s, 'passed into a byword for filth and squalor'.[9] The Reverend Rice-Jones, who lived in and ran a London Home Mission just off Drury Lane between 1882 and 1884, described what he heard every Saturday night in the area behind Jeremiah's station.

> About ten o'clock at night the street begins to wake up in earnest. The barrel-organs . . . sometimes go on playing till past midnight. On the pavements little children [are] dancing to jig music, obscene songs, and profane oaths. From the public houses . . . emanates the noise of many voices all trying to make themselves heard at the same time. But the revelry does not reach its height until the taverns are closed, and the drunkards . . . are turned into the gutter. [It] is as if the gates of Pandemonium were opened, and the demons of darkness all let loose upon the street.[10]

By three or four in the morning, the sounds emanating from the district's Bacchanalia would become more dark and disturbing. In the parched light of every Sabbath morning, the Reverend Rice-Jones listened to a continuous uproar of 'singing, shouting . . . cursing, fighting; women's voices crying "Murder!" and the voices of little children screaming with terror'.[11] Sometimes he heard violent fights beneath his window, people banging against his street door. One morning he found it 'stained with blood'.[12]

In 1881 alone, three thousand people were apprehended in E: Division for being 'drunk and disorderly'.[13] Across the city as a whole, drunkenness was a rising problem, and throughout the night, Jeremiah's fellow constables had been busy picking the souls in soak up off the pavements and shovelling them into cells.

Amidst the Saturday-night chaos at Bow Street, Jeremiah may not have heard the commotion in the black recesses of his own police yard. He may not have noticed the violent retribution meted out on the intoxicated George Broach by another Bow Street police constable. Obeying Jeremiah's order, the two officers had indeed deposited Broach outside. Being too bung-eyed to stand, Broach had found a stray chair and slumped down on it. A third policeman, Constable Tom Flawn, happened to pass through the yard and, spotting Broach, thought he recognized him as the man who had kicked him in the face, dislodging two precious teeth, a few months earlier. Constable Flawn decided to take this as his opportunity for revenge – a tooth for his tooth.[14] He crossed the yard and stood in front of Broach.

'I will pay you,' said Constable Flawn, 'for having knocked my teeth out some time ago.' With that, he punched Broach in the face, crushing his nose and spinning blood onto the yellow brick wall. Flawn's next punch blackened Broach's eye. Beneath the quickening sky, Flawn then issued Broach with an invitation – to 'fight'.[15]

It was turning into a typical Saturday night for the unfortunate George Broach. A casual labourer from Bedfordbury (to the west of Covent Garden), he already had several convictions for drunkenness and assault to his name. He was twenty-two years old. Constable Flawn was twenty-three. The two young men were evenly matched for a fight, but Flawn was not alone in the dark police enclosure.

With high brick walls and a tall black gate that led out to Bow Street, the police yard had deliberately been designed to shield incoming prisoners from the 'jeers and blasphemous jokes' of people on the street outside.[16] Previously they had suffered the ignominy of being dropped off in front of a braying public; now they were delivered into the large yard 'silently and safely', or without witness.[17]

More fast fists then came at Broach, as four or five policemen joined Constable Flawn in his attack. Cuffing, boxing, thumping, the policemen ignored cries from local resident Martha Horton, begging them to stop. Her bedroom window in Martlett Court overlooked the yard, where she had 'repeatedly witnessed assaults by the police on prisoners'.[18] A mother of twin baby boys, she was frequently up in the night. The brutal attack on Broach, she claimed, lasted 'half an hour'.[19]

Inside the police station, Jeremiah was working in the inspectors' office. This room had two windows overlooking the inner police yard, but his attention was turned in the opposite direction. A public waiting area adjoined his office, separated by a glass partition. Those awaiting the inspector's consideration were offered the sparse comfort of a deal bench and a bright fire in the grate.[20] Police notices tapestried the walls, calling attention to wanted murderers, housebreakers and vanished rogues described in minute detail: age, height, carriage and complexion, the colour of their eyes, the shape of their nose.[21] The constables on duty took their prisoners to stand by the inspector's partition in order to have their charge entered into a large ledger. On this Saturday, when George Broach was brought back inside after his beating in the yard, the task fell to Inspector Minahan.

When Jeremiah looked up, he could not have failed to notice Broach's bloodied face. Sober now, Broach pointed out Flawn as his attacker. After taking Broach's original charge, Jeremiah questioned Constable Flawn about the wounds.

'I have been reading all the orders,' Flawn said, 'and have not been in the yard at all.'

'He made a bolt for it,' the other policemen said.

'Fell up against the brick wall,' they said.

'Flawn has not been in the yard at all.'

'I have never seen the man before,' lied Constable Flawn.[22]

Who to believe: a foolish constable or a reckless drunk? Between them they would force Inspector Jeremiah Minahan into a decision that would alter the course of his life. But inside the bustling police station in March 1882, Jeremiah was simply dealing with a workaday choice: to fall in with a drunken rough or swallow a blatant lie from a young subordinate.

*

If anything, Jeremiah may have seen himself in Constable Tom Flawn. Almost two decades earlier, he too had been a police constable in his early twenties, a young man who left a country childhood in Ireland behind to conquer the greatest city in the world.

When he first arrived in London in 1863, the city's population was booming. Before the end of the decade, its inhabitants were 'nearly double that of Paris, four times that of New York, five times that of Berlin'.[23] Arriving the same year as Jeremiah, Fyodor Dostoevsky recorded his own first impression of the 'gigantic' city:

> [London is] a biblical sight, something to do with Babylon, some prophecy out of the Apocalypse being fulfilled before

your very eyes . . . Baal reigns and does not even demand obedience, because he is certain of it . . . The poverty, suffering . . . and torpor of the masses do not bother him in the slightest.[24]

Jeremiah traipsed endless muddied, gravel streets smattered with orange peel, horse manure and dust. He passed costermongers shouting their wares of fish, fruit and vegetables from carts decorated with polished brass plate. He saw street-corner stalls selling hot tea and coffee along with ham sandwiches and cake, and passed shoeblack boys camouflaged in polish, eyeing his passing 'mud pipes', or thick-soled country boots. At Jeremiah's feet ran wild dogs, while children cartwheeled alongside rolling trams in the hope of receiving a ha'penny for their spectacle.[25] One- and two-horse carriages, hackney cabs and omnibuses squeezed with Jeremiah through crooked apertures, parting and fraying the bodies that moved like mercury through a maze.

His stature made him a 'Jack of legs' (big man) next to the city's diminutive 'Jack sprats' and he would have stood out from the mob; watched by beady-eyed songbirds trapped inside their cages, by women behind the windows of their rookeries and 'gentry-kens' (gentlemen's houses), and by the street's 'mancatchers' and 'runners', out to fleece him of his cash, by 'fair means or foul'.[26] In the eyes of such seasoned city dwellers, he will have looked an easy target. No matter his size, he was still a young 'chaw bacon' or 'greenhorn' – a fresh, wide-eyed boy from the country. As far as the Metropolitan Police commissioners were concerned, this made him the perfect raw material for a London police recruit.

Young agricultural labourers like Jeremiah were believed to be healthier, better built, more obedient and more willing to accept the stringent Metropolitan Police regulations than their London counterparts. By comparison, boys bred in the degenerative and morally dubious metropolis were considered physically feeble, weak and inefficient.[27] They also had an attitude problem. One senior officer complained the London proletariat were 'loud-voiced, independent, arrogant,' and thought 'they [knew] more than the oldest officers in the service'.[28] The country recruit, however, was known to show 'no obstinacy', and could be moulded by the police 'like wax'.[29] Free from any connections or vested interests in the city, and cut off from any family or acquaintances, their loneliness and separation were considered their greatest asset.

In early April 1863, the twenty-year-old Jeremiah arrived at 'an obscure little apartment' in old Scotland Yard at 4 Whitehall Place. He joined a queue with many other young men, hopeful of signing up and finding perhaps 'a more stirring life'.[30] Clutching references from 'two respectable housekeepers', he waited with 'tailors, greengrocers, bricklayers and barmen, clerks and cooks' to pass the all-important height measurement required by the Metropolitan Force – five feet seven inches – and the 'educational test', which elicited 'a great deal of tongue-rolling and elbow squaring'.[31] Successful candidates were next provided with their uniform, then in the process of being updated: by 1864 a high-collared tunic coat had replaced the old swallow-tail style, and the heavy chimney-top hat had been swapped for a lighter custodial helmet made of cork, faced with fabric and decorated with a silver Brunswick shield.

For an ambitious, bright young man, the appeal of joining the police was its accessibility.[32] One of the first British public institutions, it provided a realistic opportunity to improve a working man's lot. As well as gaining a regular – though small – salary, Jeremiah was enlisting in a genuine meritocracy. 'Every man', stated the *Metropolitan Police Instruction Book*, 'has an equal opportunity of rising to the higher ranks if he shows himself qualified by activity, good conduct, intelligence and educational qualifications'.[33] By the late 1860s, the force was consistently over-subscribed and just twenty per cent of applicants were sworn in.[34]

New recruits were deliberately made to live apart from the rest of society. All single officers like Jeremiah were obliged to move into the police section house, which provided officers with safe and affordable lodgings conveniently near or inside the police station. They also gave senior men, including the commissioners, a perfect means of monitoring and controlling every aspect of a policeman's life: leisure hours, reading matter and even an officer's choice of wife were subject to the approval of their superiors.[35]

Constable Minahan arrived at his section house in G: Division, Finsbury, on 27 April 1863.[36] It was a tightly packed, commercial district that included Clerkenwell, 'the chief seat of watch-making and jewelry making', meaning Jeremiah's streets were a magnet for thieves and burglars.[37] His personal belongings were locked away and he was provided with a bed, a used mattress and a bolster in a room shared with several other men. Each morning he had to present himself for roll call, an inspection and the daily reading of police orders. Even off duty, he was expected to wear his uniform and to remain sober. Drunken behaviour led to dismissal and was the main reason why men were made to leave the force.[38] Jeremiah was on call twenty-four hours a day, seven days a week, and could be transferred to another area of the city at any moment. Trade unionism and strikes by officers were banned.

It was a claustrophobic life, and despite much camaraderie, tensions between the men could become unbearable.[39] Jeremiah lived for at least eight years in these houses and whether he liked and trusted his fellow workers or not, he was expected to remain absolutely loyal to them. For the next two decades, Jeremiah would refer to his colleagues as his 'brothers'.[40]

The policeman's sense of isolation was compounded by the reaction he met beyond the security of the station. From the moment he put on his uniform and stepped outside, Jeremiah ceased to be an individual and instead became a bobby, a Robert, a peeler, a copper and in less salubrious circles, a 'slop'. Each time he walked down a London street, his blue suit and helmet were a target for resentful jeers and random violence. Among the barrow-sellers of the city, 'to serve out [knock down] a policeman [was] the bravest act by which a costermonger can distinguish himself'.[41]

Soon after Jeremiah began working, a fellow officer on duty, Constable Whitwell, was struck on the head by a 'thick-set, powerful' labourer named Thomas Spiller. The 'frightfully ill-used' officer was then kicked and bitten by a local mob, rendering him 'quite unfit for duty'.[42]

Faced with such antagonism, many officers were tempted to hit back, indeed accusations of police brutality and overzealousness had peppered the newspapers since the advent of the New Police in 1829. General orders warned against 'unnecessary violence' but there were no clear rules for officers faced with a huge variety of situations, and by 1880, *Lloyd's Weekly* newspaper was referring to new cases under the headline '*More* Police Brutality'.[43] Other reports suggest attempts were made by both senior staff and commissioners to keep such cases out of the public eye; while inside the force, the men were actively discouraged by their superiors from raising concerns.[44] It was a practice that 'resulted in an atmosphere of fear', writes the police historian Haia Shpayer-Makov, 'in which the men did not dare complain'.[45] There was no place for 'grumblers' inside a station house and should a complaint become public it was regarded in official quarters 'as a sort of treason to the entire constabulary'.[46] Any man who spoke out might have his name blackened and even run the risk of dismissal.

*

Jeremiah's promotional success in the Metropolitan Force suggested he had indeed been a loyal man, that he was not a 'grumbler'. The tall recruit had been quickly requested for the 'Reserves', a special unit made up of 'cool-headed' men with 'a peculiarly imposing demeanour'.[47] For a small rise in pay, they formed the early riot squad. Within seven years Jeremiah had been promoted to sergeant and within a speedy fifteen an inspector.[48]

Crucially on that Saturday night in March 1882, George Broach and Constable Flawn were putting Jeremiah's fidelity to the test. His willingness to toe the line had so far proved unequivocal. George Broach was a violent blackguard with a penchant for 'wetting his neck' whereas Constable Flawn was a junior officer in Jeremiah's own police division. The expectation was that Jeremiah would back his brother officer. After all, he had done it before.

Six months earlier, Jeremiah had been used as a witness in the defence of two E: Division detectives named Charles Berry and William Reader, who stood accused at the Bow Street police court of violently assaulting a local man, John Hagan, in a pub in Soho.

At 10 p.m. on Saturday 1 October 1881, Detective Sergeants Berry and Reader had marched past used-clothes shops and theatrical stores on their way to the Noble Arms public house in Great White Lion Street (just off Seven Dials, by Covent Garden). This particular street harboured many thieves and coiners in its booths and flash kens, a fact known to D.S. Berry, who had been successful in convicting a good number of them.[49] Now Berry had discovered that a 'friendly lead' (a whip-round) was being held by a group of local villains in the upstairs meeting room of the Noble Arms. The meeting, chaired by a tall man nicknamed 'Long 'un', aimed to raise funds for a fellow thief, Morris Gamble, who was facing five years for felony and needed money to 'buy a mouthpiece' (procure a barrister) to represent him in court.[50] According to a constable in a different division, Gamble 'never did any work, was the constant associate of thieves and the biggest blackguard in the neighbourhood'.[51]

John Hagan, who was standing behind the bar downstairs, saw the detectives arrive and head straight upstairs. Hagan was employed as a potman by the landlord of the Noble Arms but was also a part-time coiner; his secret stash of counterfeit coin was actually hidden under the pub floorboards. Concerned about the detectives discovering his 'queer' coin or simply wanting to warn the men of the policemen's approach, quick as a flash, he ran up after them.[52]

He found several of the thieves already desperately trying to escape Berry and Reader and exit the pub.

'Any orders?' Hagan asked the panicking blackguards, with admirable nonchalance.

Berry turned to Hagan.

'Who are you kidding to?' he asked.

'To no one,' said Hagan, 'I'm doing my duty as a potman.'

With that, Hagan grabbed Berry and Reader to stop them chasing the fleeing men – or so the detectives claimed in court. Hagan, for his part, insisted he was upset by Berry's subsequent use of 'very foul language'. He was even more upset when Berry punched him in the face and pushed him down the stairs. On arriving back on the ground floor, he scuttled behind the bar, but Berry and Reader had not finished with him yet. They grabbed him and threw him out of the public house and on to Great White Lion Street, kicking him along the road.[53] When he tried to make a run for it, they beat him about the head with an umbrella, to the cries of 'Shame! Shame!' by a female witness.[54]

At the Bow Street police court a month later, Inspector Jeremiah Minahan loyally answered questions from Berry and Reader's defence barrister, Montagu Williams. While his superior, Chief Inspector Wood, watched him 'on behalf of the Commissioners of Police', Jeremiah distinctly denied his brother detectives had 'presented any signs of having been drinking' when he saw them on the evening of the alleged assault.[55] Both men, Jeremiah insisted, were of an 'excellent character' and he attested to their many years in the force. The jury was flummoxed. They failed to agree on whether Hagan had been punched, thrown down the stairs and kicked along the street or not. As the consequence, the judge dismissed the case and the following week it was dropped by the prosecution altogether – Berry and Reader were found not guilty.[56]

Faced with George Broach and PC Flawn, Jeremiah could have followed the same line. This would have been the easiest solution. Several other officers at Bow Street had already declared that Broach, who had a record for police assault, received his injuries during a failed attempt to escape custody. Jeremiah was meant to accept this version of events, but this time he chose not to. He refused to support his brother officer's spurious claims and instead gave Broach leeway to make an official complaint, first providing him with Flawn's collar number, then instructing the young constable to attend the Bow Street police court the following week. Flawn would have to answer to the charge of assault brought against him by Broach in front of the magistrate. Jeremiah had also ensured that the two constables who arrested Broach in the first place were suspended for their allegiance to Flawn. Both had denied that he was present when Broach was beaten.

After nineteen years in the London force, on a stormy

Saturday night in March 1882, Jeremiah had effectively thrown over his long, successful career by siding with a young drunk against the uniform might of a powerful institution. And having made this first small stand, he was soon to find that he had entered a new hinterland, from which there was no return. For he would no longer heed the commands of corrupt Englishmen. Instead, from now on, he would only hear the truth of his own rebel heart.

Chapter Two

The Same Old Game of Revenge and Tyranny

> Gaelic Mental Characteristics: Quick in perception, but deficient in depth of reasoning power; headstrong and excitable; tendency to oppose.
>
> D. Mackintosh, *Anthropological Review*, January 1866[1]

Jeremiah Minahan was born on 6 May 1842, in County Limerick, south-west Ireland, to Jeremiah and Margaret, small tenant farmers on the plains of the meandering River Maigue. The second son among a brood of ten, he was baptized on 16 October, in an old house with a leaky thatched roof, which served as the local Catholic congregation's chapel.[2] He was raised in a close rural culture interconnected by family and faith and rooted in the rituals of saints' feast days, hurling matches, weddings and wakes; of intoning the same prayers and sharing the same songs. Within each was a memory, as embedded in his family's Limerick souls as the grain in the wood, as the cool in the river.[3]

But Jeremiah was also born into a creed and community hardened by political and religious divides, between England and Ireland, Protestantism and Catholicism, repression and rebellion. His was a generation that would be exiled by this same unending struggle, rent by the shifting sands of alienation and belonging.

The Minahans farmed over forty acres of land in the

barony of Pubblebrien, near the village of Patrickswell.[4] This pretty, busy village had a single, winding street lined by houses and cottages. Roofs of grey slate and brown thatch hunkered against the green, low-rising fields behind the main thoroughfare. The rough walls of the cottages were painted white, with yellow or red on the windows and doors. There were two blacksmiths, three tailors, three publicans, a police station and by 1850, a National School Board elementary school in the village.[5]

Jeremiah's family lived at Lissaleen, a two-and-a-half-mile walk from Patrickswell.[6] His uncles, aunts and numerous cousins lived in Clounanna to the north-west and Lurriga to the north-east. Overlooking the Minahans' tenant farms was a cemetery, situated on top of a windswept hill, where Jeremiah's ancestors were buried. Standing here at a family funeral, Jeremiah will have seen across the flat River Maigue plain to Knockfierna Hill in the distance. The hill was said to be the home of 'Donn Firinne', the King of the Faeries, whose legend renamed Knockfierna 'The Hill of Truth'.[7] Running back from the hill to the tiny family graveyard, fields nurtured wheat, oats, potatoes and cattle. Ash trees and birches lined hedgerows clustered with singing goldfinches. Fat seawater clouds regularly traversed the Limerick skies, rolling in and back from the Atlantic and bringing salty air, heavy with rain.[8]

The novelist William Makepeace Thackeray found the Limerick landscape delightful. 'I know few [views] pleasanter', he wrote, 'than the sight of these rich, golden, peaceful plains, with the full harvest waving on them and just ready for the sickle . . . and the air loaded with the rich odour of the hay'.[9]

When it came to describing other parts of the county, however, Thackeray revealed a certain English condescension.

> High and low, in this country, they begin things on too large a scale. They begin churches too big and can't finish them; mills and houses too big, and are ruined before they are done; letters on sign-boards too big, and are up in a corner before the inscription is finished.[10]

In Limerick City, he found St Mary's Cathedral, which dated from 1111, to be a 'barbarous old turreted edifice'. 'How different', he reassured himself, 'to the sumptuous elegance which characterises the English!'[11]

Thackeray's crude sense of political and cultural superiority was typical of his time. 'One might almost say', wrote the historian L. P. Curtis in *Anglo-Saxons and Celts*, 'that anti-Irish prejudice constitutes one of the longest secular trends in English cultural history'.[12] During the nineteenth century, a stock Irish character in Establishment newspapers was typified by his dangerous emotionality and his lazy indolence; caricatured in the press as an unruly, ape-like madman, who personified the bestial, low-living reputation of the Celtic race.[13] 'In Ireland,' wrote the Dublin correspondent of *The Times* in January 1846, 'it is contrary to the national character for the mass themselves to improve. They are contented with potatoes'.[14] On the Victorian stage, in the form of 'Pat' or 'Paddy', the Irishman was a wily, feckless rogue: if he wasn't singing or drinking, then he was brawling.[15] After three centuries of English colonization, anti-Irish prejudice was so entrenched that it had become part of common parlance. To have a 'Paddy' meant to have a temper tantrum, as did 'to get up one's Irish'. To 'weep Irish' meant to cry crocodile tears and to 'go to an Irish wedding' was an expression for emptying a cesspool.[16]

When an American, William Balch, first saw the Irish for himself on a visit in 1848, he was shocked by how wrong his preconceptions were. Having been led to believe the Irish were 'exceedingly plain and ugly in their appearance' he saw that 'Ireland has been slandered'.[17] Encountering other ways in which the rural poor had been maltreated by the English, Balch came to see some justification in the native Irishman's rebelliousness, in his refusal to conform and in his emotional reaction against the English Establishment. Balch accused the English of creating 'serfs of absentee landlords, to be abused and cheated to the last inch by merciless agents, [and then taxed] to the last farthing to support lordly priests whose doctrines they disbelieve'.[18]

Though Irish Protestants were by no means immune to English prejudice, the British government had systematically discriminated against Catholics on the basis of their religion for many decades. A series of Penal Laws had prevented them from voting; from serving in Parliament and their land ownership and educational chances were severely limited: basic rights that were only fully regained in 1829; and in an overwhelmingly Catholic Ireland, the economic and political consequences of this former marginalization were ongoing.[19] When Balch visited, all Irish denominations still had to pay tithes to the Anglican Church.

Jeremiah's father leased his farmland from a Protestant and Orangeman named William Barker. Barker was a member of the rich and influential Anglo-Irish Barker-Ponsonby family, who – like many of their peers – owned hundreds of acres of Ireland. Mr Minahan's 'house, office and land' was on a sixteen-acre plot with an 'annual value' of £15. He paid 30s per acre each year, meaning his rent of £24 per year far exceeded the land's true value.[20]

By the Barker family biographer's own admission, the Minahans' landlord's character 'was not an attractive one'.[21] William Barker was quick to evict the tardy when their crops failed – families who, according to letters to Barker from his agent, had no crops and nothing left to sell and therefore 'could pay nothing'.[22] Barker's agent was called Richard Wicklow. He lived locally and was reasonably sympathetic to the tenant farmers' plight. Discussing a farm at Lissaleen, where Jeremiah's family lived, he explained to Barker why the tenants could not afford their rent: the two farms of Lissaleen and Lurriga were, he told Barker, vastly 'over-peopled' and the rents Barker charged were too high for the poor quality of the land.[23] Non-payers of rent would usually have any remaining crops sold off in return for their arrears and the fact that Wicklow was forced to hire 'keepers' to guard this stock in 1835 suggests this was the line Barker sometimes took. For the hired guards it was dangerous work, the work of a traitor. On 4 October 1835 Wicklow wrote to Barker informing him that two of his keepers had been horribly beaten, one 'almost to death'.[24] The whole county of Limerick, he explained, was in an extremely 'disturbed state'.[25] Rebellion was never far from the minds of the rural Irish poor. Nor was revenge.

Jeremiah grew from an infant to a child during the most seismic episode in the embittered history between the Irish and the English: the Irish Famine. 'If aught on earth could ever justify vengeance, and form an apology for retaliation,' wrote Balch, 'the Irishman has it':

> His starved wife and children, as they turn their glazed eyes [and] raise their attenuated hands, imploring him for a morsel of food, when he has none to give – do virtually . . . plead with him to avenge their untimely death, and punish the cruel monster who caused all their misery.[26]

Balch's 'cruel monster' was, of course, the British government, which responded to the devastation in Ireland with ineptitude.[27] When the Irish potato crop was first attacked by the blight and failed in the summer of 1845, the Tory Prime Minister, Sir Robert Peel, made short-term preparations for famine relief by importing £100,000 of Indian corn from North America and by financing a programme of public works to provide employment to the struggling rural populace.[28] These relief policies were planned to end in August 1846 in anticipation of a better potato harvest the following year, but in 1846 the crops failed again and four hundred thousand people died either directly or indirectly from want of food.[29] Yet this was only the beginning; the blight on the potato crop would not disappear completely for another five years, by which time, Jeremiah was nine.

In his home county, Limerick, the effects of the famine had first begun to be felt when he was three. During the spring of 1846, the *Limerick Chronicle* noted a huge increase in doctors reporting fever, dysentery and stomach problems. Dr Peal, who practised in Jeremiah's village, Patrickswell, wrote: 'there is more sickness this year than usual; unless public works are provided the poor will be destitute, the breaking out of disease consequent on the scarcity of food'.[30]

The workhouse for Jeremiah's district was built to accommodate 800 people, but by 1847, there were 1,397 inmates, including 496 children.[31] Others died trying to get there. A schoolteacher in the locality recalled how 'poor famine-stricken people were found by the wayside, emaciated corpses, partly green from eating docks and nettles and partly blue from the cholera and dysentery'.[32] An Englishman travelling through Limerick by train saw 'men ragged as scarecrows gazing from the fields [and] crowds of women and children, many nearly naked, climbing upon the palisades to beg at the stations'.[33]

On 23 November 1847, the Minahans' landlord, William Barker, received a loan of £2,900 from the British government relief programme, the Board of Public Works. The loan was provided for repairs to be executed in the 'townland' of 'Lurraga, Lissaleen and Clounanna' – the home of the Minahans.[34] It meant Barker could pay his tenants a small wage to work the repairs while they waited out the famine. Possibly as a result of this, Jeremiah's family survived, but so too did their memories.

During the famine one million Irish people died. Millions more failed to recover from the physical and mental effects of starvation, the disease and poverty that were its legacy. As well as the million dead, between 1845 and 1851 another million left Ireland for good.[35] By 1851 the Minahan homeland of Lissaleen had lost 50 per cent of its population and Lurriga even more.[36] Emigration became a routine expectation for the rural poor, ruined farmers and disillusioned businessmen alike. Over the next decade, most of Jeremiah's brothers, sisters and cousins headed west to America, finding work in the iron mills in the industrial port of Troy, New York.[37] Jeremiah was different. He headed east, into the heart of Ireland's ancient foe. As if to take hold of it single-handedly, he joined the Metropolitan Police, a body of men charged with keeping the British queen's peace.

In the early years of the service, 16 per cent of the force had been made up of Irish-born officers.[38] Police recruiting teams were even sent out to Ireland to encourage their applications. Jeremiah was literate and intelligent and his height and fine looks matched the ideal public image they desired.[39] Though by the time he joined, their numbers were declining, diligent Irishmen still tended to get ahead. Despite the cultural animosity of the English towards the Irish, in the London force they were twice as successful in gaining promotion as Scottish and Welsh recruits.[40] 'The fact is', wrote Sir Basil Thomson in *The Story of Scotland Yard*, 'that Irishmen have a special bent for police work'.[41]

Jeremiah's career advancement seemed to reflect the truth of Thomson's words and as a police officer, he appeared totally unfettered by his Irish background. That is, until he was transferred to E: Division, Bow Street, on Thursday 11 November 1880.[42] It was this division that brought his Limerick heritage flooding back.

There were so many Irish immigrants living in the slums surrounding Bow Street police station that the area was sardonically nicknamed 'Little Dublin' or the 'Holy Land'.[43] A fresh wave of emigration brought more incomers crowding into the area just as Jeremiah himself arrived – the result of another famine that struck Ireland in 1879. Though less severe than the famine of the 1840s, the crop failures prompted the return of traumatic memories for Jeremiah's generation, the children of the bleak years of 1845–51. Throughout the winter months of 1879/80, national newspaper appeals were made in England for aid to dispel the new distress; simultaneously, nationalist agitation for Irish Home Rule manifested itself in mass meetings on both sides of the Irish Sea, while in rural Ireland the famine led to an agrarian uprising against excessive land rents. These were years that re-ignited the 'right to rebel' in Irish culture, both at home and abroad, stirring a unique and intense defiance within the British political landscape that lasted decades.[44]

In the surrounds of Bow Street, Jeremiah could not have avoided his own memories, etched across the faces of the crowds he passed each day. As an inspector, he went regularly out into the local streets to check the beats of his constables. The majority of accents he heard even hailed from his part of Ireland, as those from the south-west largely travelled along southern routes to London.[45] Despite his success in England, Jeremiah still identified with his countrymen and later described himself as part of the 'humble', part of the 'oppressed'.[46] Contained in E: Division were the consequences of colonization and its response: resentment and insubordination.

*

A short year after his transfer to Bow Street, another huge change took place in Jeremiah's life. Having fallen in love, this weathered bachelor of almost forty was married at St Mary's Church in Lambeth, on 30 August 1881.

Jeremiah's new wife was Barbara Pennant Hughes. She was a tall 'fine woman' with dark hair, who was three and a half years his senior and well into advanced spinsterhood at the age of forty-two.[47] Her mother was an Irishwoman and her grandfather, more significantly, was Sir Thomas McKenny, a famous lord mayor of Dublin, 1818–19. McKenny was a Protestant who was also controversially sympathetic to the rights of Catholics in Ireland. Working with the political leader of the Catholics, Daniel O'Connell, Mayor McKenny held a highly contentious public meeting of Dublin Protestants in February 1819, to endorse Catholic emancipation.[48] His singular support meant that he became a heroic figure for O'Connell and the Irish Catholics.[49] Family letters reveal Barbara's interest in her grandfather's legacy. In one she asks a cousin for a key to visit his tomb in Monkstown Church, Co. Dublin.[50] The famous family legend of McKenny's stand against the Anglo-Irish Establishment may also have served, more than sixty years later, as inspiration for Barbara's new husband to challenge his own English masters, at the Bow Street police station.

*

In the days prior to Constable Flawn's appearance at the magistrates' court over his assault on George Broach, Inspector Jeremiah Minahan was repeatedly harassed by his E: Division superiors, who were desperate to stop more allegations of Bow Street brutality reaching the newspapers.[51] At one point, Chief Inspector Wood cornered Jeremiah to warn him of the futility of telling the truth at the pre-trial hearing: 'If five or six constables stick together,' he told Jeremiah, 'I don't see what you can do'.[52]

But depite Wood's menace, Flawn was formally committed for criminal trial at the hearing by the Bow Street magistrate, though he continued to deny the charge. On Holy Saturday, 8 April 1882, while Flawn prepared to sign a deposition expressing his innocence, his defence barrister asked the magistrate for one last opportunity to 'supplement' Flawn's evidence. Acting perhaps on the word of Chief Inspector Wood, he wanted to allow Inspector Minahan an opportunity to clarify his previous statement. Awkwardly for Flawn's defence, during the hearing, Jeremiah's version of events had still failed to tally with the other police witnesses. The Bow Street magistrate agreed that Jeremiah could be returned to the witness box.[53]

Continuing to display a flagrant disregard for his superior's ambitions, Jeremiah 'positively confirmed' yet again that Flawn lied to him on the night of the assault on Broach, when he declared he had not been in the yard at all.[54]

'Did he make any report?' asked Flawn's barrister.

'He did afterwards,' said Jeremiah, 'and I say that it is untrue . . . As you question my evidence, I respectfully ask the magistrate to hear the evidence of the gaoler on the night in question.'[55]

The gaoler backed Jeremiah's testimony against Flawn and two other constables who had claimed that Broach had bloodied his face by falling when trying to escape. Now several of Chief Inspector Wood's Bow Street officers had been exposed as perjuring themselves before the watching court reporters. Negative publicity was guaranteed – as was a rocky road at the police station for Jeremiah: a fact of which he was well aware.

Ten years before, a penny pamphlet entitled *The Revolution in the Police* had circulated in London. The pamphlet expressed the frustration many of the men of the force felt about working within an institution that demanded unquestioning deference. The pamphlet's anonymous author complained that the Metropolitan police were a body of men 'governed by a brutal and despotic power', which knocked down 'any individual daring to express an outspoken opinion of his own' and subjected him to a chastisement well established and known to all:

> The course pursued is, first, to shift the man to another division . . . Once there, he is watched and dodged about by all the Jacks in office, until he is caught tripping in some trifling offence, or breach of police rules, when he is at once reported and dismissed from the force, losing all chance of promotion and pension.[56]

Jeremiah can have been in little doubt about what was coming to him: 'the same old game of revenge and tyranny'.[57]

On the Tuesday following the Easter weekend and his appearance at the police court, Jeremiah stood inside the yard of Bow Street station to hear the police orders for that day, 11 April 1882. With immediate effect, 'Inspector Jeremiah Minahan 43862' was to be transferred to T: Division, King's Road, Chelsea, where his situation would become considerably worse.

Chapter Three

The Curse of Chelsea

> I soon . . . fell under [my superintendent's] heavy displeasure.
>
> Jeremiah Minahan, 1884[1]

Crossing the metropolis with all their homely possessions, Barbara and Jeremiah may at first have celebrated their good fortune. Jeremiah's transfer to Chelsea was one he had, in fact, begged to receive. Rather than await the fallout for defying his masters, he had instead sidestepped his Bow Street bosses by approaching *their* superior direct. Earnestly he had requested that Assistant Commissioner Pearson release him from E: Division, and Pearson answered his 'prayer'. As such, Jeremiah in 'no way' looked upon his move to Chelsea as punishment.[2] Rather, he may have believed he had outfoxed his institutional masters; or that his new brother officers might forget the treachery of his honesty.

Chelsea was a pretty green suburb, slowly succumbing to brick. Journeying there by boat in 1872, the French artist Gustave Doré remembered floating 'past the new bare park of Battersea on the Surrey shore, to Chelsea. We are getting away from London houses, smoke, and commerce . . . There are bits of greenery. The air is clearer . . . We are making rapidly for the grassy banks, the meadows [and the] punts . . . London is indeed pushing out of town'.[3] Granted thirty shillings removal expenses by the Metropolitan Police Receiver's office, Barbara and Jeremiah could afford a van to carry their furniture to their new lodgings at 2 Uverdale Road.[4] The most efficient route from Jeremiah's former abode near Elephant and Castle took them north of the river then west along the recently completed Chelsea Embankment.[5] Here they rolled past Cheyne Walk's Georgian, ivy-clad town-houses – the habitat of artists and writers. They skirted a post office, a shipping depot, the Aquatic Tavern public house and the skiffs and galleys at Greave's boatyard.[6] Noble trees bordered the river's edge and cast shadows across the local shop awnings, their merchandise laid out beneath. As Jeremiah and Barbara passed the shops' dark windows, they may have caught their own fleeting reflections. It was the two of them now, into the world together.

No records remain of their meeting and courtship, but it seems that Barbara and Jeremiah had married for love, and in defiance of convention. The marriage certificate shows Barbara was living in Gypsy Hill, south London, an area where Jeremiah had been stationed between 1873 and 1880, and where they must have met.[7]

Barbara's father was Joshua Hughes, an Anglican vicar. She had spent her childhood with four sisters and three brothers in the pretty rectory of Llandingat Church (St Digat's) in the small market town of Llandovery, Carmarthenshire. In 1870, William Gladstone promoted her father to the Bishopric of St Asaph, north Wales. Joshua Hughes was an unorthodox choice, as he had not received a university education. As such, some deemed him unqualified for the post, a snobbery that left him sensitized to the exposure brought by his new role and anxious about his public detractors.[8]

Though Bishop Hughes felt socially insecure, he did not want for money. A year earlier, in 1869, he had suddenly become rather rich, when his wife Margaret had inherited the huge Irish estate of her father, Sir Thomas McKenny.[9] By the age of thirty, therefore, Barbara Pennant Hughes was a potential – albeit minor – heiress, but rather than remain with her parents in Wales, she was living independently in London before she married, and appears to have been working as a teacher or governess.[10]

Jeremiah reneged on his Roman Catholic faith to marry, yet this does not appear to have appeased Barbara's father, a man once described by a family friend as 'somewhat too allied with the existing system of opinion'.[11] Although religious plurality was increasingly tolerated in late-nineteenth-century England, religious conversion was still charged with controversy. Faith was too heavily bound up with politics, particularly between England and Ireland.[12] Evangelical Protestants, for instance, had used the devastation of the Irish Famine as an opportunity to offer Catholics food alongside Protestant teachings in a conversion campaign known as 'souperism'. During the same period a number of middle-class and aristocratic English Anglicans converted to Catholicism, most notably the Oxford academic John Henry Newman (later Cardinal Newman). Conversions both ways caused outrage and division, largely because they were conceived as threatening betrayals of the dominant culture. Jeremiah's apparent conversion to Anglicanism was a demonstration of his love for Barbara, but while some of his Irish Catholic kinsmen may have considered this the act of a traitor, to some Anglicans and Protestants it will have been viewed as an expression of weakness, of a fundamental lack of devotion.[13] Jeremiah's decision was thus freighted with the religious conventions of others, however insignificant these may have felt to him.

Bishop Hughes' final response to Barbara and Jeremiah's marriage was described in the *News of the World* some years later:

> His life's romance came years ago when he met a Bishop's daughter, with whom he fell ardently in love. Despite the

> intense opposition of her family he won her for his wife. The bishop drooped at this finale, and refused to recognise the too romantic girl ever after.[14]

Bishop Hughes' will does not survive, so it is impossible to be certain whether Barbara was also disinherited. Certainly she and Jeremiah lived out their lives in rented rooms while her widowed mother and unmarried sisters 'lived on their own means' in Malvern, Worcestershire, with three house servants.[15] In the remaining family correspondence there is sparse reference to Barbara before her marriage, but afterwards she ceases to be mentioned altogether. Summers and Christmases pass without a single mention, and when Barbara's younger sister Jane was married in London in 1891, the siblings travelled to the metropolis for the wedding; with the notable exception it seems, of Barbara and Jeremiah.[16]

For Barbara, marriage had meant defying her father to keep her husband. For Jeremiah it represented further injustice at the hands of the British Establishment, made manifest in the figure of Bishop Hughes. In the spring of 1882, the weight of their defiance for love and subsequent shunning was parcelled up and carried to 2 Uverdale Road with the rest of the couple's luggage.

*

Located on a new estate at the western end of the Chelsea Embankment, Uverdale Road ran from the blackened wharfs on the river to Chelsea's central thoroughfare, the King's Road. Orderly black railings enclosed each four-storey house, laid out in terraced rows. Barbara and Jeremiah would pay approximately eight shillings a week for their rooms set over the lower two floors of no. 2.[17] A scullery window at the rear overlooked their small garden.[18] Their neighbours would come to include an urbane mix of professionals and artists: a solicitor, a dentist, a professor of geology, as well as a painter and an actress.[19] Chelsea was becoming an enclave for a more modern middle class and as a couple who flouted faith, class and convention to marry, Jeremiah and Barbara Minahan melded well with its liberal culture in the spring of 1882. The progressive character of his new district may even have tricked Jeremiah into believing he could change his world. But lingering still in Chelsea's shadowy back streets there remained a powerful relic of a passing age.

*

A few hundred yards from Uverdale Road was the leafy thoroughfare of Church Street.[20] Spaced along the street were semi-detached villas and elegant white stucco townhouses, five of which impressive dwellings were owned by a wealthy woman in her sixties. Her name was Mary Frances Jeffries. Thirty years earlier Mary Jeffries had been a lowly 'laundress' on the Dorset coast. Now she owned several opulent homes in one of the most desirable areas of London. Hers was an astonishing rise up the economic ladder, achieved by her prolific Chelsea trade in the unspeakable lusts of gentlemen.

In 1851, the thirty-one-year-old Jeffries was living in Melcombe Regis, Weymouth, and was married to a man named John, who worked as a house servant and lived independently from her at 10 Gloucester Place. She kept lodgings in nearby King Street, where she employed a nineteen-year-old maid, an unusual luxury for a laundress, though not for a businesslike prostitute.[21] Alongside 'seamstress' and 'actress', the term 'laundress' was a common euphemism for a prostitute, particularly on census records, and King Street was conveniently located close by the old port – a short walk for any lost or lonely sailor.[22]

After a brief stint as back-street publicans, the couple followed Jeffries' widowed sister Sarah and her two young children to 78 Oakley Street in Chelsea, an affluent road by the Thames. It was here in 1866 that Sarah died of consumption, leaving Jeffries sole guardian to her niece and nephew, a responsibility that created her need for greater financial security.[23] Her business acumen proved ruthless and impressive. No longer catering to sailors, Jeffries' burgeoning Chelsea empire provided discreet resorts for a wealthy gentleman's late-night 'finish'. Hers were luxuriantly furnished rooms – the kind of establishment where nothing could be ordered prior to a bottle of champagne, price one sovereign, and where the cheapest whore cost a minimum of £5.[24] As the 1870s progressed, Jeffries was earning enough money to snap up her townhouses on Church Street: nos. 105, 111, 125, 129 and the sizeable St James' Villa at no. 155.[25] Simultaneously she paid the lease on a large house at 15 Brompton Square, Knightsbridge, and had interests in other properties in Kensington and Fulham.[26] All served as brothels and houses of assignation.[27] Jeffries' rapid business expansion earned her the reputation of 'chief' of her profession and by 1880 she was the most infamous procuress in the city.[28]

With so many houses to supply, her greatest challenge lay in maintaining a regular stock of fresh young girls. It was a task she regularly meted out to others, including her maid, Maria Watts, who just a few years earlier had stood in the vicinity of Jeremiah's new Chelsea lodgings.[29] The houses on Uverdale Road to which Barbara and Jeremiah moved in 1882 did not exist when Maria Watts knew the same plot of land in 1874. Instead of brick dust, Maria had inhaled the sweet, floral air of the Cremorne Gardens, an ornate pleasure park loved by Londoners of all backgrounds since 1845. Sent by Jeffries, Maria had been at the Cremorne to mine from the leisurely crowd yet another 'nice' girl to inveigle back to her mistress' nearby brothels.[30] Despite the promise of a sweetening shilling, she felt it a sour task.

More than ten thousand people a day had poured into the Cremorne at its peak.[31] Once inside, the crowd that swarmed and flowed around the preoccupied Maria had enjoyed myriad entertainments: coffee houses, theatres, a circus, a maze and a huge dancing platform. Above the waltzers, seated in an ornate pagoda, was a twenty-five-strong orchestra. Their music jostled with the sounds of promenading players, sideshows and the 'rumble of the bowls in the American saloon, the crack of the rifles [aimed] at the little tin beasts . . . and sometimes, by young couples, the voice of love!'[32]

As well as amusements, the Cremorne provided a twilit sphere, where visitors could mix with strangers from across the class divide, enjoying the public frisson of social display.[33] For more than three decades the gardens held a world of escape and desire where for a few brief hours little heed was paid to 'cost' or consequence.[34]

Yet to the knowing gaze of Maria and to others less dazzled by the park's glittering lamps and whizz-bang fireworks, the Cremorne was associated with more venal pleasures:

> As calico and merry respectability tailed off eastward . . . the setting sun brought westward Hansoms freighted with demure immorality in silk and fine linen . . . On and around the [dancing] platform waltzed, strolled and fed some thousand souls – perhaps seven hundred men of the upper and middle-class, the remainder, prostitutes.[35]

As the years passed, the Cremorne became increasingly synonymous with sleaze; with the eighteenth-century mores and Hogarthian debauchery that was anathema to the new generation moving into the area, who soon began to count the Cremorne's 'cost'.

*

Jeremiah and Barbara's professional, middle-class neighbours were part of a generation in revolt against the traditions cherished by their parents; a revolt sparked by a confluence of critiques that opposed the tolerance of aristocratic authority, free-trade economics and narrow convention that characterized the old order. Hitherto, peace of mind had always rested on the 'tacit acceptance' that there were certain affairs that should not be explored too fully: a prudery which meant a 'vast deal of life skulks or burrows at the back of busy thoroughfares, where few know of its existence, or care to follow it'.[36]

But for the children of this conservative generation, modern reality would triumph over coy respectability. Most importantly, they grew up in a post-Darwinian world and benefited from a new-found ability to question common Christian creeds. In 1916 Edward Pease, secretary of the Fabian Society, recalled the impact of Darwin's theories on his peers:

> It is not easy to recollect how wide was the intellectual gulf which separated the young generation of that period from their parents. *The Origin of Species* . . . inaugurated an intellectual revolution such as the world had not known since Luther nailed his Theses to the door of All Saints' Church.[37]

Though Darwin's evolutionism did not destroy the religious faith of the Victorians, it did undermine their belief in divine intervention. Instead, Darwin's theory of natural selection allowed that man could determine his own progress and destiny. The late Victorians realized that they no longer needed to wait for God, they could go out and change the world for themselves.

Simultaneously, they experienced the apparent failure of free-trade economics and the onset of a global Great Depression that lasted from 1874 until 1896.[38] The distribution of wealth and the economic distance between classes in the United Kingdom was more pronounced than ever before.[39] In 1870 the economist and politician Henry Fawcett (a staunch defender of Darwin's work) placed the blame for this growing disparity squarely on the unregulated, free-trade policies of the mid-century. Though free trade had initially generated prosperity, Fawcett wrote, 'unhappily in this prosperity were the germs of future poverty'.[40] During the 1880s, Fawcett's 'germs' grew and under-employment, poverty and distress reached chronic proportions.[41] In London particularly, over-crowded city streets meant that even the wealthy found the economic divide difficult to ignore. While walking in the glitzier thoroughfares of London's theatre district the social investigator James Ewing Ritchie noted 'the questionable gentleman who . . . eases you of your pocket-handkerchief or purse; the poor girl who, in tawdry finery, walks her weary way backwards and forwards in the Strand'.[42] Ritchie, who had started his investigations in the 1850s, retained the attitude that the slum dwellers he observed were victims of their own fecklessness. Such people, he wrote, were 'accustomed to filth, they have no objection to overcrowding, they must have a public-house next door'.[43]

Now a new swathe of social reformers were starting to reject this apathy. *The Bitter Cry of Outcast London*, a pamphlet subtitled *An Inquiry into the Condition of the Abject Poor*, was published in October 1883 and created a national sensation. Written by the Reverend Andrew Mearns, a Congregational minister living in Chelsea, it described the real conditions of London's slums in shocking detail.

> Here is a poor widow, her three children, and a child who had been dead thirteen days . . . Here is a mother who turns her children into the street because she lets her room for immoral purposes . . . Where there are beds they

> are simply heaps of dirty rags, shavings or straw . . . Wretched as these rooms are they are beyond the means of many.[44]

Unlike Ritchie, Mearns recognized the cyclical nature of poverty, the ever-recurring drama of low life.

> Habitual criminals would never have become such, had they not . . . been packed together in these slums . . . Who can wonder that young girls wander off into a life of immorality, which promises release from such conditions? Who can wonder that the public-house is 'the Elysian field of the tired toiler?'[45]

Within days, Mearns found an ally in the son of another Congregational minister, William Thomas Stead. Stead was a young Northumbrian replete with the earnest determination of his peers. As the newly promoted editor of the *Pall Mall Gazette* newspaper, Stead wielded significant influence and ambitiously seized on *Outcast London* as the first major coup of his crusading editorship.[46] On 16 October 1883, Stead reprinted Mearns' findings, accompanied by a leader insisting that 'one of the grimmest social problems of our time should be sternly faced not with a view to the generation of profitless emotion, but with a view to its solution'.[47]

Floods of letters poured into Stead's office in outraged response to Mearns' words, while the *Daily News* remarked that 'every day there grows . . . the utter disbelief in the absolute necessity of the existing conditions'.[48] By the end of the week, unscrupulous slum landlords were firmly held to blame and condemned by Stead for making a 'fortune out of the suffering and degradation' of others.[49] His words echoed the philosophy of T. H. Green, an influential Oxford don who espoused the necessity of moral capitalism. According to Green, property rights came with a responsibility to the common good. After all, he said, 'it is only through the guarantee which society gives him that he has any property at all'.[50]

The desire for moral social reform gained further impetus with the emergence of a powerful new force, the urban professional class. The smooth operation of England's booming cities had become dependent on those working in medicine, law, education and government. Via like-minded newspapers and the lecture-hall circuit, these professionals espoused the values of 'selfless public service' and inspired generations of middle-class children to follow their creed.[51] Self-sacrifice and social reform came to replace self-restraint, and by the 1880s, good deeds were cutting-edge.

This search for new ideals had found a natural home in the modish quarter of Chelsea, whose enlightened, bohemian reputation was further enhanced by the ostentatious lives of two local residents, Oscar Wilde and James McNeil Whistler. In choosing Chelsea as their home, Wilde and Whistler followed many ground-breaking Victorian writers and artists including Thomas Carlyle, Elizabeth Gaskell, George Eliot and Gabriel Rossetti.

Politically too, the area was a hotbed of radical activity, and working men's clubs flourished. Edward Pease recalled his own indoctrination into an embryonic Fabian Society in 'a bare room somewhere in Chelsea' in 1883.[52] The Fabians advocated intellectual socialism and were early lobbyists for women's rights, a national health service and the abolition of hereditary peers. Their members included the sexologist Havelock Ellis, the suffragette Emmeline Pankhurst, the playwright George Bernard Shaw and later, the authors H. G. Wells and Virginia Woolf: individuals who, as Pease described, were 'cut adrift from the intellectual moorings of [their] upbringings'.[53]

*

Set within this increasingly progressive atmosphere, the Cremorne Gardens, with its coarse, old-fashioned 'entertainments', began to appear seriously outmoded. During the 1870s, Chelsea residents started complaining about the gardens in earnest, declaring them a 'pestilential hotbed' where even the flowers drooped their heads in 'shame' over this 'curse' of the parish.[54] Letters in *The Times* had long demanded an end to the Cremorne's so-called delights.[55] Petitions were signed by a combination of Christian moral reformers and local 'tradesmen, mechanics [and] professional men' concerned about the value of their properties and impatient with drunk visitors howling through their streets.[56] It was not only common costermongers who irked Chelsea's locals, upper-class bucks schooled in Bullingdon rules and bent on having their 'sport' also meant the Cremorne had become a by-word for gentlemanly licentiousness and violence.[57]

The tradesmen and professionals eventually won out. Despite opposition from hackney-cab drivers, publicans and, interestingly, several Chelsea policemen, by 1877 the Cremorne was gone, the land sold for re-development, and the Cremorne's feudal epoch covered over by the new-fashioned, clean estate now enjoyed by Jeremiah, Barbara and their up-and-coming neighbours.[58] In his 1881 guide to the London suburbs, W. S. Clarke shared a retrospective view of the gardens with his middle-class readers: 'Of Cremorne – nothing need be said,' Clarke wrote, 'as a place of public amusement its history is scandalous . . . and contains little more than a recital of the frivolities of a past generation.'[59]

During the controversy over the Cremorne's closure, one comment, however, was to prove prophetic. 'Does anyone', wrote one journalist, 'suppose that the vice against which this crusade is directed will disappear with the disappearance of the Cremorne?'[60] Indeed, the pleasure gardens' reach had long ago rolled with the river mists beyond the limits of the compound and into the surrounding district. Wherever there were crowds of moneyed swells seeking the 'dark blue eyes . . . freshest cheeks [and] the richest curls' there was money to be made in Chelsea by middlemen and women like Mary Jeffries, who had no intention yet of shutting her gates to vice.[61]

*

If not the Cremorne, Jeffries sent her maid, Maria Watts, to visit local mothers who she had spotted walking abroad with attractive daughters. 'Mrs Jeffries' wanted to look the girl over at home, Maria told them, about some 'needlework' – or so went the line.[62] Some of the mothers, fraught with poverty, might choose to swallow Maria's falsehoods and send their pretty daughters to their fate. Soon Maria's conscience began to buckle beneath the weight of all her witnessing.[63]

The events that finally spurred her to depart from Mary Jeffries' scene began with a knock on the door of no. 121, another Church Street property Jeffries once owned, but sold before Jeremiah Minahan moved into the area.[64] Outside, Maria found another of Jeffries' employees, a Chelsea inhabitant named Mrs 'C', with a shockingly 'little girl' beside her. Having dazzled her with metropolitan promises, Mrs C had procured the girl in Worcestershire, over one hundred miles away.[65] She claimed to Maria that the girl was in fact Mary Jeffries' 'niece', come to London for a rare visit. Torn between her shillings and her scruples, Maria allowed the two visitors inside. The country girl will have seen that Jeffries decorated her houses just 'like any respectable person would have'.[66] On the ground floors were neat parlour rooms. One of these usually contained a 'nice little dining room' table. The girl did not yet know that this was where the men laid their money.[67]

Maria gave the girl a bath. As she heated the water, her memory may have returned to her very first day in Jeffries' household. In an upstairs room she had discovered another young woman languishing in bed. Her name was Moncrieff; she was eighteen years old and had been invalided through 'the venereal disease' – syphilis.[68] During the secondary stage of the disease a syphilis sufferer will experience symptoms such as a body rash, usually on hands, feet and genitalia, headaches, fever and swollen lymph nodes. As she nursed Moncrieff with hot water and ointment, Maria unpicked her tale. She had been given £15 by Jeffries for her virginity and was sold to a gentleman already infected.[69] There was still a belief that intercourse with healthy virgins of either sex could rid a man of disease, especially syphilis, which was highly contagious and had no certain medical cure.[70] Jeffries herself pocketed £10 for Moncrieff's defilement. The gentleman had paid £25 for his 'remedy' and Moncrieff's slow death sentence.

Not only were men drawn to young prostitutes in a bid to avoid or cure syphilis, there was also something of a cultural obsession with innocent little girls. It was a trend anticipated by the pornographer William Dugdale, who between 1850 and 1860 reissued a sleazy read called *The Battles of Venus*. Though the tome originally dated from 1760, Dugdale clearly understood that its chapters on 'Virgins' and 'The pleasures of rape' chimed with the sensual fashion of his day:

> [The] time when a virgin should be enjoyed . . . seems to be a year ere the tender fair find on her the symptoms of maturity: whilst yet no ringlets deck the pouting mount, but all is like her lily hand, both bare and smooth.[71]

Another gentleman named 'Walter' documented over a thousand of his sexual conquests in eleven volumes during the 1880s, which he called *My Secret Life*. In reality 'Walter' was an outwardly respectable family man and successful city merchant named Henry Spencer Ashbee.[72] Several of his tales reflect the prevailing fixation on seducing virginal girls. One conversation he recorded took place on a foggy night in the metropolis, after 'Walter' walked past three 'juvenile punks' and managed to accost two of them:

'How old are you?' Walter asked.

'Fifteen.'

'Have you any hair on your cunt?'

'Only a little, Sir, but she has none – have you Louey? . . . Come to a house with us . . . and we'll both strip naked.'

Walter took both girls to a hired room and 'took the hairless one' because 'fear seized me'. By fear, Walter meant his dread of syphilis.[72]

During the 1880s young virgins were the most sought-after commodities on the sex market.[74] A parallel industry also sprang up, supplying fakes – the not-quite virgins who used strategically hidden bags of pig's blood to fool their customers.[75] In response, medical men and self-proclaimed 'experts' formed a lucrative sideline in issuing paperwork attesting to a virgin's authenticity.[76] Men who preferred not to risk the streets passed their money to reputable purveyors like Mary Jeffries.

The Worcestershire girl being prepared for her defloration by Jeffries' pliant maid was thirteen years old. She had arrived in Chelsea wearing her village apparel, a 'country dress and nail boots'.[77] Despite her youth, her presence in Jeffries' brothel was perfectly legal: the age of carnal consent in 1874 was still twelve, though the following year it was raised to thirteen. One law that might have been applied to the procuress Mrs C, who had inveigled the girl from her village, was that of the 'Abduction of Unmarried girls Under Sixteen'. This was predicated on the defendant knowingly taking the girl out of the charge of her parent or guardian without their consent, or by *false pretence*; yet it did not effectively cover finding and luring a vulnerable girl on the street.[78] Even if Mrs C was caught out for lying about 'Aunt Jeffries', her charge would only be that of a misdemeanour, with a maximum of two years in prison. This was because the girl from Worcestershire was poor. A far stronger abduction law, a felony punishable by fourteen years' imprisonment, applied to the seduction of a girl under twenty-one if she was 'entitled to property' and it could be suggested she was abducted 'through motives of lucre'.[79] In other words, English legislation valued an upper-class girl with money over a working-class girl with nothing.

The presence of children in London brothels was therefore increasingly commonplace. In July 1881, one police superintendent told a Lords Select Committee about a house of 'low description' he had visited in London's West End:

> In each of the rooms of that house I found an elderly gentleman in bed with two of these children: I asked their ages [all were under fifteen], and got into conversation with them. They knew perfectly well that I could not touch them in the house; and they laughed and joked me.[80]

The police had no legal powers to interfere with brothels. Any prosecution had to be brought by the local vestry and they in turn required two complaints about a brothel's public 'nuisance' from unembarrassed, tax-paying householders before they could act.[81] The superintendent also informed the Lords Committee that the prostitution of very young children (meaning twelve or thirteen years old) was 'a new thing', that had worsened 'within the last two years'.[82] Mass poverty in the cities made young girls available, while male fears and fantasies of the day made them desirable.

Once the thirteen-year-old from Worcestershire was clean and dry she departed in a cab for the shops with her new-found 'aunt' – Mary Jeffries. On their return, Jeffries took off the girl's country clothes and dressed her in their new purchases. She was then left in the 'best bedroom' overnight while the maid, Maria, was sent off to bed. When Maria went up with breakfast next morning, she found the little girl in a flood of tears. A 'great big gentleman', she said, had come to bed with her in the night and 'hurt her very much'.[83]

With a fury fuelled by her own complicity, Maria turned on Jeffries when she appeared in the house at midday.

'What have you been doing to that little girl?' she demanded. 'She is crying her eyes out. You ought to be horse-whipped!'

'It is all nonsense,' replied Jeffries with practised insouciance. 'Don't believe what she says. Here, have a glass of wine.'[84]

Maria swallowed Jeffries' bribe, but left her employ the same day. This, of course, did not deter her mistress, whose operation continued to flourish unfettered by either the morality of her servants or the inadequate eye of the police, who in Chelsea were to prove particularly blinkered.

*

On a stinking bend at the wrong end of the King's Road, halfway between Jeffries' Church Street enclave and Jeremiah's Uverdale Road, lay Chelsea's police station.[85] Inspector Jeremiah Minahan ascended the four steps leading into his new brown-brick workplace at 10 a.m. on Wednesday 12 April 1882, an overcast spring morning. Standing in the station's narrow hallway, his vision adjusted blinkingly to the dimly lit interior, and while his eyes took in the dishevelment inside, he intuited perhaps something rotten, something dark about the building's atmosphere. He may too have noticed a hint of hostility in the eyes of his new brother officers as they glanced him up and down, or worse, turned away. And alongside the creeping acknowledgement of his cool reception, the triumph of his clever escape from Bow Street may have come crashing down like 'Groof, The Flying Man', who fell to his death before a cheering Cremorne crowd.[86]

The S-shaped curve at 389 King's Road once marked the poorly lit, rural brink of London's reach and was the location of a tavern named accordingly, the World's End.[87] The public house opposite the police station, the Man in the Moon, remained a terminus for the city's horse-drawn omnibuses. From here it was possible to travel to Hoxton, Bethnal Green and Bank, via Fleet Street and Piccadilly, every five minutes.[88]

T: Division, Chelsea, was a district in flux; caught between the green fields and setting sun of the west and the bright new dawn of plate-glass windows, telegraph poles and railway tracks slowly encroaching from the east. At the top end of the King's Road near Sloane Square, the plumbing merchant Thomas Crapper had recently shocked Chelsea pedestrians by flagrantly exhibiting his flushable water closets in an open, modern showroom. Just around the corner, the draper Peter Jones was busy extending his empire from two shops (nos. 2–4 King's Road) to ten between 1880 and 1890.[89] Halfway between Peter Jones and the police station was located the most famous of Chelsea's many nurseries, owned by the Veitch family. A renowned horticulturalist, Harry Veitch would later inspire thousands of suburban gardeners by originating the Chelsea Flower Show. He would also become a friend to Inspector Minahan.[90]

Yet Jeremiah's new station remained a long mile from Chelsea's forward-thinking entrepreneurs. Built in 1852, both the building and its occupants had failed to keep pace with the changes in its locale, with the tall, robust policemen squeezed into a space designed for daintier, rural times.[91] Seventeen young officers slept in rooms on the upper floors. In the basement there was space for three or more prisoners. On the ground floor, on either side of the hallway were two small offices, twelve feet square. One was probably used as a public waiting room, the other as the inspectors' office. At the rear, beyond the central staircase, was a long open room, most likely used as the policemen's reserve room or canteen.[92]

During his first few months in the division, Jeremiah tried to embrace his work. He investigated a spate of burglaries in a pleasant enclave just north of the Fulham Road called the Boltons. Inhabited by merchant bankers, landed proprietors and barristers, the Boltons' wide thoroughfares were graced with garden villas and opulent red-brick mansion blocks.[93] One Boltons resident, a lawyer named Joseph Haskett, observed Jeremiah at work and found him 'most intelligent and obliging'.[94] The Liberal MP Joseph Firth, who was burgled, remarked that Jeremiah dealt with the crime with 'much intelligence' and when offered a half-sovereign for his trouble declined, insisting 'he had only done his duty'.[95] But back inside the station next to the malodorous bus stop, Jeremiah's efficiency was rather less welcome.

Optimistically, he initially thought he might begin to rectify its filthy interior. An ageing constable named William Hide and his wife, Gertrude, were employed to keep the building spick and span, something they had obstinately failed to do for many years. Despite Jeremiah's entreaties to tackle the mess, they remained stubbornly inert. Frustrated, he mentioned the matter to the other inspectors. Straightaway they cautioned him against chastising Hide.

'It's no use,' one inspector warned Jeremiah, 'Hide is a favourite with the superintendent and you will only get yourself in hot water.'[96]

They were right. When Jeremiah – prompted by a visit from the assistant commissioner – suggested the station needed cleaning, the superintendent, William Fisher, sided with Hide against him, gathering a group of officers together to ensure his message was clear.

'The Commissioner complained,' Superintendent Fisher announced, 'that the station was dirty and saw me about it. Inspector Minahan has made a long report to me. I don't find fault with you [Hide]; you have been here many years and always done the work very well.'[97]

In moving to Chelsea, Jeremiah had entered a distorted world where lax or transgressive behaviour was openly favoured above effective police work.

It was not always so. When Fisher first took over T: Division in 1868, he had made an effort to clean up his officers' misconduct. Demonstrating a short-lived zeal, he forced two police constables to resign for abusing their positions and ignoring his authority. Both men had been caught 'borrowing money' and repeatedly 'incurring debt' from local publicans, which the policemen then refused to pay back.[98] Pub landlords courted police constables because they collated residential complaints, which might later negate a publican's licence, so the boredom of a constable's beat would commonly be relieved by a refreshing glass of beer, donated by dubious innkeepers. Less diligent officers took root in their local tavern, where they sat 'soaking under the pretence of making enquiries' and it was a problem of which superintendents were well aware.[99]

Fifteen years on, a more jaded Fisher took a completely contrasting approach to his officers' relations with Chelsea publicans. In fact he now appeared thoroughly complicit in his own men's corruption. Unfortunately for Fisher, Jeremiah also discovered this when he began investigating a local pub himself. Having received a complaint about the noisy 'drunkenness and obscene language' emanating from an old inn by the river named the Magpie and Stump, Jeremiah – ignoring more warnings from his colleagues against interfering – decided to pay a visit in person.[100] The pub's landlord, presuming Jeremiah was a regular Chelsea peeler, attempted to soften his demeanour with a refreshing 'bribe' but was rebuffed, several times.[101]

When it became apparent that Jeremiah was next to attend the annual Chelsea meeting for the renewal of local licences and would therefore be requested to disclose any residents' complaints about public houses, Superintendent Fisher suddenly telegraphed an order instructing him to desist. Charles Ross, a third-class inspector to Jeremiah's second, and Fisher's most loyal henchman, was ordered to attend instead. Reliably, Inspector Ross failed to mention any complaints about the Magpie and Stump, and – though his pockets may have been lighter – the landlord's licence was successfully renewed for another year.[102]

A fearlessly candid policeman like Jeremiah was no asset to Fisher's dissolute division, so it had been a curious move by him to accept Jeremiah's transfer from Bow Street in the first place. 'You can see with half an eye,' one Chelsea inspector told him bluntly, 'the superintendent does not like you'.[103] But the evidence suggests that Fisher – who was angling for a promotion to chief superintendent – may have been keen to impress his superiors by taking control of a perceived troublemaker and dissenter.[104]

Since it took four years to fully train a new recruit and yet most men left the service within five or six, the strategy of the Metropolitan force was geared towards enticing experienced officers to stay on the job.[105] A transfer such as Jeremiah had received was therefore the preferred 'punishment' or solution for men who were challenging, but had not blatantly broken the rules. The undertaking of senior officers then appears to have been to test the troublesome officer's mettle. Fisher's task was to push Jeremiah and 'dodge him about' in order to divine whether he was truly reconciled to rebellion or might yet be coerced back into conformity.[106] At the same time, Jeremiah was expected to turn a blind eye to his colleagues' shadier doings, if he wanted keep his career. Over the following months, the play between the superintendent and the inspector was to become as intense as any chess match held at Gatti's on the Strand, but these two were not the only players with a stake in the Chelsea game.

Chapter Four

It Is Not in London Only that I Carry on the Business

> I cannot wonder that the majority of the British public scarcely credits that such a thing as this horrible traffic exists, but from my own bitter experience and the history [of] others, it is alas only too true.
>
> Adelene Tanner, 1880[1]

A voice came to him through the blue of an August midnight.

'It is no good,' she said, 'for the police to watch my houses. As I only do business with gentlemen of the highest rank in life.'[2]

Jeremiah paused on his Chelsea beat and turned. He knew who she was. Her reputation was far greater than her physical stature: standing in the shadows of 125 Church Street, she looked a little old lady with a stoop. But to London's sex industry in the summer of 1882, Mary Jeffries remained a colossus. A shameless show-off, she relished the reverberations she caused in fine society, habitually frequenting respectable night haunts with her entourage: gaggles of 'fallen girls' in flashy silk and young boys 'whose fingers glistened with diamond rings, and whose feet were covered with patent shoes'.[3]

Two years earlier, her infamy had become celebrity. In January 1880, a journalist named Clement Scott found himself at the centre of a widely reported libel trial following his review of an October ball in the *Era*, a theatrical magazine. Scott was accused of causing reputational damage to the dance's organizer after describing the mere presence at the ball of one 'Mrs. Jeffreys [sic], of Church Street, a notorious procuress' with her 'semi-levy of young men and young women'.[4] The Old Bailey jury found his revelations to be 'severe but honest', and Scott was found not guilty. Jeffries' fame, meanwhile, was sealed in history.[5]

Curious, Jeremiah chose to stop with her awhile, in order, he wrote, to 'obtain all the information [he] could'.[6]

'Good evening,' she said, '. . . you have not been here long.'[7]

He saw a well-dressed woman whose firmly set chin and slightly raised eyebrows bore a look of resigned inevitability.[8] A sixty-two-year-old widow, nearing the end of a long career immersed in all manner of sexual desires, there was little perhaps that surprised Mary Jeffries. Her hooded eyes appraised the 'well favoured' police inspector before her.[9] The best London courtesans and brothel-keepers 'would study every lech, whim, caprice, and desire of her customer'.[10] In Jeremiah, Jeffries saw a powerful man buttoned tightly into his smart blue uniform. And what she surmised about his 'caprice' impelled her, misguidedly, to boast.

'I keep eight houses,' she said, 'I pay my taxes and keep my houses in good order . . . the police have watched my houses and only found I conduct them well.'[11]

Soon after this meeting, Jeremiah quietly began investigating Mary Jeffries. To ascertain exactly how many properties she owned in the area, he checked the Chelsea Vestry Rate Books. She was telling the truth: her taxes had been paid on time for many years. By now Jeffries had begun focusing her operation on three adjacent properties on Church Street: nos. 125, 127 and 129. All three were single-fronted, terraced townhouses.[12] Having sold nos. 121, 111 and 105, Jeffries had re-invested her money in the redecoration of these three and had them 'ingeniously arranged for the purposes of [her] business':

> Nos. 127 and 129 are connected internally by doorways on the upper floors and the other one [125] by an entrance through the garden. Practically the three houses are only one set of premises; for persons entering one may leave by another, the object . . . being to escape the notoriety and odium attaching to visiting houses of this kind.[13]

And there were rumours of more: 'a flogging-house . . . in Hampstead, a house of assorted perversions near the Grey's Inn Road, and a white slave clearing house [for trafficking girls] conveniently situated on the river near Kew'.[14]

Although the whispers that snaked in Jeffries' wake were often far more imaginative than the truth, wealthy men continued to be drawn by her cosmopolitan antics and professional acumen. She also offered them what they wanted.

One lucrative London sex trade was sadomasochism. According to the pseudonymous chronicler of late-nineteenth-century eroticism, Pisanus Fraxi (who was also Walter, author of *My Secret Life*), one successful 'whipper' was Madam James, who had a house at 7 Carlisle Street, Soho and had retired with 'a good fortune and dwelt at Notting Hill in luxury'.[15] Fraxi also listed the numerous women in London willing to 'take any number of lashes' including: 'Miss Ring . . . One-eyed Peg, Bauld-cunted Poll and a black girl, named Ebony Bet'.[16] Generally though, he found Englishmen 'experience pleasure in receiving rather than administrating the birch'.[17]

While idling at the Serpentine in Hyde Park, Jeffries confided to her coachman, George Bellchambers, that she had usurped or 'trod on the toes' of Fraxi's Soho 'whipper' Madam James, and the two had fallen out over a client: none less than the Belgian king, Leopold II.[18] To be so interchangeable, Mary Jeffries and Madam James must have offered similar services.

Jeffries communicated with her high-ranking customers by driving about the gentlemen's clubs of Piccadilly in her smart brougham carriage. Her regulars included the Turf Club, the Guards Club, the Army and Navy and the Marlborough. Taking messages and leaving replies at their front doors, she would arrange meetings for her patrician clients, and leave Bellchambers to liaise with the girls.[19]

Her business model fed on the increasing polarity between upper-class men and their female peers. Criticized by contemporaries for their 'germination of selfishness and isolation', the gentlemen's clubs reinforced this gendered segregation, which often now began at public school.[20] Conversely, the education of upper-class girls was limited, according to the writer Elizabeth Lynn Linton, to sitting 'still in solemn decorum' all 'tricked out in ribbons and frocks' while the 'mind [was] left absolutely vacant of all interests'.[21] Even Linton, a conservative who later railed against late-Victorian feminism, suggested in an 1868 article, 'Foolish Virgins', that though an insipid girl nurtured to make a good marriage may have suited 'the veriest blockhead who ever lounged in Pall Mall', it was yet possible that 'the most eligible *parti* of the season might dislike the idea of taking a female idiot to wife'.[22]

High-born men and women were estranged further still by the Married Women's Property Acts (1870 and 1882), which meant women no longer had to give up their earnings and property to their husbands. Some male 'providers' felt their often arranged marriages were becoming a raw deal and were tempted to flee domesticity altogether.[23] 'Nowadays', remarked the marriage writer Edward Hardy in 1886, 'it is often said that [young men] are giving up matrimony as if it were some silly old habit suited to their grandfathers'.[24]

If he did commit to marriage, a gentleman found other ways to keep himself away from feminine influences at home. Country houses were increasingly equipped with male-only areas – the library, smoking room and billiard room. More modest homes also often provided a single room for the man of the house to 'escape' to.[25]

Even within their own minds, late-Victorian gentlemen tended to separate traditionally held male and female traits. Affections and emotions were suppressed in favour of the stiff upper lip and manly self-control. Some applied a similarly simplistic dichotomy to women, dividing restrained female relatives and accessible prostitutes into symbolic opposites: the saint and the sinner, the goddess and the whore.[26] Mary Jeffries' typical client was thus a rather warped creature, a cultivated man's man for whom genuinely intimate relations with the opposite sex were almost impossible. The poet Edward Carpenter described him as 'man the ungrown', whose 'passion is the little fire with which he toys, and which every now and then flares out and burns him up'.[27]

Carpenter was echoing the concerns more plainly put by John Stuart Mill in his seminal essay, *The Subjection of Women*, almost thirty years earlier. According to Mill, the entire social system of England was bent to this male perception of distinction and superiority: from the law courts to marriage, men benefited from the 'right of the strong to power over the weak' and were backed on this assumption by their gentleman judges.[28] As such, the law delivered a wife to a man as a 'thing', towards whom husbands were in no way 'expected to practice the [same] consideration [as they would] towards everybody else'.[29] Mill felt lower-class husbands particularly viewed their wives as 'fair game', ripe for mistreatment and brutality.[30] But in April 1878, in a famous essay, *Wife Torture in England*, the Irish writer and social reformer Frances Power Cobbe insisted that: 'wife-beating exists in the upper and middle-classes rather more . . . than is generally recognized'.[31] 'After all', she wrote, if 'eloquence should fail, there is always an *ultima ratio*, [the sense] that that final appeal lies in their hands'.[32]

Jeremiah would shortly discover a young woman in just such a predicament. Sophie Mackintosh lived at 5 Redcliffe Square, Chelsea, a six-storey house, with her parents, two sisters and her husband, John McEwen Mackintosh.[33] Mackintosh, a stockbroker, had married Sophie when he was twenty-nine and she was twenty-one. Jeremiah was to learn that he had treated his young wife with 'cruelty and neglect' from the off.[34]

As if to demonstrate his discontent with female frippery, Mackintosh first struck Sophie with a bouquet of flowers, at their marital home just off Grosvenor Square, in 1875. A year later, he held her up against the wall, 'tried to take her wedding ring off and threatened [her] life'.[35] While she was pregnant with their son Angus in 1877, Mackintosh repeated his threat. On holiday on the Isle of Harris, he pulled off Sophie's cap 'with great violence . . . tearing out her hair'.[36] Avoiding the disgrace of battering her face, he went for her arms, which he regularly covered in bruises. By 1879, Mackintosh had ceased caring about scandal and his threats to Sophie were so bad she had sought 'refuge in the servant's room'.[37] Eventually, for her own safety, Sophie managed to move herself, her four-year-old son and her aggressive husband back in with her parents at Redcliffe Square.

In 1883, Sophie applied for a divorce from Mackintosh citing mental cruelty and adultery, an accusation for which she needed proof. Her husband's mistress was said to be a 'woman unknown' at 125 Church Street – the brothel belonging to Mary Jeffries.[38]

*

Jeffries' gentlemen paid £5 for a girl. Of which, she informed Jeremiah during their extraordinary night-time conversation, 'she received £2 . . . and the girls would receive £3.'[39] Jeffries' 'eight' houses entertained around three customers a day, earning her a tidy average of £336 a week. On top of this were the special requests from one-off clients: rich men like the brutal colonialist Leopold II, King of the Belgians, who spent astonishing sums.

Leopold II once put '£800 a month' into Jeffries' pocket.[40] When this sum was later revealed in court, no one disputed its viability. The question was, what did Leopold spend it on? Jeffries was quick to sate Jeremiah's curiosity with a disturbing answer. 'It is not in London only that I carry on the business,' she told him, 'but I send young girls to Paris, Berlin and Brussels'.[41] Leopold had been paying Jeffries to traffic young Englishwomen to him in Belgium.[42]

Unlike England, in most Western European countries prostitution was strictly controlled by a system introduced by Napoleon Bonaparte in 1804 and entrenched by the French doctor Alexandre Parent-Duchâtelet in 1836, the year he published *Prostitution in the City of Paris*.[43] Parent-Duchatelet argued that prostitution was a social necessity to be contained and regulated. He also believed prostitutes were lazy and unstable and advocated that they should be strictly kept within *maisons closes*, under the direct supervision of the *police des mœurs* – the vice squad – and other authorities such as the doctors who conducted twice-weekly checks for venereal infection. Brothels were also compartmentalized according to class in a scheme comprehensible to both the police and the clientele: in Brussels, for example, a high-class brothel was demarcated by a red light; the class below used yellow.[44]

Most importantly, no new prostitute could register herself with the *police des mœurs* unless she was proven to be over twenty-one years old.

City authorities in France, Italy, Spain, Holland and Belgium all adopted a form of the Parent-Duchâtelet system.[45] But English law only toyed with the French doctor's theories by introducing the controversial Contagious Diseases Acts (CD Acts) in 1864. In a supposed effort to protect soldiers from venereal disease the CD Acts subjected perceived prostitutes in English ports and garrison towns to compulsory medical examinations. However, the more useful European over-twenty-one age limit was never adopted, and adolescent English girls tended to fall into the gap between these two systems.

Young girls of all nationalities were traded for prostitution throughout the Continent, but certain cultural differences made gullible English girls particularly attractive to international *placeurs*. Firstly, those of the poorer class were exposed, in their overcrowded lodgings, to human sexuality from an early age and adolescent experimentation was the norm.[46] 'Their own low-class lads', grumbled Walter, 'had them before anyone else'.[47] A girl willing to go further and dabble in the casual prostitution common to English cities could earn the equivalent of a week's wages in a single encounter.[48] According to one *placeur*, one in three of the English girls he sold overseas were already 'prostitutes'.[49] Tempted by the adventure of working abroad, they only realized that the Continental *maisons closes* stripped them of their liberty and 'kept [them] in as prisoners' when it was too late.[50] Paradoxically, the *placeur*'s remaining 'two thirds' were obtainable for the opposite reason. Their Victorian ignorance about sex, or as one French policeman put it, their 'strictly prudish' education, meant that they inadvertently offered 'themselves the easiest prey imaginable': utterly unsuspecting of the *placeurs*' luring lies.[51] Finally, a weakness in government bureaucracy meant that all under-age English girls could be provided with official-looking paperwork certifying that they were over twenty-one. In exchange for 3s 7d, anyone could go to the General Register Office at Somerset House, select a random woman's name with a suitable birth date from the public index and apply for a copy of her birth certificate – 'no questions asked'.[52] So however young an English girl might appear to the authorities overseas, this 'formal looking instrument with a large red seal [and] a stamp on it' quickly dispelled any suspicion or concern.[53]

This aspect of Jeffries' business commanded serious money. Just how much was revealed in a letter posted to her from an Italian gentleman connected to King Leopold's court. Addressed to 'Signora Maria Jeffries, Londra, Inglaterra', the letter was delivered in error to another, completely innocent Mrs Jeffries, who passed it on to a journalist in 1885. The correspondent requested that Jeffries forward him 'a lively young girl of sixteen years, nice complexion, with pretty throat, to live with [me] as my mistress. Price down to be £240, with £60 for the one who shall bring me the girl'.[54] For a shrewd businesswoman who had once shared the intimacy of south-coast sailors, purveying English girls to Europe was not only easy and lucrative – it was also legal.

As the Earl of Dalhousie had explained to the House of Lords a few years before, *placeurs* like Jeffries knew they 'could ply their trade [in] London and elsewhere with perfect security'.[55] Against the immoral traffic of girls abroad, 'Statute law was powerless' and 'Common Law equally useless to check the evil'.[56]

In exchange for his £800, Leopold could have enjoyed two or three English girls a month. What happened to them after he had disposed of them remains unrecorded, but the fate of numerous other trafficked girls had recently been brought to the attention of the British public. These girls were taken to Belgium, France and Holland by a different set of *placeurs*, who lacked Jeffries' high-born, private clientele. Instead the gang had used ordinary transport to shuttle their *coulis* (packages) into public-access, government-regulated *maisons closes* and as a consequence they were caught. Their undoing owed much to the testimony of one victim, Adelene Tanner, who detailed exactly how a naive girl might be ensnared by a *placeur* and once trapped, discover that her situation could quickly, horribly deteriorate. Whether in the hands of an opportunist gang or a cool professional like Mary Jeffries, the outcome for most girls was the same. Once fallen, there could be no return to respectability, no reprieve from the dark sway of the netherworld.

*

It was a snow-filled Christmas Day, 1878, when Adelene Tanner stood alone at Tulse Hill railway station.[57] She was eighteen, though those who saw her swore she appeared much younger.[58] Wanting to warm her wet clothes, she went into the station's waiting room to stand before the fire in the grate. Her back to the room, she did not see the man watching her countenance: catching her loneliness, marking her worth.[59]

Adelene was working as a lady's companion, her first situation since the sudden death of her father Edwin the year before in the family's home town, Bristol, of an 'apoplexy' (a sudden loss of consciousness, usually a haemorrhage).[60] Originally a hatter, Edwin became a commercial traveller and with his wife, Sarah, had five children, four daughters followed by a son. Adelene was the youngest girl. She later recalled her family as having a 'nice home life'.[61] Her eldest sister, Emily, described her as a 'well-behaved, quiet girl, of great simplicty of character'; a perfect example of modest middle-class girlhood.[62]

The Victorian notion of a virtuous girl advocated obedience, innocence and sexual ignorance. Unmarried daughters were expected to serve as the 'centre of morality' in the family, and in an environment of frightening industrial change, of 'steaming torrent' and 'fiery locomotive', were charged with sitting sweetly still.[63] In his 1881 novel, *Portrait of a Lady*, Henry James reflected upon the damage this stultification inflicted on a girl's personality. His heroine, Isabel Archer, is increasingly disturbed by her repressed new stepdaughter, a 'good little' adolescent named Pansy, to the point where she finds her 'absence of initiative, of conversation, of personal claims . . . unnatural and even uncanny'.[64] More pointedly, James alluded to the peril in Pansy's ignorance, worrying that her 'cultivated sweetness' made her an 'easy victim of fate', vulnerable to manipulators and predators both within and without her closeted world: 'she would have . . . no sense of her own importance; she would be easily mystified, easily crushed: her force would be all in knowing . . . where to cling'.[65]

As with Pansy, Adelene's elders had conspired to maintain her innocence. So much so that she was even unaware she had been born with a genital defect, identified in her infancy, and which meant she 'would not be fit for marriage'.[66] She was later diagnosed as suffering from an unusually small vagina and primary vaginismus. Though this was long known to Adelene's parents and to her married sister, it was too delicate an issue to ever be 'communicated to Adelene' herself.[67]

With her father's early death, her sheltered existence was shattered. Her mother, left in an impecunious state and grieving for her lost husband, fell to drink and within three years had entered the workhouse. Adelene was left to flounder alone.[68]

On Christmas Day in 1878, while she dried off before the fire, the man who had noticed her made his approach.

'Your waterproof is burning,' he cautioned and the two then 'entered into conversation'.[69] His accent was foreign, possibly French. To Adelene he appeared a 'respectably-dressed man' in his early forties, whose dark, greying hair gave him a 'remarkable, even commanding presence'.[70] To the adults who later knew his game, the foreigner's strong demeanour was more accurately defined as the frightening physiognomy of a 'common' thug.[71] But before he could fasten his fingers around Adelene's lonely heart, her train bore her safely away into a billowing cloud of snow. It was a brief tryst, though not in vain. When she saw him again, Adelene would feel this stranger her friend.

The man was John Sallecartes. Though born in Belgium, he lived in London at various lodgings close by Soho Square. In this dilapidated neighbourhood, political refugees escaping the revolutions on the Continent lived side by side with economic migrants and criminal fugitives; and numerous coffee houses, bakeries and tobacconists catered to their homesick tastes.[72]

Like Jeffries, Sallecartes was in the business of trading English girls overseas. He and his fellow *placeurs* would promise their victims a glamorous job abroad or even the romance of a foreign marriage. Sallecartes's business partner was Frederick Schultz, who, unlike Sallecartes, was noticeably handsome with brown eyes and dark hair, a countenance he enhanced by always wearing black.[73] But just like Sallecartes, who had been imprisoned several times for assault, Schultz' polished veneer camouflaged a volatile personality. By 1881 he was wanted by the Dutch authorities for murder.[74]

Between 6 and 7 p.m. on 22 September 1879, nine months after their first meeting, Sallecartes spotted Adelene again, this time walking along the Tottenham Court Road. He may have remembered her face, or simply noted the same artless potential he had spotted in Tulse Hill, but Adelene certainly remembered him, and allowed him to walk beside her through the early autumn evening. He told her his name was 'Sullie'. She told him she had recently left her situation in south London and was looking for something new. 'Sullie' took this as his cue.

'Would you like to go to Paris?' he asked.

'That depends on the circumstances,' said Adelene, somewhat coquettishly, 'and who takes me.'[75]

In seeking her next place and wandering the metropolis without a chaperone, Adelene represented a new cultural phenomenon: the independent 'shop girl' or 'working girl'. Young, single and self-supporting, these girls' new-found liberties stirred great anxiety amidst contemporary commentators. Some suggested they risked becoming 'fast'; corrupted by the sensuality of consumerism and an 'excessive love of dress'.[76] Others, like the novelist George Gissing, described them succumbing to the city's immoral undercurrent and meeting a tragic end. In the case of Adelene Tanner, Gissing was close to the mark.

In reality, Adelene was a confused young girl. Losing her parents, she had also lost the status and security to which she had been accustomed and was no longer certain of her place. Her sister stated that she was 'easily influenced' while others said she was 'weak-minded' or had been turned by a 'bad crowd' in the city.[77] In essence, all of these statements were true. Adelene was vulnerable, and open to anyone who might offer a lead.

Sullie kept guiding her towards Soho. At a 'kind of hotel' he introduced her to a 'well-dressed' Frenchman named Edouard Roger. He was a failed Parisian businessman, who, facing ruin, had fled to Belgium and set up a high-class brothel in Brussels.[78] Having been offered young girls for his 'stew' by Sullie, Roger had arrived in London to pick up 'a fair pretty girl and a dark girl' just that month.[79]

The two men insisted Adelene enjoy a glass of wine with them at a Soho cafe, and throughout the evening, plied her with drink until she 'scarcely remembered what [she] said'.[80] Through the bottom of her glass, Adelene found Roger 'stylish', 'fascinating and courteous'.[81] When she staggered off out of earshot, Roger raised a concern with Sullie. 'She looks quite young,' he said, worried that he would not be able to register her with the Brussels *police des mœurs*.[82] But Sullie could reassure him that a birth certificate from Somerset House could 'prove' otherwise.

Adopting the stance of translator and go-between, Sullie told Adelene that Roger had taken 'a great fancy to [her]; that he would take [her] to Paris, and if after seeing his grand house, carriages &c. [she] would like to be his wife, he would marry [her]'.[83] Like all other *placeurs*, Sullie espoused the promises that would most appeal to guileless girls, as he later explained to a journalist:

> You get the girl to listen to you, and persuade her to anything. [That] they will have good situations, fine clothes . . . high wages and all the inducements which would enable a sharp girl to smell a rat. But . . . they swallow the bait like gudgeons.[84]

Having persuaded Adelene to lodge with his 'wife' overnight, the following morning Sullie gave her breakfast – a gin – quickly swallowed at a public house then delivered her back to Roger's hotel. It was a grey day, full of unrelenting rain. As well as Roger, Adelene was introduced to another Frenchman, named Emile Regnier. Roger and Regnier gave Adelene more liquor then promised her some much-needed breakfast, leading her to Regnier's home nearby. Instead of food, Regnier's wife gave Adelene coffee laced with brandy, until at noon a 'doctor' arrived. Together he and Regnier's wife forced a bewildered, drunk Adelene back onto a large trunk and held her down while the doctor lifted her skirts and examined her with 'an instrument'. Owing to the 'extreme smallness of [her] person' Adelene almost passed out with the pain.[85]

When the strange ordeal was over, she demanded her hat and coat, but Regnier's wife refused and chivvied her about until finally she was hustled into a cab outside. Inside the carriage was her 'husband-to-be', Roger, his middle-aged maid and to Adelene's surprise, two more English girls: Emily Ellen, aged twenty, and Lydia King, aged nineteen.[86]

The cab bore them all through the rain to Victoria Station, where Adelene saw Sullie had reappeared and was waiting for them. He too clambered aboard the London, Chatham and Dover boat train and pressed a small note into Adelene's hand.

'Learn this on your way,' he whispered.[87]

Then, as the train began to jolt and move off he suddenly jumped back out onto the platform. He had been at the station purely to deliver three birth certificates for the girls and to collect payment. Roger paid him 900 francs, 300 for each girl.

Dismayed, exhausted and still drunk, Adelene fell asleep on the train. When she woke she read Sullie's note, and burst into tears.

> Ellen Cordon . . . Oldham Road, Manchester. Father's name Ralph Corden a forgeman. Mother's name, Ellen Jones Cordon.[88]

This was the name on her new birth certificate, and as official passports had largely fallen out of use at the frontiers of Western Europe, a name was all that was required to cross the border.[89] 'Adelene Tanner' no longer existed. Despite her tearful pleas, Roger refused to let her turn back. He was determined to have a return on his investment. At Dover the boat train pulled up onto Admiralty Pier, where the steam packet was waiting. From the pier, Adelene could see the lights of Dover town clustered beneath the cliffs; a few yards from her feet the seawater swelled, black and greedy. With no money, no friends and no clear idea what was happening, she kept going forward.

At 10 p.m., the steamship lurched into the Channel.[90] Only now was Adelene informed their destination was not Paris, but Ostend in Belgium. It was the first of Sullie's promises that would be revealed as a vicious lie.

On route, Roger's maid warned her to state that her name was 'Ellen Corden' at the Ostend Custom House. 'If we made even the slightest mistake,' recalled Emily, we were told we 'would go to prison'.[91] No girl dared refuse.

Roger's brothel was situated at 3 Rue du Commerce in the Quartier Léopold in Brussels, a prestigious neighbourhood that included 'some of the best Belgian and foreign families'.[92] Outside the building glowed a discreet red light. Gradually, Adelene began to understand that Roger's was a 'bad' house. Once inside, credulous girls had this truth 'broken to them by degrees . . . Little by little she [is] allowed to see where she [is] and [coming] to accept her fate . . . submits'.[93]

The following morning, Adelene, Emily and Lydia were registered as prostitutes at the Brussels *police des mœurs*, a wholly corrupt division that colluded with local *placeurs* and brothel-keepers.[94] According to the Brussels authorities, the real point of this department was not to vet for underage girls, but to protect men from the 'impudent provocation' of street 'nymphs' like Adelene, who 'soiled the nuptial bed' with their 'dangerous poisons'.[95]

In registering herself as 'Ellen Corden', Adelene committed a criminal act. Over the coming weeks at Roger's brothel all the girls were threatened with arrest for presenting false documents should they try to escape. Their fear of a foreign prison, together with the 'debt' they incurred from their sale, kept them captive in the house.[96]

Detained behind the brothel's locked front door, in rooms with blacked-out or heavily curtained windows, Adelene was given only a petticoat and dressing gown to wear. Her 'smallness of person' was then offered as a kind of sport for Roger's wealthy clients, who resorted to violence, alcohol and even lard in their base attempts to defile her. Emily, a far more fiery character than Adelene, loathed Roger's house so much she resorted to banshee-like fits to gain her freedom. In response she was bitten by Roger's wife and beaten until her ribs were broken, then she was permanently dressed up – as punishment – in a baby's outfit and nicknamed 'Baby Nelly'.[97] She later recalled listening to the debauched attacks on Adelene through the locked bedroom door. Her cries were so distressing, Emily said, that she had wanted to 'kick the door down'.[98]

*

A few weeks after Adelene disappeared from London, a Quaker reformer named Alfred Dyer exited the Friends' Meeting House in Clerkenwell. Dyer was thirty years old, but frail and thin. When he passed under the Meeting House's lamp, it revealed his long brown beard, his angular features and his sloping, sympathetic eyes. A fervent evangelist too shy to readily look a fellow in the eye, Dyer advocated Christian social purity and moral reform via the furious power of print. A pamphleteer, author and newspaper editor, he ran a publishing office for many years at 1 Amen Corner on Paternoster Row, close by St Paul's Cathedral in the City.

Once outside on the cobbled street, an unnamed friend joined him. Secluded in the darkness of the wintry Sabbath night, the friend told Dyer the story of another acquaintance who had recently had a troubling experience in Brussels. In a *maison close* he had encountered a young English girl so distraught by her entrapment that she was contemplating suicide. Her name was Newland. She had been courted in London by a handsome gentleman and on the promise of marriage had accompanied her 'lover' to the Continent. Once there, she had been sold into a licensed brothel in Brussels under a false name.[99] The dark-haired romancer who had sent her to the devil was Frederick Schultz, John Sallecartes' (Sullie's) partner.[100]

Alfred Dyer's feeble physique camouflaged a stubborn spirit and a determination to turn his beliefs into living action. Disturbed by his friend's anecdote, he wrote to a contact in Brussels and managed to orchestrate Newland's rescue. On her return home, he verified her tale. In the process, he came to believe that an entire commerce, trading English girls across the Channel, was operating with impunity. To prove his theory, he decided to investigate the iniquity in Brussels for himself. During his crusading visit in late February 1880, he incurred the ire of the crooked police and suffered the violent threats of several brothel bullies, but he also found Adelene Tanner.[101]

*

Trapped inside Roger's brothel, Adelene was repeatedly beaten and abused until a visiting doctor from the *police des mœurs* recognized that she was ill.[102] He diagnosed an 'acute case of urethritis' (an inflammation of the urethra most commonly caused by chlamydia) and noted that she had 'pustules on her vulva'.[103] She was sent for mandatory treatment at the St Pierre Hospital, where Dyer found her several months later. As well as being a lock hospital for prostitutes – meaning a hospital where prostitutes were prohibited from leaving until they were treated for their venereal infections – St Pierre formed part of the medical school at the University of Brussels. Its leading doctor, named Thiry, had a tendency to use prostitutes for his experimental trials.[104] Adelene was soon cured of her urethritis, but she remained under Dr Thiry's 'care' because he was interested in 'instrumentally' destroying her virginity.[105] This is what she remembered.

> They commenced to operate upon me for the purpose of making me capable of prostitution. They did not give me chloroform, but the students held my hands and feet, whilst the operator [Thiry] seemed to tear away at my living flesh, inflicting upon me agonies I can never describe.[106]

Adelene never recovered from her treatment under Thiry. She vomited blood for many months and completely stopped menstruating.[107] As soon as he could, Dyer arranged her safe return to England. When she arrived in April 1880, she looked, according to one witness, like 'a crushed worm'.[108]

Yet there was still some fight in her, a desire to prove that she was 'sinned against, not sinned'.[109] She provided Dyer with a full account of her experiences, which he published that summer, rallying repeated petitions from the public for a government inquiry. Before the year was out, Dyer and his supporters had not only necessitated a Home Office investigation, but had gained the assistance of the Treasury solicitor in instigating the prosecution of eighteen *placeurs* and brothel-keepers in Sallecartes' network. Two trials took place in Brussels in December 1880 and April 1881.[110] Charged with offences ranging from the debauchery of minors to bodily injury, illegal detention and forgery, all the defendants were found guilty and imprisoned, including Edouard Roger (three years), Emile Regnier (six years) and John Sallecartes (six years).[111] Frederick Schultz escaped prosecution and disappeared.

Though Adelene did not attend the trials for fear it might 'overthrow her reason', her case remained pivotal to the prosecution's success because her 'smallness of person' attested to her original virginity.[112] It proved she had been a 'genuine' victim and not, as was often alleged, a girl of already questionable morality who had 'volunteered' for her fate. The *Daily Telegraph*, a newspaper read by Jeremiah Minahan, stated in its report of 17 December 1880 that Dyer had also been a 'chief witness' in the courtroom. Another man present at the December trial was an astute barrister named Thomas William Snagge, sent on behalf of the Home Office. In his report, Snagge wrote that it was 'beyond all doubt that for many years a trade or traffic has been carried on, [involving] a very large number of English girls'.[113]

His report also revealed that thanks to Dyer's campaign, more than a dozen girls were rescued, most from Belgium. These included an eighteen-year-old from Gloucestershire named Hephzibah Smart and another named Ada Higgleton. Both died soon after they reached home, suffering illnesses either caused or exacerbated by their maltreatment abroad. Louisa Hennessey, who was trafficked at seventeen, returned pregnant with the child of an unknown client.[114] One hundred and fifty others flocked to an English rescue home opened in Brussels in the wake of the trials.[115] Adelene was taken in personally by Dyer and his wife to live with them as their housekeeper. Despite their kindness, Adelene's experiences, wrote Mrs Dyer, had permanently reduced her to an afflicted 'wreck of her former self and an unspeakable grief to her friends'.[116]

Snagge's findings for the Home Office led directly to the instigation of a Lords Select Committee on the Protection of Young Girls, which in July 1882, just the month before

Inspector Jeremiah Minahan met Mary Jeffries in Chelsea, had reported its conclusions in the newspapers. Convinced of the 'shocking trade' between London and the Continent, the Lords had recommended a raft of anti-vice reforms, which included raising the 'age of irresponsibility' (consent) from thirteen to sixteen.[117] Nonetheless, it would be another ten months before their suggestions were even introduced in Parliament. So standing coolly chatting across her Chelsea garden wall in August 1882, Mary Jeffries could rest easy. She could open all her Church Street secrets to Jeremiah and boast about selling girls to 'Paris, Berlin and Brussels', for he had no power to stop her. The justice of a Brussels courtroom may have wiped out Sallecartes' network, but this clearly did not bother Jeffries. So confident was she in the shielding influence of her powerful patrons that she felt she operated beyond the haphazard scrutiny of the police or any other righteous hindrance. She was, she believed, unstoppable.

That same August night, Jeremiah saw Jeffries' latest housemaid, Ann Lewis, appear at the brothel's front door with another young prostitute at her side. As they scuttled past him, in his full uniform, Jeffries turned and chided them for dawdling. 'Make haste,' she said, 'there is a gentleman at St James Villa.'[118] Jeremiah watched as they melted away, unable to intervene or protect the girl.

Then, when he turned back to Jeffries, he saw, glinting between her fingers, gold, 'a sovereign or half sovereign'.[119] But this time Jeffries had misjudged the man and Jeremiah refused her smoothing tip.

'You are not like the other inspectors,' Jeffries harrumphed and disappeared back inside her house.[120]

The bizarre conversation was over. Armed with further insights into the dubious habits of his brothers at the Chelsea police station, Jeremiah walked on. A few months later he would assist Sophie Mackintosh with her divorce from her brutish husband by providing a statement of evidence about Jeffries' brothel to her solicitors. She was finally released from her violent marriage on 20 January 1885.

But for now Jeremiah continued on his beat, mindful of Jeffries' brazen admissions. It was too soon for him to envisage the devastation she would wreak on his own life. Too early to understand that in daring to dwell on one old woman's debauchery, he would unleash the wrath of one of the mightiest men in England.

Chapter Five

They Called Me A Fool

Be careful what you are saying.
Superintendent Fisher to Inspector Jeremiah Minahan, 9 April 1883[1]

On Thursday 22 November 1883, Inspector Jeremiah Minahan was ordered to attend the bureau of the Assistant Metropolitan Police Commissioner, Lieutenant-Colonel Douglas Labalmondiere.[2] So he journeyed back to 4 Whitehall Place, the headquarters where he had queued to join the great organization more than twenty years earlier. As he headed round to the rear entrance in Great Scotland Yard, he may have encountered more anxious striplings clustered outside the old recruitment office, but he will not have lingered; the weather that day was agitated, vacillating between showers and hail, wind and storm.

Seven days earlier, Jeremiah had submitted – at the behest of both Superintendent Fisher and the District Superintendent – a report listing fifteen examples of obstruction and malpractice that he had witnessed in Fisher's Chelsea division over the previous eighteen months. These were written to substantiate Jeremiah's claim before District Superintendent Howard that under Fisher, the King's Road station was maintained in a 'state of insubordination'.[3] In doing so, Jeremiah felt reassured by the Metropolitan Police rules, which '*allowed*' [JM's italics] policemen 'to make complaints of superior officers', should they be obstructing the proper discharge of police duties.[4] But he had failed to weigh the principles of an institution against the politics of its people; or to see that Fisher had laid him a trap.

Within two hours of submitting the requested report, Jeremiah was suspended. His future in the force now lay in the hands of Assistant Commissioner Labalmondiere.

*

As his months in Chelsea passed, Jeremiah's troubles at the station had only worsened, particularly in his relations with Inspector Charles Ross, who had proved his most recalcitrant adversary. Ross continually defied his authority and refused to obey 'Inspector Minahan's orders'. Since their stand-off inside the police station six months earlier, Ross's insistence that 'no other superintendent would have [him] in his division' left Jeremiah in no doubt that in the show of brotherhood between the men, he had been allocated the role of outcast: a part created for him by Fisher.[5] 'I have to fight,' Jeremiah noted, 'against a spirit of insubordination manifested towards me . . . by many of the men . . . which seems to spring from the manner in which the Superintendent treats me'. One inspector, for example, demonstrated his dislike of Jeremiah by regularly passing him 'without exchanging a word'.[6]

During his confrontation with Inspector Ross that spring evening, Jeremiah had insisted – in front of the other officers – that he would report Ross's 'conduct to the Superintendent'.[7] Even if he suspected it was a futile endeavour, he had to be seen to follow through with his threat. Nine days later, the two antagonists stood before their chief. Having heard their complaints, Fisher ambiguously suggested that 'there must be a recommendation', and that he would send Jeremiah's briefing on Ross' impertinence up to the District Superintendent. Ross, believing he had forced his master's favour too far, quickly begged Fisher not to punish him with a transfer. Jeremiah, 'having pity on Inspector Ross as he had lately taken a house, and has a young family', suggested that if Ross apologized, he would rather let the matter drop, but Ross refused and his 'insolent conduct' continued, while Fisher, conveniently enough, 'lost' Jeremiah's report.[8]

Ross's enthusiasm for challenging Jeremiah stemmed from his desire to please Fisher and even perhaps in the pleasure of vexing Jeremiah's probity, but there was another underlying issue that may have heightened his antipathy. Like Jeremiah, Ross was an Irish immigrant, but unlike Jeremiah he was of Protestant stock. Even if Ross knew about Jeremiah's conversion or had seen him in the local Anglican church with Barbara, 'Minahan' remained a surname that betrayed his Catholic roots; and it is pertinent that in 1882 and 1883 anti-Catholic sentiment in London was reaching a newly hysterical level.[9]

On 6 May 1882, less than a month after Jeremiah arrived in T: Division, Lord Frederick Cavendish, the newly appointed Chief Secretary of Ireland, and his permanent undersecretary were assassinated with surgical knives in Phoenix Park, Dublin, by a gang named the Invincibles.[10] The group members were all former Fenians, Irish republicans agitating against the British government for an independent democratic Ireland. By this time, the Fenian notion of a people's army fighting for Irish self-governance had moved away from insurrection on the home front to targeting the 'imperial enemy' direct, through terrorist campaigns across Britain.[11]

The letters of the Liberal Home Secretary, Sir William Harcourt, reveal that during the early 1880s American-trained terrorists were being regularly shipped back across the Atlantic to England. Fenianism in the United States was fuelled by fierce nostalgia and bitter memories of Ireland's poverty and famine.[12] Despite Home Office protests, the US government did nothing to stop Fenians publicly soliciting Irish American money. The editor of one American newspaper, the *Irish World*, made an impassioned appeal in 1883 for terrorist funds:

> If we are determined to keep up the fight on the Irish side we should resolve to *fight to win* at all hazards . . . England and Ireland have been for centuries at war . . . What is England's mode of warfare? . . . Ask Cromwell . . . Ask the Chinese . . . the Afghans, the Zulus. Ask every unfortunate people over whose cloven liberties [England] planted her pirate flag.[13]

The most famous terrorist of the day, Jeremiah O'Donovan Rossa, aka the 'O'Dyamiter', also owned an anti-English newspaper, the *United Irishman*. The English had tortured Rossa before deporting him to America in 1871 for plotting a Fenian uprising. In his paper, Rossa advertised courses in bomb manufacture. Students paid $30 for a thirty-day programme on dynamite, which was said to contain more force than a 'million speeches'.[14]

A secret agent working for the Home Office described attending such a bomb-making course in New York in 1883. Every Tuesday evening the scholars learned:

> How to make the explosive . . . used in [London's] Underground Railway . . . It was chloride of nitrogen and phosphorous dissolved in bi-sulphide of carbon. The chloride of nitrogen was contained in a large glass bottle, having a smaller one with the phosphorous attached to it. The two bottles [were] thrown on the ground [causing them] to explode.[15]

Once students were 'ready to proceed on their missions' they travelled from America to Antwerp, Bremen or Hamburg. Here they waited until they received 'instructions to proceed to the United Kingdom'.[16]

At the behest of O'Donovan Rossa, in January 1883 two large bombs had destroyed a gasometer in Glasgow's city gasworks, injuring eleven people.[17] On the night of Thursday 15 March, a huge bomb went off amid new government buildings in Charles Street, Westminster.[18] A few minutes later, a watchman found another bomb behind the offices of *The Times* newspaper.[19] Shortly before Inspector Ross completely stopped obeying Jeremiah, *The Times* summed up the mood of many Englishmen and women.

> Now the public . . . will come to know with whom it has to deal . . . Men who will hesitate at nothing . . . in the satisfaction of their own wild demands . . . In Manchester, in Leeds, in London, the feeling of the English workman towards his Irish companions has become cold . . . a few more cases of dynamite [will] turn it into angry hostility.[20]

In his subsequent reports, pamphlet and letters, Jeremiah never mentions his 'Irishness'. In the climate he may have preferred to distance himself; or felt, with the great majority of Irish Catholics in England, Canada and Australasia, that he was a loyal subject of the crown whose background was irrelevant.[21] Yet the early 1880s were so charged with violence and counteractive coercion between Ireland and England that, writes the historian Roger Swift, 'every Irishman of spirit [in Ireland and abroad] was a sentimental Fenian' with rebellion running through his veins.[22] It appears that Jeremiah was also now finding it more and more difficult to contain his own need to question and defy.

When the Fisher-led antagonism was directed solely at him, Jeremiah remained in control of this desire. But the following October, he had delegated work to an able young constable, who in turn attracted the other men's chagrin. On the evening of the 24th, Jane Richardson, a dressmaker from Pimlico, was travelling down the King's Road aboard a London Road Car Company (LRCC) omnibus. It was the end of a grey day, beset by drizzle and soot, making the outside back steps of the omnibus slippery. Whatever the weather, it was a dangerous way to travel. 'The reckless racing and competition daily witnessed between these unwieldy vehicles', wrote one journalist, meant that 'scarcely a week passes without the occurrence of accidents'.[23]

Jane became the latest victim, thrown from the lurching vehicle. Her injuries did not require a hospital visit, but she did want to make a complaint about the omnibus driver and arrived at Chelsea police station to find Jeremiah on duty. Inspector Ross was also lurking. 'It's useless,' he warned Jeremiah in front of Jane, 'you trying to find the driver and conductor of the car.'[24] Jeremiah ignored him. Five or six similar accidents had been reported at the King's Road station in the last few months, yet no coachmen had ever been brought to account.

So Jeremiah chose PC Thomas Hocken to watch the buses pass the next day. At 6 p.m., when PC Hocken was in position, Inspector Ross tried to swap him for a constable of his own preference. This determination suggests he may have been in the pay of the bus company. Accidents were so frequent and compensation costs so dear that bribing a police inspector to help keep cases out of the courtroom could have been considered a cheaper alternative by the LRCC, which was in financial difficulty.[25] But this time Jeremiah insisted that Hocken remain and he easily found the culprit. A trial was set for 29 October at the Westminster police court.

Honor Watson was called as a prosecution witness. While she waited at the courthouse, an off-duty constable from

Jeremiah's station approached her. His name was James McIlwain.[26]

'There is a lot,' he told Honor, 'to be brought out in people's characters.'

McIlwain may have been known to Honor, she had a son his age and had lived in the same Chelsea parish.[27] McIlwain may have harboured some gossip about Honor's respectability; or he may simply have been chancing an empty menace. Either way, he was threatening to use his position to her future detriment.

'It is just as well,' he continued, 'to keep out of things.' He then offered Honor her 'omnibus fare' with his parting shot: 'Don't say you have seen me.'[28]

Honor obviously did, because Jeremiah eventually reported it, though not until he had nothing left to lose. What incensed Jeremiah more than Ross's and McIlwain's efforts to 'obstruct instead of assist a police prosecution' was that afterwards Hocken was subjected to 'petty persecution'. When Hocken told him that McIlwain had threatened him too, Jeremiah's control finally broke.[29]

For over eighteen months in the dirty, poky police station, Jeremiah had faced insolence from fresh-faced constables who wounded his pride and made a mockery of his two decades' experience in the force. Clearly it was the policemen who flouted the law in Chelsea who were rewarded: with money from bribes and the favouritism of Fisher.

His response, in November 1883, had been to write the first of three reports complaining about the 'unprecedented' way Fisher handled the men. Each served as an example of 'insubordination' that confirmed Fisher's belief that Jeremiah's non-conformity had become a permanent fixture – and as such he was no longer a fitting asset to the Metropolitan Force.

*

Yet as he edged past the 'books piled up on staircases . . . piles of clothing, saddles and horse furniture' that cluttered the overburdened interior of Scotland Yard, Jeremiah still hoped to discover the actual reason why he was being punished for submitting these reports, an act both requested and *allowed*.[30]

It was Assistant Commissioner Labalmondiere's task to provide him with a response. A sixty-eight-year-old man with lively eyes and a thin, tightly drawn mouth, Labalmondiere was, wrote one wry journalist, a man 'most remarkably obtuse and discourteous'.[31] The son of a retired sugar planter, at sixteen he left Eton to enter the Royal Military College at Sandhurst, joining the 83rd Regiment of Foot, which travelled through Canada, India and Ireland.[32] In 1850, he was offered his senior post in the Metropolitan Police and returned to England. By the time Labalmondiere encountered Jeremiah he was one year short of collecting his pension.

Inspector Minahan's reports presented him with a problem. As a literal-minded man, he may have agreed that Jeremiah had adhered to the police rulebook and was entitled to raise concerns about a superior who appeared corrupt. Yet his military experience meant he recoiled at the thought of a man of low birth and junior rank being granted the right to exercise such liberties. After all, a gentleman of Labalmondiere's generation and social standing expected unquestioning deference from a man like Jeremiah Minahan. While Jeremiah, equally, was becoming increasingly disinclined to give it.

Though Jeremiah was ordered to return to Labalmondiere's office two days later, on 24 November, and again on 26 November 1883, he still remained unable to fathom the actual reason for his punishment.

'Under what grounds,' he eventually asked Labalmondiere outright, 'are you suspending me?'[33]

By way of response, Labalmondiere picked up Jeremiah's report. Ignoring the first thirteen careful examples of Chelsea impropriety, he fingered point fourteen. The offending paragraph referred to a woman named 'Jeffries – the keeper of several brothels for the nobility in Church Street'.[34] Jeremiah had noted the appearance of Jeffries' 'youthful prostitutes' and described how in April 1883 he had supplied evidence about the procuress' Church Street activities to the solicitors acting for Sophie Mackintosh in her divorce from her violent husband.[35]

What had really concerned Jeremiah about Jeffries was the reaction of his brother officers at the mere mention of her name. To assist Sophie Mackintosh's case, he had asked a fellow Chelsea policeman named Sergeant Cox, who once kept observation on Jeffries' houses, to corroborate his findings. Cox refused. He was 'not going to say anything', he told Jeremiah ominously, for which 'action might be taken against him'.[36] Jeremiah's disclosures met with an equally cool reception from Superintendent Fisher and his brother inspectors, who appeared 'exceedingly' annoyed he had provided any information about Chelsea's infamous madam.[37] It fell to his most ardent adversary, Inspector Ross, to sum up the mood of the men inside the King's Road police station.

'You are a fool,' Ross told him, 'for not taking [her] gold.'[38]

Yet these suggestions of coercion, bribery and bullying did not flummox the assistant commissioner; instead, the *only* reason Labalmondiere would give Jeremiah for his suspension was a line in his report that paraphrased Mary Jeffries: 'I only do business', she had told Jeremiah, 'with gentlemen of the highest rank in life.'[39]

' "Brothels for the nobility",' Labalmondiere read back to Jeremiah, 'that is highly improper.'[40]

*

As Jeremiah absorbed Labalmondiere's shameless retreat behind a shield of gentility, he may have remembered Fisher's warning six months earlier. When he heard about Jeremiah's encounter with Jeffries, Fisher first joined the others in laughing off Jeremiah's outrage, then suddenly he was serious. 'You had better be careful,' he warned, 'what you are saying.'[41]

His caution stoked Jeremiah's curiosity. Bruised at being treated as the station's 'laughing stock', he returned to Church Street again and again like a moth to a flickering flame.[42] For six months he observed Jeffries' doxies go to and fro with her grey and eminent clients, whose names he duly noted. An assiduous investigator, he recorded his findings in a small book and locked it away in his office at the police station. He did not reveal this surveillance to his brother officers, but they were watching him. Around the time Jeremiah stood frustrated before Labalmondiere, one nameless officer stole the precious notebook from his locked desk drawer.[43]

*

Faced with Labalmondiere's pretence to horror at the very mention of 'brothels for the nobility', Jeremiah kept his counsel, but his superior's brazen denial of upper-class immorality left a sour residue that fuelled him through the cold months to follow.

Jeremiah was not alone in his bitterness. Political radicals and Christian petitioners alike were now expounding the link between prostitution, poverty and class, and in doing so had broken the 'invisible sanitary cordon' surrounding the subject of fornication.[44] 'We rebel!' cried Josephine Butler, a leading female reformer whose campaign work during the 1870s to repeal the Contagious Diseases Acts (CD Acts) had brought together a consortium of emergent feminists, politicized members of the working class, religious puritans and civil libertarians.[45] 'We are systematically brought up to be silent upon the evidences of vice and impurity which confront us', she stated in a rousing speech, but 'our eyes can no longer be closed [to the] foul realities of life'.[46]

The CD Acts covered eleven ports and garrison towns in England including Dover, Plymouth and Portsmouth and were intended to reduce the incidence of venereal disease in soldiers and sailors by forcing *suspected* local prostitutes to submit to a vaginal examination. Infected women could be incarcerated in a lock hospital for up to nine months. In essence, the CD Acts entrapped and sequestered the woman, while the man who 'sinned with her, [went] free'.[47]

Josephine Butler had rallied wide support for the repeal of the CD Acts by kindling the antipathy of the respectable working class to the 'Old Corruption' of the Victorian aristocracy.[48] She characterized the political defenders of the CD Acts as licentious upper-class rakes who conspired to control women through the law, while perpetuating their 'slavery' through prostitution.[49] In her public speeches Butler frequently referred to the five-hundred-year-old story of Wat Tyler, who violently avenged his daughter's rape by a government official and in doing so sparked the peasants' revolt of 1381.[50] She illustrated her pamphlets with parallel tales of contemporary abuses: one told the story of a girl confined by a magistrate under the CD Acts. The girl later told her, 'It did seem hard ma'am that the magistrate . . . who [ordered] my imprisonment had paid me several shillings a day before to go with him'.[51]

More damagingly, Butler's attack on the debauched patrician archetype garnered approbation from respectable working-class men who now had the right to vote. Indignant letters from men aligned to trade unions and radical political societies appeared in pamphlets, denouncing the CD Acts as 'class legislation' and as 'un-English'.[52] Her agitation translated into a loose alliance between working-class male radicals and middle-class, early feminists in protest at 'the corruption by aristocrats of young [lower-class] innocents'.[53] Many gentlemen, not unnaturally, registered these growing demands for social and moral reform as a direct attack on their birthright, their very sense of self; and they were quick to snarl back.

Butler, who came from a genteel and prosperous Anglican family, was subject to 'ridicule . . . in the press, [to] social ostracism . . . abuse and violence' and was labelled the leader of the 'shrieking sisterhood'.[54] Undaunted, she saw progress in this vitriol. 'Persecution and violence [are] a welcome sign', she wrote, 'that the enemy is roused to bitterest hatred . . . because his sovereignty is about to be overthrown'.[55]

Nor were the men who aligned themselves to Butler's feminist critique safe from derision. Most commonly, they were represented by the satirical figure of the 'suburban clerk' which personified men who tried to distance themselves both geographically and culturally from working-class miseries – and memories – by aspiring to (lower) middle-class respectability.[56] Known as the 'black coats' (later white-collar workers), they were men who worked away at the lowest rung of the professional ladder – men like Jeremiah Minahan, family people who espoused the values of hard work, sexual morality and individual responsibility. They despised aristocratic idleness.[57] The male elite dismissed them as a bore, and accused them of being emasculated by their enjoyment of home life.[58]

In 1879, the writer and expert on the royal court T. H. S. Escott deplored the suburban or middle-class 'right of five-o'clock tea' as a 'symbol of the ascendancy of the softer over the sterner sex'.[59] Soon thereafter, the Liberal Home Secretary, Sir William Harcourt, complained about the 'depressing

. . . joyless monotony' of 'the class of people [who] consider that the whole duty of man is summed up in going about . . . in a black coat' and who inflict their 'dreariness . . . on others who are willing to be merry'.[60] Like many of his peers in Parliament, Harcourt was particularly suspicious of petty-bourgeois reformers like Alfred Dyer, who was regarded as an irrational, even fanatical moralist. Harcourt was kinder to Josephine Butler, yet he openly believed that all the middle-class reforms of the nineteenth century had been achieved at the expense of pleasure and enjoyment.[61]

The haughty attitudes revealed by Escott and Harcourt did not go unnoticed by Jeremiah or his peers, particularly as the women such gentlemen paid to debauch were closer in rank to their own kin than any daughters of the upper class.

On 20 April 1883, the CD Acts were suspended by a parliamentary vote. This was a small political triumph for the 'black coats' over real aristocratic rakes like George Cavendish-Bentinck, a Tory MP and grandson of a former Prime Minister, the 3rd Duke of Portland. While Butler and her friends sat listening in the House of Commons before the late-night vote, Cavendish-Bentinck had loudly bemoaned their religiosity, their 'exaggerated ideas concerning the rights of women' and their radical links to foreign revolutionaries.[62] Five months later, the October publication of the Reverend Mearns' pamphlet *The Bitter Cry of Outcast London* intensified the fiery indignation already fanned by Butler's campaign and brought with it a call to further action. By the time Jeremiah Minahan encountered Assistant Commissioner Labalmondiere at Scotland Yard in November 1883, sex was not only conspicuous, it was charged with the perilous whiff of revolution.

Labalmondiere may well, therefore, have sniffed insurgency in Inspector Minahan's note about Jeffries' 'brothels for the nobility'. He may too have felt the threat of exposure of Jeffries' high-ranking clientele. But more than this, Labalmondiere experienced the uncomfortable chafe of his own dark secret.

Soon after his return to England in 1850, a much younger Captain Labalmondiere had sired an illegitimate baby girl. She was born on 24 May 1851 and her name was Lina. When the child was baptized on 11 August 1851, her parents were registered as Douglas William Labalmondiere and a woman named Caroline.[63] At the time, Labalmondiere was thirty-six and unmarried. No further records of the girl or her mother or of their future relations with Labalmondiere appear to exist. If Lina did survive she would have been five years old when her father married a different woman, one Margaret Doveton Paget – the daughter of a landed Somerset magistrate – in October 1856.

Like many of his peers, Labalmondiere hid his moral transgressions beneath a well-tailored exterior and it was in part the fear of their revelation that fuelled his anxiety over Mary Jeffries' brothel. While the report reveals that Jeremiah was concerned with Jeffries' wholesale corruption of Chelsea police officers, Labalmondiere – unsettled by the disquiet of the times – registered him instead as a meddler, intent on scrutinizing the private lives of the powerful.[64]

Still, the official reason given for Jeremiah's punishment was eventually altered to something far less incendiary than his report on 'brothels for the nobility'. Instead, on the morning of Saturday 1 December 1883, Jeremiah was demoted for the entire document, in which – it was now alleged – he had made 'false accusations against his Superintendent and brother inspectors'.[65] Beyond consulting Superintendent Fisher, however, Labalmondiere had concluded Jeremiah's 'accusations' were 'false' without making any inquiry at all. He was degraded from inspector to sergeant and his pay was cut accordingly – almost in half – from around £187 per annum to 38 shillings per week.[66] He was also ordered to transfer again, this time to the furthest outskirts of north London, to Y: Division, Highgate.

The bleak night following this news must have been fraught with indecision for Jeremiah. Aside from the humiliation, he knew that his brother officers in Highgate might mete out similar treatment to those in Chelsea. He was a marked man, a thorn in the side of any superintendent who preferred conformity to veracity. 'To continue to speak the truth and discharge my duties faithfully to the public', Jeremiah explained, would inevitably lead 'to further reduction in rank'.[67] Yet if he decided to resign from the force in protest, there was a great deal to lose.

Jeremiah would not only forfeit his job but also his police pension, to which he had contributed 2.5% of his wages for over two decades. He was still fit and healthy, but at forty-one no longer young; in addition, the policeman's lot of long hours, shift work and walking the beat meant that even officers of strong physique were soon 'worn out men'.[68] The automatic right to a pension after a certain period of service was not established, nor yet was the state pension: old age could mean destitution and poverty. One in three workhouse inmates in 1891 were over sixty-five; in London the figure was closer to one in two.[69] Jeremiah was not yet at the end of his working life, but turning away from the force now, in the midst of an economic depression, might jeopardize the future security of both himself and Barbara.

By the Sabbath morning, 2 December 1883, he was ready to report his decision. 'I beg respectfully', he wrote, 'to be allowed to resign my situation as a police sergeant in one calendar month from this date, having been degraded for speaking what I believe to be the truth'.[70]

Superintendent Fisher allowed him to leave immediately. On Monday 3 December 1883, a dull-eyed winter's day, the now ex-Inspector Minahan returned to his lodgings in Uverdale Road a free man. His decision had been prideful, even petulant, but was not irrational. He had decided to gamble his future on government justice.

'I resigned', he explained, 'in consequence of the unjust punishment inflicted on me [and] if I had remained in the force, I should have no right of appeal'.[71]

*

A tradition had long existed within the Metropolitan Police for disgruntled former officers to bypass the authority of their commissioners and appeal direct to the Home Secretary.[72] This was Jeremiah's intention. He also desired to open the corruption of the Chelsea police to scrutiny through an independent inquiry. Jeremiah still retained the faith that beyond T: Division, truth and honour prevailed in the institutions of government.

At the end of 1883, the Home Secretary serving under Gladstone and the Liberal government was still Sir William Harcourt. To improve his chances at the Home Office, Jeremiah first petitioned the support of his two local Liberal MPs, Joseph Firth (a Quaker) and Sir Charles Dilke (a progressive, upcoming star in the Liberal Party). In the first week of December 1883 he submitted to each a long memorial outlining his experiences at the King's Road station and an appeal against Assistant Commissioner Labalmondiere's punishment. In addition he gathered the signatures of twenty-six 'Influential Persons' of Chelsea who were 'well acquainted with Inspector Minahan' and found him 'an intelligent, energetic, steady and courteous officer'.[73] Jeremiah's signatories comprised the professional class of his neighbourhood: the magistrate, a solicitor, several clergymen and doctors, the artist C. J. Lewis and Mr Harry Veitch, the horticulturalist who established the Chelsea Flower Show.

Joseph Firth MP, whose burglary was ably investigated by Jeremiah during his time at the King's Road police station, responded within the week.

> New Court, Temple, December 11th 1883
>
> Dear Sir
>
> I have read your papers and the memorial to the Home Secretary . . . I will do anything I can to assist you in the matter. I very much regret that the police force should lose the advantage of your services.
>
> Yours truly, JFB Firth[74]

Jeremiah's hopes must have soared the very next day, when Firth wrote again.

> I took the opportunity yesterday, when at the Home Office, to arrange that a full inquiry be made into your case, and I think Sir Charles Dilke has given an intimation to the same effect. I expressed the hope that they would be able to accede to your suggestion.[75]

All Jeremiah and Barbara could do now was wait and pray.

The Home Secretary, Sir William Harcourt, was an able and hard-working minister. He had been appointed to the Cabinet by Gladstone in 1880 as a useful 'pile-driving power' to hold divisions within the party, between Radicals and aristocratic Whigs, in check.[76] Half of Gladstone's 1880 Cabinet were peers. Under pressure from Harcourt, Gladstone granted the Radicals an appeasing foot in the door, by appointing Joseph Chamberlain (the son of a Unitarian shoemaker) as President of the Board of Trade.[77] Harcourt's ability to mollify disparate party members did not stem from an innate diplomacy, but rather a complete lack of long-term ideology. In April 1880, the *Pall Mall Gazette* referred to him as the 'Swiss of politics . . . encumbered by no political principles whatsoever'.[78] His Cabinet colleague Lord Derby wrote in his diary on 27 November 1884 that 'Harcourt harangues . . . more than anybody, but is seldom in the same mind two days running'.[79]

Harcourt's capriciousness was rooted in a deep-seated insecurity. Though proud to come from a well-connected Anglican family who counted the Plantagenets in their ancestry, he was nevertheless born the younger son of a younger son. He could never depend on inheriting the family estate in Oxfordshire and his social position was a hindrance that sharpened his snobbish pride and embarrassed him among his aristocratic friends. Unlike them, Harcourt had to make his own way in the world. After graduating from Cambridge University, he first made his name as a political journalist and later as a successful barrister. Both trades suited his argumentative nature and his sharp tongue, and his legal practice was so successful that by his early thirties he was earning £20,000 a year.[80] A decade later he was ready to accept the offer of a political constituency and in the 1868 general election was voted in as the Liberal MP for Oxford City.

Like Jeremiah Minahan, Harcourt was a big man. At six foot three he was half an inch taller, but by the time he became an MP had already grown stout. A once striking youth, his features had grown fleshy. He bore a doughy nose, a full mouth and a double chin barely disguised by his 'chin-strap' whiskers. Having been raised as a child in an austere household without 'variety or amusement', he embraced gratification in later life.[81] He was impulsive and impressive, delighting in 'yachting and deer-stalking' while consuming 'something like sixteen cigars a day'.[82] This 'hearty appetite for the pleasures of life' resulted in his bulky physique, which, alongside his bullish manner, contributed to his political nickname: Jumbo.[83]

Twelve years after becoming an MP, Harcourt was appointed Home Secretary. As head of the Metropolitan Police and responsible for the prison service and the courts, he received countless petitions against harsh sentences and perceived miscarriages of justice, including the one delivered by Joseph Firth MP in December 1883 on behalf of Jeremiah Minahan.[84]

Their timing was unfortunate. As well as overseeing a department struggling to keep pace with its workload, Harcourt had also grown to distrust the Irish and Roman Catholicism.[85] By December 1883, he believed his suspicions wholly warranted, for he had spent the entire year utterly obsessed with stopping the Fenian Terror, rushing through legislation to stop their activities and setting up Scotland Yard's 'Irish Special Branch'.[86] But still the bombs came.

On 30 October 1883 two infernal machines exploded on the London Underground injuring seventy-two people: 'workers and assistants returning home'.[87] Five weeks later, the Irishman and former police inspector Jeremiah Minahan submitted his petition for 'mercy' to the Home Office.

According to practice, Jeremiah's memorial was first sent to Police Commissioner Henderson, who simply rubber-stamped Labalmondiere's decision and returned Jeremiah's papers to the Home Office. A letter dated 31 January 1884, from Henderson's offices to Jeremiah's solicitors, gives some suggestion as to what his report contained:

> I . . . must decline to enter into any discussion of the case referred to; merely observing that, while it is a matter for regret if any person feels himself aggrieved, I cannot entertain the notion that the present application has either law, fact or propriety to support it.[88]

Commissioner Henderson was clearly unwilling to support any suggestion that his own organization was corrupt or dissolute. The memorial, with Henderson's opinion, was next passed to Harcourt's permanent undersecretary, who in turn showed it to the Home Secretary. In a letter sent via Joseph Firth on 6 February 1884, Jeremiah finally discovered where his future lay:

> I am directed by the Secretary of State to acquaint you that he has had before him the petition praying for the reinstatement of Jeremiah Minahan . . . He has inquired into this case, and ascertained that Mr Minahan's resignation was voluntary, and consequent of his reduction to the rank of sergeant after a most careful inquiry by the Assistant Commissioner into a series of charges brought by him against the Super of his division, all of which proved to be without foundation . . . Under these circumstances, the Secretary of State sees no reason for interfering with the decision of the Commissioner.[89]

The institution had turned its back on its former employee. Jeremiah had tried for government justice and failed.

Whether Harcourt's decision against the ex-inspector Minahan was informed by his impatience with Irishmen, his empathy with Labalmondiere's anxiety or the fact that he had simply received Jeremiah's plea at the end of a trying week in office was as yet unclear. In the following weeks and months a new understanding would come to sharpen Jeremiah's disillusionment and push him further down the path of retribution. But for now, he instinctively focused his fury upon the man who had extinguished the last embers of his innocence: Harcourt. This was Jeremiah's desperate reply:

> The Home Secretary bases his answer simply on the

> reports of the Assistant Commissioner . . . and by refusing to investigate the matter further, he practically denies my right to appeal against himself. As one of her Majesty's subjects I protest against this injustice on the part of the Home Secretary, and I demand a full inquiry into my case, by some tribunal totally unconnected with the police.[90]

No inquiry or tribunal was forthcoming. The clean, modern Chelsea lodgings taken by Barbara and Jeremiah two years earlier were suddenly rendered unaffordable, just as their progressive hopes now seemed unrealizable. In the forlorn month of February 1884, the Minahans were left to face the abyss alone.

Chapter Six

How Do You Do Ducky?

> You can fancy, now, the hoards of vengeance in his heart against the employers. For there are never wanting those who . . . find it their interest to cherish such feelings in the working-classes; who know how and when to rouse the dangerous power at their command and who use their knowledge with unrelenting purpose.
>
> Elizabeth Gaskell, *Mary Barton*, 1848[1]

It is impossible to know when the black cloak of vengeance settled upon the broad bones of Jeremiah's shoulders, or exactly how he discovered the new friends who helped him wrap it to himself more tightly: men and women prepared to work for a better world. For within the month, Jeremiah was returned to the feverish heart of the city. In February 1884 he stood close by the straining crowds of Ludgate Hill, at the west end of Paternoster Row, the core of London's publishing business. High above the rooftops he could see the swelling dome of St Paul's Cathedral, while at street level along the Row was a long line of bookshops, wholesalers, publishing houses and printers. Hurrying under the canvas awnings that closed over this narrow, gloomy thoroughfare were the ruling 'despots of literature', men who fashioned the ideas of the scrawlers into poetry, long tale and legend.[2] In medieval times the merchants on Paternoster Row sold 'God' in the form of religious tracts, prayers and graces.[3] Now that they were modern, these men sold dreams.

Stripped of his uniform, Jeremiah adopted instead the smart dress of sombre respectability: a well-brushed coat, a clean collar and tie and a soft bowler hat.[4] As he stepped inside the tight little printing house he cut a striking figure; a droll contrast to the fellow he was about to meet. The herculean Jeremiah and the runty, reforming publisher Alfred Dyer made a rum couple. Yet the shadowy alliance they formed in the spring of 1884 would be strong enough to haunt and pester England's ruling elite.

Neither man would reveal precisely how they came together. When asked directly about meeting Dyer, Jeremiah only allowed, vaguely, that he had gone 'to a printer, a gentleman who afterwards turned out to be a printer'.[5]

Immediately following his disappointment at the hands of Sir William Harcourt, Jeremiah had posted copies of his Home Office petition with a covering letter to the editors of several newspapers: the *Daily Telegraph*, *The Times*, the *Daily Chronicle* 'and two others'.[6] None took up his tale. So he decided to have his reports more professionally printed up. The cheapest, quickest and most popular way to achieve this was to produce a pamphlet – the Victorian social medium of choice for sharing ideas, experience and opinion. Into his, *How an Inspector of the Metropolitan Police was punished for faithfully performing his duty to the public*, Jeremiah copied his allegations of the corruption in Superintendent Fisher's division, his odd meeting with Mary Jeffries and his failure to find justice from Sir William Harcourt at the Home Office.[7] In the right hands, it was explosive material.

The printer and publisher he found to help him was Alfred Dyer. Jeremiah regularly read the then liberal *Daily Telegraph* and may well have been aware of Dyer from its columns.[8] Unlike Jeremiah, Dyer knew how to catch a newspaperman's eye and was shamelessly adroit at kindling controversy. Over the previous four years he had provoked at least two national scandals in the press and his regular pamphlets – full of condemnation for a myriad of lusty sins – were widely digested.

By the time the April blossoms were floating through the city streets, a copy of Jeremiah's pamphlet – anonymously sent – had alighted on the desk of the Home Secretary.[9] As Harcourt scanned the thin paper and its revelations as to his own mishandling of Jeremiah's affairs, he will have spotted in the line: 'Printed by the Dyer Brothers, 1 Amen Corner, Paternoster Row', an irksome opponent.[10]

Dyer had already embarrassed the Home Secretary in 1880 with his shocking revelations about Adelene Tanner and the traffic in English girls to the Continent. In doing so, he had effectively forced Harcourt into commissioning Thomas W. Snagge's report, after both he and Butler exposed a previous Home Office investigation, denying the widespread existence of an immoral traffic, as inept and erroneous.[11] Dyer had next proceeded to engage Harcourt in an unseemly public spat – much enjoyed by the newspapers – over the Contagious Diseases Acts and Harcourt's thoughtless treatment of a seventeen-year-old orphan girl from the garrison town of Dover. Her name was Elizabeth Burley.

At 12.30 p.m. on Tuesday 15 March 1881, several witnesses saw Elizabeth, who was a tall, dark-haired servant girl, being chased through the Dover docks by two local policemen.[12] Basing their beliefs on piecemeal observation and scurrilous assumption, the two constables suspected young Elizabeth was a practising prostitute. Desperate to avoid the ignominy of their approach, Elizabeth, who always claimed her innocence, ran away. Guilty or not, a woman was marked for life by the public taint of a CD Act enquiry. Her character was destroyed and she became thereafter the subject of 'insult, cruelty and outrage of the most degrading kind'.[13] So Elizabeth fled.

Pursued not only by the two policemen but also a group of jeering boys to the dead end of Dover's Granville Dock, Elizabeth jumped fully clothed into the cold sea. Seeing her below, floundering in the waves, the constables simply turned, walked away and left her to drown. It fell to a railway porter and a master mariner named John Barber to save her, and Barber was so angry about one officer's inaction he later stated that 'if I had had a pistol I feel sure I should have shot him'.[14] The following morning the Dover police vindictively charged Elizabeth with attempted suicide. During the ensuing row, Dover's local magistrate refused to prosecute the girl and denied the constables' charge that she was fallen. Elizabeth's only crime, in fact, was to have been seen stepping out in public with a soldier sweetheart.[15]

With the assistance of both Josephine Butler and Alfred Dyer, Elizabeth's case found its way into the local, then national newspapers. By 5 May 1881, it had reached the Home Secretary in the form of a question in the House of Commons. An expedient politician who had always supported the CD Acts, Harcourt responded with the easiest line of defence, which was to blame the girl rather than his unjust and increasingly unpopular system. Utilizing the policemen's flimsy reports, Harcourt vehemently insisted that the seventeen-year-old had indeed been 'leading an immoral life' in Dover, that she was in fact a prostitute.[16] To patrician cries of 'Hear! Hear!' Harcourt thus succeeded where the Dover police had failed: he had sullied Elizabeth's reputation in public and permanently stained her character. The girl's defamation at the hands of the Home Secretary was duly repeated in the national news the following day.

Harcourt may not have been aware, when he batted back this ordinary Commons question, that Elizabeth now had a dogged protector. Shortly after her release by the magistrate, Alfred Dyer's wife had arrived in Dover to offer Elizabeth the sanctuary of their small country home in Hillingdon, Middlesex, where she joined the family's other rescued soul: Adelene Tanner. With the Dyers' support, Elizabeth now found the courage to respond to Harcourt's abasement. In a public letter she demanded that *he* apologize to her for his low insult. Several more newspapers now made room for her indignation.

> It is not enough that an innocent girl should be chased through the streets . . . for nothing at all; but I am now to have my character blackened in Parliament by Sir W. Harcourt. I suppose Sir Harcourt is a great man, and I am only a poor girl; but my character is as much to me as a lady.[17]

Harcourt never stooped to apologize to Elizabeth, nor to respond to Dyer's accompanying letter, which harangued him for his 'cruel charge' against a 'friendless girl'; though he did quietly have the two Dover constables censured and removed to different stations.[18]

In consequence of his careless, combative style over the case, Harcourt hooked himself long-term enemies in Dyer and other radical reformers who decried his 'smug self-complacency'.[19] They held up the Home Secretary's actions as typical of a ruling class both indifferent to and ignorant of the lives they governed. Together, Dyer and Butler succeeded in turning Elizabeth's tale into campaign gold and the public outcry led directly to the suspension of the CD Acts in 1883. Or, as the *Daily News* asserted, Elizabeth Burley did more to hasten the demise of the CD Acts 'than reams or columns of inflated rhetoric'.[20]

By the time Jeremiah Minahan arrived at his offices in February 1884, Alfred Dyer was focused on his latest campaign, to raise England's age of consent, still just thirteen, and push other anti-vice legislation through Parliament. The new measures, labelled the Criminal Law Amendment Bill, had been introduced into Parliament in May 1883 and indifferent ministers on both sides of the House of Commons had failed to offer it much support or enthusiasm. Until the Bill became law, Dyer's efforts to stop the traffic of girls like Adelene Tanner to the Continent would come to nothing. He was therefore on the hunt for his next national scandal, a little something to hurry the House of Commons along. Fortuitously, as well as the ex-inspector, Dyer had also just received some interesting news from Hastings.

*

Dr Elizabeth Blackwell, the first registered female doctor in both America and England, had arrived in the seaside town in 1879.[21] Dr Blackwell was in her late fifties and moved to the East Sussex resort, with its 'warm nooks' and 'bracing breezy walks', for the benefit of her health.[22] It was then a fashionable lodging-house town boasting a smart Regency veneer, a long esplanade and discreet bathing rooms tucked beneath the south cliff. Visitors also found amusement in the Assembly Rooms and the recommended Hastings sights: the candle-lit caves up on West Hill and the auctions held at the Fishery on Hastings' shingle beach.[23] The local fisher-people ran over 120 boats between them, some as large as thirty tons. These were vessels big enough to journey as far as Plymouth, three hundred miles to the west, or Great Yarmouth, almost two hundred miles north.[24] The boats could easily cross the narrow English Channel to France. They could easily carry a discreet cargo of girls to the devilish Continent.

Dr Blackwell was a lifelong friend to Florence Nightingale and a mentor to the early feminist Dr Elizabeth Garrett Anderson. She was also a close associate of Josephine Butler and campaigned with her for the repeal of the CD Acts. By February 1884, she had officially retired, but took great interest in her adopted seaside community. She tried to close down brothels in Hastings and attended dull municipal meetings in an attempt to curtail local political corruption.[25] Her organization of the Moral Reform Union brought her into contact with young people in the resort, whose doings the Union attempted to maintain as chaste. About the seafront Dr Blackwell was also a well-known figure, a frequent walker in a 'chest protector' who always carried carrots for the horses and made friends with the gossiping cab drivers.[26]

The 'South Coast' information Dr Blackwell alerted Dyer and his friends to in February 1884 was of a 'confidential character', which concerned a 'trafficker in girls'.[27] The suspected trafficker was one 'Mary Jeffries, of Chelsea' – the woman named by Jeremiah Minahan as successfully running 'brothels for the nobility', also in Chelsea.[28] London's most notorious flesh-trader had thus materialized before Dyer twice in a single month. Was the 'nobility' funding her vicious trade in virtue both at home and abroad? God was surely calling him to find out.

A brief, whispered exchange between Dyer and Jeremiah at 1 Amen Corner would have been enough to instil in the moral reformer the feeling that this tall Irishman might offer far more than another turn of his printing press. Although Jeremiah's old notebook, recording his private observations of Jeffries' Church Street brothels, had been filched from his desk at the King's Road police station, Jeremiah had a policeman's memory. He had not forgotten the distinguished patrons of Jeffries' brothel, watched during his private surveillance of Church Street. Some were the most celebrated and respected gentlemen of the day. That February, the scandal Dyer needed to propel the politicians into action over the age of consent had just walked in through his office door.

Dyer and several other social purity reformers, who by now had formed a new campaign group, the London Committee for the Suppression of the Foreign Traffic in

British Girls, rapidly agreed to engage the services of the ex-inspector.[29] Throughout the spring of 1884, Jeremiah was dispatched to return to Church Street and renew his observations upon Mary Jeffries. For his efforts Jeremiah was offered the sum of £2 a week, only two shillings more than the sergeant's wage he had thrown over, but he needed the funds and despite the hazards of the task proved an 'active, intelligent and thoroughly reliable' private investigator.[30] Nevertheless, he was still chary of Dyer's religious motives. Later he was careful to emphasize that he worked purely 'as a servant' for the London Committee and did not share their moral intent.[31] But in playing the reformer's 'private detective', Jeremiah at least kept alive any furtive desires he may have harboured to settle his own scores.[32]

And Dyer himself was motivated by much more than rescuing hapless girls from seduction and sin. Long ostracized as a practising Nonconformist, his reforming activities during the 1880s formed part of an ongoing collective struggle for social and political inclusion, equality and even power.[33] The movement insisted that moral authority enter into all matters of public policy, and one tactic of this struggle was to expose the existent political hegemony as iniquitous and dissolute, and as such, unworthy of the privilege of governance.[34]

Quakers and Unitarians, being largely 'professionals and owners of sizable economic enterprises', formed the upper social tier of the Nonconformists; Methodists tended to be drawn from the lower and lower-middle classes; while other Baptists and Congregationalists were 'predominantly shopkeepers, small-scale entrepreneurs and [also] professionals'.[35] The Unitarians in particular were Nonconformists who exerted a significant influence on British intellectual life: a cerebral denomination with little shared dogma beyond the insistence that Jesus was not the Son of God, a position that was illegal until 1813, their central tenet was their rigorous commitment to civic duty and social responsibility.[36] They campaigned for legal reform, sexual reform and female education. They fought for female suffrage and a woman's right to work, for primary and infant schools and the dissemination of new parenting techniques.[37] They even espoused the novel notion that fathers should share the care of their children with mothers. William Shaen, a radical lawyer and the son of a Unitarian magistrate, believed that a tender relationship between a father and his child ought to be the educating motive of a moral and intellectual man. 'There are such things as domestic men', he explained in a letter to his sister, 'I am one myself'.[38] As the legal representative of Dyer's London Committee, it was Shaen who organized Jeremiah's wages during his investigation of Mary Jeffries.[39]

As early as the 1840s, Shaen and a fellow Unitarian, James Stansfield MP, who led the parliamentary campaign to repeal the CD Acts, had declared the female franchise as an essential element in political reform.[40] Victorian women born into Unitarianism enjoyed a significant amount of respect and freedom and many flourished. William Shaen was married to Emily Winkworth, the great friend of the successful author Elizabeth Gaskell (who herself was the daughter of a Unitarian minister). Shaen acted as Elizabeth Gaskell's lawyer following the publication of her biography of Charlotte Brontë. Other Unitarian women in the same network included Florence and Parthenope Nightingale, the women's rights activist Barbara Bodichon and the journalist and social investigator Harriet Martineau. Bodichon's circle included Dr Elizabeth Blackwell (the daughter of a Quaker) and the author George Eliot (who came from a Methodist family).

The Nonconformists' 'conscience' also influenced the values of the wider British middle-classes. The *Manchester Guardian*, which espoused liberal but moderate values to local readers, was established by a group of Nonconformist businessmen in 1820. From 1872, under the editorship of the Unitarian C. P. Scott, the *Guardian* became more radical and went national. On a similar scale, thousands of mid-Victorian readers of the much-loved Charles Dickens absorbed his increasingly radical critique of the inequalities in British society. Dickens was also a Unitarian.

With the extension of the British franchise in sight, William Ewart Gladstone began courting middle-class Nonconformists in the 1860s and brought them into the Liberal Party fold. Some historians argue that late-nineteenth-century Liberalism became 'the political projection of the Dissenting [Nonconformist] experience' or that the 'Dissenting tail [wagged] the Liberal dog'.[41]

But in the spring of 1884, as Jeremiah began watching Mary Jeffries again, there remained a major challenge to the radical Nonconformists' drive for change: the Liberal Whigs. These were the traditional aristocratic supporters of free trade and laissez-faire governance who still dominated Gladstone's Liberal Party between 1880 and 1885. The Whigs valued freedom as much as conscience and believed state interference, particularly into the moral choices of men, to be highly suspect.[42] Though they sympathized with Nonconformist grievances and in public were increasingly expected to dance to the tune of their morality, for the Whigs, a man's private life – his *free* time – was still a separate sphere.[43] A wealthy elite, they did not wholly share the Nonconformist notion that 'what is morally wrong can never be politically right'.[44] In this atmosphere, it was little surprise that the Criminal Law Amendment Bill failed, once again, to make it through Parliament in the spring of 1884 and by July, Gladstone's Liberal government had withdrawn it altogether. Left in the lurch, the Nonconformist reformers had no other viable political force to turn to. So Dyer, who believed he operated in tandem with 'God's providential working', decided to adopt less orthodox methods to achieve his aims.[45] In the case of Mary Jeffries, Dyer believed that exposing the sins of her powerful clients might provide the public leverage necessary to embarrass Parliament into bringing back the Bill and raising the age of consent for good.

*

The stretch outside Mary Jeffries' enclave was quiet and empty, only echoing the clatter and call of the King's Road, which segued across the bottom of the street. The greenery of Church Street's villa gardens provided the sole camouflage for a lurking private detective. Jeffries and her girls must have soon been aware that the tall, 'square up and down' Irish policeman was returned to his former haunts.

Over many months, the ex-inspector observed Jeffries walking between her three terraced brothels at nos. 125, 127 and 129, and at no. 155, the semi-detached villa where she also kept her brougham carriage and horse. Jeremiah also pursued her across London, noting her at more houses in Fulham and South Kensington. Through the spring and summer of 1884, he constantly skulked in the brothel crone's shadow.

Having returned one spring day to his regular station outside 125 Church Street, Jeremiah watched two more of Jeffries' prostitutes arrive by hansom cab. While he waited, one of them descended the cab's step and sauntered towards him instead of the house. Taking in his splendid physique, she opened her expert eye and said: 'How do you do Ducky?'[46]

Jeremiah did not reveal his response to such a sugary solicitation from a 'bit o' jam', but he remained long enough to watch her sashay slowly back into Jeffries' lair without him.

Knowing his face was too familiar, Jeremiah also employed a painter named George Brokenbro to vary his watch. On Thursday 3 April 1884, Brokenbro began relieving him of his evening shifts from six in the evening until two in the morning. On one evening alone in April 1884, Brokenbro observed one couple go into no. 155, then three more ladies and four gentlemen going in separately; at no. 129 he 'saw a gentleman and lady go in together. Then I saw two ladies go in separately . . . and one gentleman go in'; at no. 125, 'four gentlemen and six ladies' entered the house. In total Brokenbro saw eleven clients and thirteen prostitutes enter Jeffries' Church Street establishments, which, taking Jeffries' average earnings of two pounds per girl, meant she had taken at least £26 over eight hours on just four of her eight *known* houses.[47]

As well as employing Brokenbro, Jeremiah charmed the local servants into assisting him with his investigation. As a former policeman, he understood the value of their knowledge and gossip.[48] He befriended the current maids and traced the former staff of Mary Jeffries as well as those who worked nearby. One was a cook whose kitchen window lay opposite Jeffries' headquarters. The cook, named Anne Clark, had seen for herself that Jeffries ran 'gay houses' and had noticed 'a great number of different gentlemen going in both at night and in the morning' including 'two policemen'.[49] Jeremiah was keen to continue his surveillance through Anne's kitchen window, but her master, Mr Bailey, refused to be 'mixed up in this business', and even denied Jeremiah leave to interview his servants, warning that 'if he pursued his inquiries . . . he would not only handle him roughly, but give him into custody'.[50] He was a man of his word. On one occasion at least, Jeremiah managed to sneak below stairs and when Bailey discovered he had been hoodwinked, he dismissed Anne instantly. Then he set off for Jeremiah's new house, south of the river in Clapham, where he brought his horse to a hurried halt, marched up to the front door and punched the man who opened it. Jeremiah disposed of his hot-headed assailant by hitting Bailey right back.[51]

Actually, irate neighbours were the least of Jeremiah's worries. His former brother officers in Chelsea had also begun intimidating his informers and witnesses. A twenty-five-year-old horse-keeper named Harold Baring was harassed and eventually arrested for being 'drunk and disorderly' by two Chelsea constables who 'had boasted that they meant to have him the first chance they could get'.[52] Baring had been 'prepared to depose' in the Jeffries' investigation 'that he had seen [the Chelsea officers] receive money'.[53] Jeremiah also found that many local witnesses were too afraid of the 'evil one's [Jeffries'] wrath' to assist him.[54] It was a dangerous game to meddle in the twilit world of brothel-keepers and *placeurs* and there were plenty of cautionary tales.

*

In January 1881, Josephine Butler had employed another private detective named Monsieur de Rudder, a Belgian living in Bloomsbury, to assist her in finding the violent *placeur* and Sallecartes's partner, Frederick Schultz. For months Schultz had evaded the authorities, escaping the first trial of his cohorts in Brussels the month before. Unlike the men of the Metropolitan Police who failed to find Schultz, Butler's detective – a 'feeble' seventy-one-year-old – tracked him down within days.[55] On 26 January 1881, he followed Schultz and his tall, fair-haired mistress all night through their Soho haunts and back to their lodgings above a tailor's shop at 47 Newman Street, north of Oxford Street. Monsieur de Rudder watched them light a candle in the first-floor window before scurrying through the darkness with his findings. Next day Butler telegraphed Schultz's new address to the police. It was Assistant Commissioner Labalmondiere who handled her information. Strangely, by the time his officers arrived two days later to arrest him, the *placeur* and his mistress had fled, leaving a trail of silk dresses and an expensive Newfoundland dog in their wake.[56] Six months later, as the wily old Belgian detective walked nearby on the Tottenham Court Road, he was struck down by a forceful blow from behind, which cut open his head. Before leaving him half dead on the ground, his assailant made clear his reasoning: 'C'est vous donc,' he said, 'qui a donne à Madame Butler tous ces renseignements.'[57] ('So you are the one who gave all this information to Mrs Butler.') When Dyer's London Committee engaged Jeremiah in 1884, the old man was still 'dying from the effects of the blow'.[58]

*

Standing beneath Church Street's whispering trees week after week, Jeremiah brazened out his task. He appears to have adopted the neutral air of any seasoned investigator, coolly collating evidence about Jeffries' web of vice. There was one client, however, who piqued his curiosity and whose depraved libidinous appetites, once learned, haunted him. But for now, he trusted once again to English justice, and in September 1884 handed his report on Jeffries over to Dyer and the London Committee. His new red-covered notebook contained enough facts as to 'the traffic carried on by Jeffries with dealers and wealthy patrons at home and abroad' to shock even Dyer, who concluded that it revealed such a 'state of moral corruption, heartless cruelty, and prostitution of authority [that it was] almost sufficient to goad the industrial classes into revolution'.[59] On 25 September, the London Committee gathered with William Shaen to consider their legal options. With the Criminal Law Amendment Bill in abeyance and the age of consent still at thirteen, there was no legislation in England to stop Jeffries' traffic overseas: girls who were minors (eight years before their Continental peers), and who were perceived to go 'voluntarily', could not be protected. But the London Committee could derail Jeffries' London business by invoking a century-old statute against brothel-keepers whose houses were said to cause a 'common nuisance' in the vicinity.[60] This legal action had to be initiated by at least two of Jeffries' neighbours, two local ratepayers. After some struggle, Dyer's Committee eventually found a cabdriver and a paper-stainer (wallpaper-maker) brave enough to take a complaint about the 'nuisance' of Jeffries' brothels to the local magistrate.[61]

Late in March 1885, an inspector from Jeremiah's old police station arrived at 129 Church Street with a warrant for Mary Jeffries' arrest. Her detention on the charge of keeping 'four bawdy houses' in Church Street was a triumph for the London Committee, who at last had an opportunity to expose both Jeffries and her clients in open court.[62] Her first pre-trial hearing was set for the following week. During his investigation, Jeremiah had discovered that peers, politicians and princes frequented Jeffries' stews, and the Committee was resolved to bare to the world the ungodly lusts of every last lord.

Chapter Seven

I Will Have It My Way

I say it is a 'got up' prosecution by the man Minahan.

Montagu Williams, Mary Jeffries' defence barrister, 16 April 1885[1]

Shortly before half-past eleven on Thursday 2 April 1885, Mrs Mary Jeffries arrived at the Westminster police court in the brougham carriage bestowed to her by an earl.[2] She was to attend the first of three pre-trial hearings, revealing the full scope of evidence that Jeremiah Minahan and the London Committee had gathered against her brothel business over the past twelve months. They would need to prove that Jeffries' Church Street properties were indeed being used as bawdy houses and that they caused a disturbance in the neighbourhood. Unlike the two girl thieves who had stood and quivered in the shaming dock that same morning, upon Jeffries' entrée into the courtroom, she was immediately offered the respectful comfort of a chair.[3]

During the three hearings on 2, 10 and 16 April 1885, the Westminster magistrate, Mr Louis Tennyson D'Eyncourt, a cousin of the poet laureate Alfred Tennyson, needed to decide whether Jeremiah had chivvied enough witnesses and gathered sufficiently sound testimony to send Jeffries to trial at the Middlesex Sessions in Clerkenwell. The hearing also provided an opportunity for Jeffries' defence barrister, Montagu Williams, to destroy Minahan and the London Committee's case before it even sullied the ears of the quarter sessions judge. Should Williams succeed, Jeffries might dodge a trial altogether. More essentially, her clients might also avoid the damage of having their private peccadilloes paraded through the public mire.

Situated in Vincent Square, the Westminster police courtroom was 'exceedingly lofty and light', with hints in its construction of the most 'superior courts'.[4] Seated regally at the centre of the room, Jeffries appeared 'elderly' but 'elegantly dressed' and was accompanied by her regular about-town entourage. Directly behind her sat a 'long row of fallen girls', while close by stood 'eight or nine young men' all bejewelled and replete in the 'flash' fashions of the day.[5] The relative comfort of the accused was in marked contrast to the tight, purgatorial perch occupied by Jeremiah Minahan.

He was in the small, incommodious waiting room, crowded with all those 'compelled to wait their turn' on the slow mechanisms of local justice.[6] It was linked to the courtroom via a central door, which banged on opening against the limbs of those in waiting, much to their 'constant annoyance and danger'.[7] Every 'word and laugh' from Jeremiah's position could be 'distinctly heard' inside the courtroom, and likewise he will have caught much of what was said by the barristers in their boxes and the witnesses on their stand.[8] As a result, it will soon have been clear to all that Jeremiah's investigation of Jeffries had been so watertight that Montagu Williams was forced to resort to a single line of defence: to attack Jeremiah's person again and again. In heaping aspersion on his character, Williams hoped to undermine the fidelity of his detective work. Jeremiah Minahan was on trial just as much as Chelsea's wicked procuress.

Montagu 'Monty' Williams was one of the most famous and successful defence barristers of his day. An Old Etonian, he had been an army officer and a stage actor before accepting the family calling to the bar. His good looks, sense of the ridiculous and easy-going attitude made him the defender of choice for the lowest of London's deviants, including a number of Metropolitan Police officers.[9] On behalf of the prosecution, William Shaen's office had engaged the services of two reputable barristers, Messrs H. F. Purcell and Edward Thomas Besley. A seasoned counsel of the Middle Temple, Besley 'disdained fireworks in court and relied instead on sound advocacy'.[10] By 1885, this florid-faced, portly prosecutor had been doing legal battle with Monty Williams for almost two decades.[11]

Busying themselves between such estimable gentlemen were the usual 'writ-pushers and briefs' (clerks), the circling penny-a-liners (reporters), opposing solicitors Messrs West and Dutton, Jeffries' phalanx of iniquitous youths and, taking notes in the public gallery, two determined black coats: Alfred Dyer and one other of his crusading cohorts, Mr James B. Wookey, a reformed alcoholic and righteous preacher on social purity.[12]

*

On 2 April 1885, the first of Jeremiah's witnesses was Elizabeth Bromwich, Mary Jeffries' Essex-born former maid. Now sixty-two, Bromwich had worked for Jeffries for a vague 'six or nine years' as her doorkeeper and cook.[13] She was a cagey old woman who appeared torn between snitching on her former mistress – seated just a few yards off – and remaining loyal to her handsome new friend, Jeremiah Minahan. A combination of poor memory and intermittent deafness enabled her, in the end, deftly to evade many of the barrister's questions.

In Jeffries' brothels, she said she 'sometimes' saw 'Mrs Jeffries and the men and women together – sitting [having] tea'. Of the gentleman who came, 'Mrs Jeffries called [them] friends that she had known for a long time'. 'Sometimes and sometimes not' Bromwich saw the flash of the gentlemen's money.

'Did you think these ladies and gentlemen met for immoral purposes?' the magistrate D'Eyncourt eventually asked outright. 'Was that your supposition?'

'Yes sir,' replied Bromwich.

Mr Purcell, the prosecuting counsel, followed D'Eyncourt with a question of even greater delicacy.

'Did you attend to the beds. I mean to say did you make the beds and that sort of thing?'

'Sometimes,' Bromwich replied, 'not always.'

'Well did you ever have occasion to go into the bedroom after these persons had been up there?'

'Yes.'

'What state did you find the beds in? Had they been used?'

'Yes.'

When Monty Williams' turn came to cross-examine Bromwich he went straight to the core of his defence.

'Who asked you to come here?'

'I can't tell who it was,' replied the shifty Bromwich.

'Do you know a man named Minahan?' asked Williams.

'I have known him lately.'

'Did he come and see you about this little matter?'

'No,' said Bromwich, who perhaps detecting a threat in Williams' tone, sought to prevent her new friend finding trouble.

'Eh? Be careful,' Williams cautioned.

'I think he did come,' she recanted.

'I thought so. Don't let us have any mistake about him,' Williams announced pointedly. 'Call him in.'

Jeremiah then appeared through the awkward waiting-room door and stood inside the courtroom to be judged by all.

'Is that the man?' Williams asked the elderly maid.

'Yes,' said Elizabeth Bromwich.

'Have you been out with him?'

'No.'

'Never been to tea with him?'

'No sir.'

'What did he tell you that he was?'

'He said he was the gentleman who had got this case in his hands,' she replied.

The prosecution's next witness was far less chary than Mrs Bromwich. He was Jeffries' former coachman, George Bellchambers, who had left Jeffries' employ a year earlier 'in disgust'.[14] Bellchambers was positively fizzing with a dangerous desire to unleash defamatory information. During the course of his testimony, he ignored the barrister's entreaties *not* to mention client names and disclosed financial detail about Jeffries' most valued patron, King Leopold II of the Belgians. Jeffries later confessed that in addition to peddling female flesh to Leopold in Belgium, she had once delivered a girl to his royal yacht, the *Alberta*, while it docked in the River Thames during a visit to the Queen.[15] Bellchambers also listed the many gentlemen's clubs where he delivered Jeffries' messages in Piccadilly and Pall Mall as well as the women he delivered to Church Street on their behalf. But he was wholeheartedly refused another opportunity to reveal any more clients. Recognizing the peril of Bellchambers' cockney effusiveness, Williams kept the defence's cross-examination cursory.

'Do you know Minahan?'

'Yes.'

'Been about with him?'

'Yes sir.'

'Did he take your evidence down?'

'Yes sir.'

'I have done with you, you can stand down.'[16]

With the dismissal of George Bellchambers, the hearing was adjourned until the following Friday, 10 April, when Jeremiah would face Montagu Williams man to man.

The most striking aspect about the first day of proceedings against Jeffries was the repeated demands by the barristers that no client names were to be revealed in the courtroom. 'Although the names of well-known courtesans . . . have been freely given', noted the *Echo*, 'a veil has been thrown over the identity of [Jeffries'] male aristocratic clientele'.[17] Leopold II, king of a foreign realm, was too untouchable to be worried by the word of an oik like Bellchambers.[18] It was those whose social position was far less assured who had the most to lose, and it was their fear of social scandal that hovered over the courtroom in April 1885, like a vulture over an ailing beast.

Besley and Williams had both been present in this kind of case before. They were fully aware of the utter destruction the mere whiff of public disgrace could wreak upon a man's reputation – however large his fortune, however celebrated his name, however innocent his claim.

*

Like many others of their generation, Besley and Williams remembered the notorious case of Risley, sixteen years before. On 17 August 1869, between twelve and one in the afternoon 'Professor' Richard Risley, a celebrated international theatre impresario, was loitering close by Piccadilly Circus beneath a skittish sky.[19] Once an athlete and gymnast whose agility had astonished audiences all over the world, Risley had grown fat, though he was tall amongst the teeming crowd and dapper in his gentlemanly dress. His fleshy fingers glittered with rings.[20] At fifty-six years old, Risley had travelled far from his beginnings as a circus boy from New Jersey: his showman's ability to charm high society coupled with a talent in spotting new acts for sensation-hungry audiences meant that by now he was extraordinarily rich.[21] His greatest success had been to introduce all of Europe to the 'Japanese Troupe', an astonishing group of jugglers and acrobats from the recently opened eastern empire. Their arrival with Risley at the Paris World Exposition of 1867 intensified the fashion for Japonisme, which inspired such radical new painters as Manet, Degas and Gauguin.[22] During the summer of 1868, Risley's Troupe crowded London's Lyceum Theatre 'every night'.[23] 'We cannot question', reported the theatrical journal the *Era*, 'that the speculation of bringing this troupe over here will be a highly remunerative one'.[24]

Risley had enjoyed a lifetime in the spotlight, yet he was plagued by shadowy desires. He still wanted something money could rarely buy: the smooth blossom of a child, untouched and unwilling.

He saw her again that morning: Maria Mason, alone, waiting for the Fulham omnibus to return her home. She was 'a very pretty, neatly dressed little girl' who was twelve years old, but looked to be about nine or ten.[25] Her older sister Caroline had just bid her goodbye and returned to her own lodgings close by in Soho.[26] When Maria noticed Risley watching her through the throng, she remembered him as the strange old man who had followed her a month before, round and about the low courts of Soho until she chanced upon her omnibus and was driven safely away.[27]

Wishing to escape his renewed attentions, Maria started walking, her cape flapping behind. But again Risley followed. She passed east through the shoppers towards Coventry Street and Leicester Square. At Windmill Street she shot across the road 'almost at the risk of her life in consequence of the vehicles' in a desperate bid to lose him, but still Risley came on.[28] The girl's fearful recklessness caught the attention of a hawk-eyed, ambitious journalist – a younger Henry Hales, now living in London and employed on the *Morning Star* to sell advertising space, with occasional work as a reporter.[29] Standing near Leicester Square, he first observed the fleeing girl, then the large man in her wake. Intuiting that something was amiss, Hales decided to follow them both. When he saw Risley accost the little girl, 'several times [taking] hold of her cape, and [endeavouring] to lead her down some of the lowest slums', he felt certain of his instinct.[30]

Maria repeatedly shook off the heavy-set stranger as they engaged in their tense dance through the streets of Soho. Finally, in Greek Street, she spotted a familiar door: her sister Caroline had once lived at no. 27.[31] Running across the road and knocking 'hard' at the door, she quickly escaped inside. While the disappointed Risley backed away, Hales also knocked at 27. Ensuring Maria was secure with a female lodger, he went in pursuit of Risley.

This uncommon Soho scene, which thanks to Hales was widely reported between August and October 1869, bears an intriguing resemblance to the opening chapter of Robert Louis Stevenson's classic novella, *Strange Case of Dr. Jekyll and Mr. Hyde*. The famous tale of the double life of a respectable middle-aged gentleman who had 'once made the happiness of many' was published in January 1886.[32] Stevenson had feverishly written the story at the end of 1885, a year marked, month after month, by ever more depraved revelations of the moral debauchery of England's wealthiest men; all begun by the trial hearing in April 1885 of Mary Jeffries. Or, as Stevenson put it in *Jekyll and Hyde*, 'you start a question, and it's like starting a stone. You sit quietly on the top of a hill; and away the stone goes, starting others'.[33]

Back in the summer of 1869, while Hales watched Risley pursuing Maria Mason, Stevenson was a lonely, disengaged student at Edinburgh University.[34] Dividing his time between the enlightened order of the city's New Town and the dark tangle of the Old Town, Stevenson soon became the 'habitué of some of the most disreputable dives' of his double-sided city.[35] Mesmerized by wickedness, he spent his empty student days dabbling in brothel-going, boozing and inhaling hashish.[36] Yet this night-time deprivation continued to torment his day-lit Presbyterian conscience; engendering a personal battle between 'the difficulty of being good' and 'the brutishness of being bad' that inspired both his canon and his muses.[37]

In his later writing, Stevenson also recalled many stories from his childhood and his student days, fictionalizing incidents years after the events themselves.[38] And as if to hint at the possible source of his inspiration for the first chapter of *Jekyll and Hyde*, entitled 'Story of the Door', he ends it with the line: 'I shake hands on that, Richard.'[39]

In the opening scene of his book, Stevenson introduces Mr Hyde, who dwelt in Soho, via a conversation between the 'well-known man about town', Mr Enfield, and his dry old friend, Mr Utterson.[40] Like Henry Hales, whose journalistic endeavours entailed that he was his own 'man about town', Enfield begins his 'very odd story' with his recollection of noticing two figures in the street.[41]

'All at once', Enfield recounts to Utterson, 'I saw [a] man stumping along eastward at a good walk, and a girl of maybe eight or ten who was running as hard as she was able down a cross street'.[42]

Just as Richard Risley pursued Maria eastward before mauling her in a Soho street, Stevenson's Hyde 'trampled calmly over the child's body and left her screaming on the ground'. Incensed, Enfield 'took to [his] heels' after him.[43]

Hales too, having seen Maria's plight and found her in a similarly 'agitated state', angrily set off in pursuit of Risley, determined 'to get the man's name'.[44] He soon found him accosting other young girls in the street, one 'not more than seven'.[45] Hales then watched as some local Soho 'women came and tossed over [Risley] dirty water'.[46] With the assistance of a passing policeman, Hales took this as his opportunity to catch hold of Risley and the angry, jostling women quickly surrounded the men.

In Stevenson's version, the 'hellish' sight of such a 'damned Juggernaut' misusing a child also impelled Mr Enfield to collar Hyde.[47] Rather than a policeman, a doctor assisted Enfield in Hyde's apprehension, while a 'group' of women also gathered round them.[48] 'As we were pitching it in red hot,' Enfield tells Utterson, 'we were keeping the women off him as best we could, for they were wild as harpies'.[49]

Under the careful eye of Hales and the policeman, Risley was forced to provide the newspaperman with his real name and address. Hales resolved to ensure that Risley's good name was ruined. In the same way, Enfield threatens Hyde:

> We told the man we could and would make such a scandal out of this, as should make his name stink from one end of London to the other. If he had any friends or any credit we undertook that he should lose them.[50]

Risley responded to Hales by offering to buy his silence. 'I hold a very good position,' he told Hales, 'and would like to talk with you about the matter . . . Money is no object to me'.[51] In *Jekyll and Hyde*, Stevenson allows Hyde a similar line: 'Name your figure', he tells Enfield and then bears out his promise with a cheque.[52]

Enfield's 'reputational blackmail' of Hyde reflected a common cultural anxiety and literary theme of the period, which obsessed over the revelation of black secrets and their subsequent threat to a person's good character.[53] From Charles Dickens' *Bleak House* (1853) to George Eliot's *Middlemarch* (1874) and now Stevenson's *Strange Case of Dr. Jekyll and*

Mr. Hyde (1886), each novel featured characters suffering the all-pervading dread that their fragile veneer of respectability might at any moment shatter and reveal them to be undeserving of 'friends or credit'. Stevenson understood this fear more than most. He had been subject to a real blackmail attempt, by a former lover, in 1877.[54]

According to the cultural historian Stephen Kern, the fear of blackmail 'became for the mid- and later Victorians a greater preoccupation in law and in fiction than either before or since'.[55] Among the middle classes, moral conservatism and the new zeal for social purity fed an industry of advice books, household manuals and morality tales, while for public figures the growth of cheap, sensationalist newspapers meant that moral transgressions were increasingly played out on a national stage.

On 25 October 1869, the celebrated Professor Risley was forced to attend London's Old Bailey for the attempted kidnap or abduction of Maria Mason, a child under sixteen. There were no other laws extant under which he could be charged. At Hales' instigation, Risley's prosecution had been pursued by the Society for the Protection of Women and Children with the assistance of their lawyers, Mr William Shaen and Mr West – the same men who prosecuted Mary Jeffries sixteen years later. Similarly, the prosecuting barrister at Risley's trial was Edward Besley, while Risley's defence barrister was Montagu Williams.

On the day, it was Williams who triumphed. The Central Criminal Court's all-male jury concluded Risley was not guilty, prompting a spontaneous burst of applause from his gentleman friends.[56] But no matter the verdict, the social damage was done. Like Stevenson's tortured Jekyll, Risley's personal torment had only just begun.

The following Sunday, 31 October, Hales' future employer, the *Lloyd's Weekly* newspaper, printed a letter from Risley in which he revealed the insidious, damaging legacy of a Victorian scandal.

> Though the verdict was unanimously . . . given in my favour, there still seems a taint of suspicion remaining . . . I address the public with a view to assure all . . . that I am guiltless, not only in deed, but in thought, not only legally but morally. The accusation of 'unlawfully taking hold' of a young child fell on me like a thunderbolt. It has caused me mental agony indescribable.

Despite his entreaties, Risley's fame and fortune never recovered from his humiliation at the hands of Henry Hales. Nor did he ever escape the public suspicion that he harboured an abhorrent sexuality. The 'indescribable mental agony' he claimed to have suffered found its echo in Stevenson's angst-ridden story, and like Dr Jekyll, Professor Risley eventually succumbed to a Hyde-like insanity. 'Broken down in constitution', he died penniless in a Philadelphia lunatic asylum on 25 May 1874.[57]

Strange Case of Dr. Jekyll and Mr. Hyde became, in 1886, an instant classic.[58] Stevenson's exploration of the dual existence of a Victorian gentleman touched a raw cultural nerve. 'I hope the day is past', wrote Josephine Butler, 'for a man who was corrupt in his private life and character to be a useful, just or beneficent ruler'.[59] Among others, she was arguing against the ideas of Cardinal John Henry Newman, who had, in his influential 1864 autobiography, *Apologia Pro Vita Sua*, reiterated the case for duality: 'A just indignation would be felt', Newman wrote, 'against a writer who brought forward wantonly the weaknesses of a great man, though the whole world knew that they existed'.[60] Newman argued for the tacit acceptance of 'the double' to the social good. To gossip or *know* of men's 'weaknesses' was inevitable in society, but to ratify such knowledge in print or in the courtroom was a far greater crime than the transgression itself.[61] It was far more honourable to those who, as Gladstone believed, 'ruled out of a sense of duty and in the national interest' to protect the innocence of the British public by drawing a veil over the sins of other gentlemen, as well as ensuring to cover up one's own.[62]

Butler, Dyer and their supporters disagreed. They believed this entrenched duplicity only served to protect the guilty rich at the expense of the innocent poor. They walk 'amongst the pure', said the preacher James B. Wookey, 'as if there was nothing in their soul-and-body murdering life of which they need be ashamed'.[63] By exposing Mary Jeffries' clients in a public courtroom, the London Committee hoped to pull back the patrician 'veil' and reveal the abuses it concealed. The events inside the Westminster courtroom during April 1885 were but one round in an ongoing contest for social pre-eminence between the old ways of the ruling elite and the values of the morally minded, rising middle-class.

*

'What *are* you?' Monty Williams asked Jeremiah, abruptly opening his cross-examination of the London Committee's private detective on Friday 10 April 1885.[64] Jeremiah hesitated. Throughout the day, rain had drummed against the flat courtroom roof and its geometric windowpanes. 'That is a very simple question,' prompted Williams.

'No occupation at present,' replied Jeremiah, 'I am employed by solicitors.'

'Who?'

'Messrs [William] Shaen and Roscoe.'

'Are they the solicitors to the society prosecuting this case?'

'Yes.'

'Did they seek you or did you seek them out originally?'

asked Williams, wanting to imply that the ex-police inspector had offered Shaen and the London Committee information in exchange for personal vengeance.

'Ah!' replied Jeremiah. 'That's a question.'

'It is a question you will have to answer.'

'Not in that shape sir,' said Jeremiah.

'Did you find them out or did they find you?'

'Neither.'

'Did you communicate with them first or did they you?'

'I went to a printer.'

'I will have an answer to my question,' insisted Williams.

'I am telling you,' replied Jeremiah, equally bullish.

'You'll get it if you let him finish,' D'Eyncourt chastised Williams.

'I like it my way,' Williams responded petulantly.

'And I'll have it my way,' Jeremiah said quietly.

This second pre-trial hearing came to be dominated by Williams' hostile questioning of every aspect of Jeremiah's past life and present motivation. Williams accused him of making 'wholesale charges against his brother inspectors of being bribed'; 'conspiring against his superintendent' and of producing evidence about Jeffries that 'carried with it the greatest improbability'.[65]

'When do you say you had this conversation with Mrs Jeffries when she told you about the houses?' asked Williams.

'About August 1882.'

'It was a long time ago then, were you in uniform?'

'Yes I was on duty.'

'And being an Inspector of the district and in uniform you say that she volunteered this statement to you?'

'Yes and offered me gold, offered me what I took to be gold.'

'I am asking you. Did she volunteer the statement to you?'

'Yes she would tell anybody.'

'Did she tell you it was no good for the police to watch her houses?'

'Yes.'

'As she only did business with gentlemen in the highest rank of life?'

'That is it sir.'

'It was all part of the conversation?'

'Yes sir.'

Several contemporary commentators picked up on this information, including the editor William Stead, the man who had publicized Reverend Mearns' pamphlet, *The Bitter Cry of Outcast London*. 'Just think what this amounts to', he wrote in the *Pall Mall Gazette*:

> Here is an ex-police inspector who swears that a certain creature – we refuse to call her woman – kept no fewer than eight houses of ill-fame, from which she was in the habit of exporting English girls to foreign voluptuaries . . . Yet because [she was] patronized by 'persons in high life' [her activities were] systematically overlooked, and when [the] inspector . . . reports the case to his superiors, he is laughed at and snubbed . . . for refusing a bribe. The matter cannot be allowed to rest here.[66]

Which is of course exactly what Williams and Jeffries' clientele most feared.

'You have got a "lingering fancy" for this case,' said Williams, insinuating that Jeremiah's motives were dubious.

'I have got a "fancy" for anybody who pays me for my work,' was Jeremiah's swift retort.[67]

'You are testing his credibility, not trying the Inspector,' D'Eyncourt eventually interceded: one of his several attempts to curtail Williams' aggression.[68] The Old Etonian QC's desire to destroy Jeremiah's character will have been intensified by his concern over the knowledge the 'private detective' carried against the brothel-keeper's clients. In terms of reputational blackmail, Jeremiah and his little red notebook of names were a walking liability, to be feared and reviled by any man who had once skulked up the steps to Jeffries' townhouse door.

By the third and final pre-trial hearing on Thursday 16 April 1885, word of the revelations to be heard in the Westminster courtroom had spread. 'The proceedings', reported *Reynolds's Newspaper*, 'seem to occasion extraordinary interest, judging from the number of persons who endeavoured [to enter] the court'.[69] Seated now close by Dyer and Wookey in the crammed public gallery was a mysterious civil servant named Mr Batchelor, from the Solicitor's Department of the Treasury (the legal arm of the Home Office).[70] He too heard the questioning of another batch of Jeremiah's witnesses: servants, neighbours and surly prostitutes who repeatedly testified to Jeffries' 'gay' houses in Church Street. Mr Batchelor had been sent to observe the final day's events at the behest of the Home Secretary, Sir William Harcourt. When Harcourt was later asked why he needed a spy at Jeffries' pre-trial hearing he was unable to provide a coherent explanation.[71]

Thanks to Mr Batchelor, Harcourt will certainly have known within a matter of hours that in the face of Jeremiah Minahan's comprehensive evidence, the magistrate had no choice but to commit Jeffries to trial at the Middlesex Sessions House in three weeks' time. It would appear that Harcourt did not welcome Mr Batchelor's news. For within a few short hours he seemed to be making his own attempt to scupper Jeffries' forthcoming trial, by picking up where Montagu Williams had left off and publicly traducing Jeremiah's reputation.

Shortly after four o'clock that day, Edward Sheil, a popular Irish Nationalist MP, broke his habitual reticence to query

Harcourt in the House of Commons.[72] Sheil was an eloquent man who suffered the misfortune of a rather squeaky voice. He normally reserved his political persuasions for his quieter, backroom manoeuvrings as a Home Rule Whip.[73] But after the final hearing of Mary Jeffries, he felt impelled to make an exception and confront Sir William Harcourt direct.

'Has the Secretary of State's attention been called,' he asked, 'to the statement of Mr. Minahan, ex-police inspector of the T division, a witness called for the prosecution of Mrs Jeffries, of Chelsea, [who] was laughed at . . . for refusing to accept gold as a bribe? And have you taken any steps towards ascertaining the truth of his statement?'[74]

Rising from his position on the front bench, eye-glasses lightly swinging from his outstretched right forefinger, Harcourt mustered his response. 'I have made inquiry into this matter [and] from the information I have received [Jeremiah Minahan's] statement is not true.'[75]

In advance of Jeffries' criminal trial, in a case based largely on Jeremiah Minahan's evidence, the Home Secretary had just risked prejudicing the prosecution's chances by publicly pronouncing its key witness a liar.

Harcourt knew he was protected from contempt of court by parliamentary privilege and that Jeremiah could do little to counter his public affront. What Harcourt was less aware of was the actual impact of his words on Jeremiah. Where Harcourt was a man who 'always seemed singularly insensitive to the pain and offence that his hard words could not fail to give', Jeremiah was a man unable to forget these same 'hard words'.[76] Instead, he began gathering Harcourt's repeated insults together, as fuel for his revenge. Now he was certain the Home Secretary was out to debunk Mary Jeffries' forthcoming trial.[77] He also thought he knew why.

*

Undeterred by the cold and rain and 'elaborately dressed in black', Mary Jeffries made a brief announcement on the morning of her trial to all those gathered outside the stately Middlesex Sessions House on Clerkenwell Green.[78] It was Tuesday 5 May 1885. 'Nothing can be done with me!' she boldly declared once again. 'As my clients and patrons are of the highest social rank.'[79]

While the old bawd nonchalantly walked up to her fate, Alfred Dyer was rebuffed from even ascending the grand sessions-house steps. 'Jurymen only,' a policeman told him and his 'three other friends'. The ever-nettling Dyer insisted on 'his right as a representative of the press' and eventually gained access.[80] Other 'friends' were informed that the court was already overcrowded, only to discover inside that the public gallery was empty.[81] The busiest area was actually the long, curving magistrates' bench, which groaned under the 'unusually large' number of beaks present to ensure that Assistant-Judge Edlin made the right decision.[82] At ten thirty, before the court had even formally opened, Montagu Williams arrived and demanded that his old adversary, the prosecuting barrister Edward Besley, retire to a back room with him for a 'private consultation'.[83]

Half an hour ticked slowly by. The architecture of the courtroom with its lofty ceiling and its three elegant windows mirrored the lordly homes inhabited by many of Jeffries' clients.[84] Jeremiah, Dyer and the London Committee waited. Their witnesses waited too. All were 'ready to swear to the presence of exalted personages and high officials' at Jeffries' brothels, 'princes and dukes, minsters of the crown and members of parliament were said to be among her customers'.[85] Also in attendance was Maria Watts, who once nursed two adolescent virgins through their violation and disease in Jeffries' Church Street houses. When the two barristers returned at eleven, Mary Jeffries was put in the dock.

'Say you are guilty,' Monty Williams ordered.[86]

'Guilty,' repeated Jeffries, to the paradoxical horror of those who had wrought her prosecution. They wanted Jeffries found guilty, but not before the names of her clientele were revealed to the public. As Williams and Besley well knew, Jeffries' guilty plea 'prevented the prosecution bringing forward the evidence . . . which would have startled the nation'.[87] Worse still, Besley, who had just pocketed a sizeable portion of the London Committee's fee for his part in the prosecution – the total cost of the case was over £300 – then made a speech apparently in support of Jeffries.[88] 'If he had been retained by the defence,' fumed Dyer, 'he could not have succeeded better.'[89]

'The case really resolved itself into allowing people to assemble together for improper purposes,' insisted Besley, as if discussing an unorthodox prayer meeting. 'There was no opportunity for outsiders to notice.'[90] Except of course, the 'outsider' Frederick Beale, butler to the Reverend Povah of 123 Church Street, who would testify to being woken at 'all hours of the night' in answering the door to 'gay' women who mistook the clergyman's home for a brothel.[91] Or George Cook, who was to lose his Church Street tenants because 'the nuisance caused by Mrs Jeffries' houses [was] as bad as ever'; or even Jeremiah Minahan, who in daring to report Jeffries to his superiors had lost his career and his pension.[92]

Taking on board Williams' accompanying plea that Jeffries was 'sixty-six' and 'of ill-health', the judge chose not to opt for the maximum penalty of two years' imprisonment. Instead Mr Edlin charged Jeffries a not inconsiderable fine of £200 and bound her over to be 'of good behaviour for two years'.[93] Yet in the very same court, one woman had recently been condemned to five years' penal servitude for filching a ham, while another received the same for pilfering a pair of trousers.[94] By comparison, Jeffries' two decades of stealing virtue received light punishment. With some aplomb she paid off her fine immediately, then swept down the courtroom steps and away into the barbarous city of unrepentant lust and liberty.

Part Two

MARYLEBONE 1885

Chapter Eight

I Want One Younger Than You

> Why should the procuress be let off practically scot-free, while the policeman whom she attempted in vain to corrupt was practically ruined?
>
> William Stead, editor of the *Pall Mall Gazette*, 1885[1]

With her singular side-rolling gait, Rebecca Jarrett pushed through the crowds on Monday afternoon, 25 May 1885.[2] Using her domed walking stick to plot her course across Waterloo Station, she parted the day-trippers and the porters with barrows, the damp parasols and shifty pocket-divers. At the exit by York Street she turned towards Waterloo Bridge, away from the sulking blue stacks of the slums and manufactories to the south.

Northumberland Street lay just over the river, close by Trafalgar Square. At no. 2, she saw a terraced office block, seven sash windows wide.[3] She heard the rumble of the printing presses in the building's machine-room, as, one stair at a time, she lurched into the inky darkness above. In a grubby office, tucked amidst a clutter of papers, a desk, table, tallboy and an overstuffed armchair, she found the stranger she had travelled from Winchester to meet.[4]

He went by the name of 'Charles Kennedy'. Their meeting on that afternoon was to remain secret, their relations known only to a rare few. It was Whit Monday, a public holiday for most but not for 'Kennedy', who rarely sat still or stopped working. He had daily deadlines to meet, and when moving about the city preferred to go at a sprint, 'running full-tilt' down Pall Mall or up Regent Street to free his pent-up energy, like a spring wound 'too tight' and suddenly released.[5]

Settling herself before him, Jarrett saw a man in his mid-thirties with a reddish beard and thick, bushy hair. His piercing blue eyes animated a careworn face and his barely repressed vigour, his impetuous and frank manner, were candidly sensual: the journalist Elizabeth Lynn Linton once described him as a man who 'exuded semen through the skin', and the early sexologist, Havelock Ellis, reported that the 'mastery of [his] sexuality was [his] great problem'.[6] An old bawd like Rebecca Jarrett will have attuned herself to his restlessness, but she was also wary of the man's true purpose.

She was right to be on her guard. He had summoned her to his office on Whit Monday after consulting Jeremiah Minahan. It was Jeremiah who suggested that in the wake of Mary Jeffries' trial, the procuresses and Continental *placeurs* would 'accommodate no one but their old customers'.[7] Any new face or fresh 'inquiry for virgins and little girls by one who had not given his proofs', Jeremiah explained, inevitably 'excited suspicion and alarm' in the netherworld.[8] Acting on his advice, Kennedy had found Jarrett. It was because of Jeremiah that she was chosen, because of him that the momentous events unfurled as they did.

Kennedy had been informed that the toxic spirit of the slums still coursed through Jarrett's veins, however much she had dampened the fever with gin and however much now she cast her hopes to God. She was brittle, but she would do.

*

In the three weeks since the disappointment of Mary Jeffries' trial both the religious and the radical press had loudly pronounced astonishment at the 'absurd' leniency of Judge Edlin's sentence.[9] Amidst the accusations that this had been a 'mockery of justice' came several calls for the Home Secretary, Sir William Harcourt, to re-investigate Minahan's original claims.[10] If by pleading her guilt Jeffries had blithely admitted the truth of her several bawdy houses, then surely it was true that she had also bribed her local police officers? 'If the demand for a thorough and impartial investigation of the charge of Mr. Minahan against the police is not acceded to,' warned the *Christian*, 'the inevitable assumption by the public will be that the authorities are afraid of the result'.[11]

Yet when the Liberal MP for Hackney raised this very point in Parliament, the Home Secretary's set response only added further insult to Jeremiah's gathering pile of Harcourt-inflicted injury.[12] The MP was a Scotsman named James Stuart, who asked Sir William why Mary Jeffries had been subjected to a fine for her disorderly houses in Chelsea when in the same courtroom, ten days later, one James Barrett had received a sentence of six months' imprisonment with hard labour for exactly the same crime?[13] He also suggested Harcourt should now 'grant an impartial investigation into the whole of this case and also [that] of Inspector Minahan, the circumstances attending to his dismissal from the Police Force, and how far these were connected with the woman Jeffries'.

'With head thrown back and chest well forward', the gladiatorial Harcourt embarked on his lengthy reply.[14] He read to the Commons a private letter that he had sent to Jeremiah's Chelsea MP, Joseph Firth, the year before, which gives some insight into his personal take on the case, as well as his irritation with Jeremiah's tenacity.

> He had been an Inspector, and in consequence of the unfavourable reports of his conduct he was put down to

> the rank of sergeant, whereupon he resigned; and he afterwards put pressure in all sorts of ways upon me to reinstate him.[15]

Having reiterated that Jeremiah's allegations against the officers of T: Division 'proved to be without foundation', Harcourt then added some fabrications of his own, implying that Jeremiah was actually a meddlesome and habitual liar. 'Minahan', he explained, had made similar false charges 'in another Division in which he had previously served [Bow Street], and on that occasion, was merely transferred to a different Division [Chelsea]'. According to Harcourt, Jeremiah had even 'expressed gratitude for the leniency' of this punishment. He then rounded up with his expressed belief that any suggestion of the Chelsea police having 'connived or desired that the [Jeffries] case should be hushed up' was groundless.[16]

The following day, Friday 22 May 1885, Harcourt capped his previous day's performance by destroying any chance of the Criminal Law Amendment Bill being passed in the Commons before the imminent general election. This was the *third* version of the Bill, which aimed to increase the age of consent in England to fifteen (reduced from sixteen to appease opponents), and in essence its purpose was to protect 'young girls from the wiles of notorious procuresses like the infamous Mrs. Jeffries'.[17] Though he had been against the repeal of the Contagious Diseases Acts, Harcourt had appeared in public to support this legislation. He had played an active role in setting up the Lords Select Committee on the Protection of Young Girls in 1881 and in a private letter to the journalist Arnold White, written from his yacht during the recent Whitsun recess, had claimed he attached the 'highest importance' to the Bill. An expedient politician, the Home Secretary understood that 'the poorer classes' had the protection of girls most 'fully at heart'.[18] Nonetheless his actions in Parliament betrayed a strange, private ambivalence.

Harcourt's death-blow was to introduce the Bill's second reading late on the Friday afternoon before the Whitsun recess. The House was relatively empty, with just over forty MPs present – barely enough for a quorum (the minimum number of MPs to vote). These forty dwindled as the afternoon disappeared to a hopeless twenty men.[19] The Conservative MP George Cavendish-Bentinck, or as Josephine Butler called him, the 'brothel-keeper's representative' in the Commons, then added the final strike by prolonging the debate until the time to vote had run out.[20] At seven in the evening the Criminal Law Amendment Bill was postponed by Parliament – indefinitely. For Alfred Dyer and his fellow members of the London Committee, some of whom had gathered that afternoon in the Commons' gallery to hear the debate, the verdict marked the failure of five years' work and toil. The age of consent in England was to remain at thirteen.

Jeremiah's efforts and sacrifices, his investigation and hopes for justice had all come to naught. No longer required by Dyer, he was reduced to working as a 'rent and debt collector' to survive, an occupation that was generally despised.[21] Though 'more paying' than the £2 a week he had pocketed from the London Committee, such employment was a humbling reduction in circumstance to a former inspector and to his wife.[22] 'It is *not* a genteel calling,' insists a lowly lodging-house keeper in Charles Dickens' *Bleak House*, 'and most people do object to it'.[23] But there were new lights on the horizon.

*

While Sir William Harcourt's harsh words further bruised Jeremiah's pride, in others they aroused curiosity. People wanted to know more about the former policeman and to assess his integrity for themselves. The *Christian Commonwealth* newspaper published an article about him on 4 June 1885, under the front-page headline 'WHO IS EX-INSPECTOR MINAHAN?' 'Probably', the journalist gushed, 'there is not in that force a man of finer physical appearance and proportions. [Jeremiah Minahan] stands over six feet, his frame is massive and he is in the prime of his life'. He also appears to have been persuaded by the truth of Jeremiah's tale and his reasons for leaving the Metropolitan Police. Jeremiah 'had to resign', he declared. 'This was his only chance of getting his case inquired into, the rule of the force being that resignation must precede inquiry. But . . . he was, as anybody can see, practically driven out of the force'. As the man ultimately accountable for the activities of the Metropolitan Police, Harcourt was responsible for removing Jeremiah's status and security. 'He is suffering solely for his brave exposure of wrong,' continued the *Commonwealth* report, ' . . . and Members of Parliament and electors are content to sit down with this!'

Moved by the ex-inspector's predicament, the paper issued an immediate call for donations from its readers to compensate Jeremiah for the sacrifice of his pension. Over the following week, contributions flowed into the London offices of the *Christian Commonwealth*, the *Christian* and to the *Sentinel* on Paternoster Row, where Alfred Dyer was running a similar campaign. 'One or two communications' received by the *Commonwealth* suggested some readers had 'faith in the Home Secretary' and sided with the view that Jeremiah was motivated solely by revenge upon his brother officers at Chelsea.[24] But the paper's socialist editor, the Reverend George Brooks, chastised the dissenters: 'SIR W. HARCOURT says brave things from his place in Parliament where he cannot be contradicted, but why does he not make the enquiry?'[25]

One reason was that Harcourt was too distracted in May

1885 by the imperilled state of Gladstone's Liberal government to worry much about Jeremiah Minahan. The Cabinet were split over their disastrous endeavour to evacuate British citizens from an Islamist insurgency in the Sudan, which had resulted in the murder of General Gordon in Khartoum in January. Flouting orders, Gordon had stayed on in Khartoum to valiantly assist the Egyptians in fighting off the Mahdi. The government prevaricated, eventually sending troops to assist Gordon's rogue antics, but they arrived too late and found the severed head of this popular English hero shamefully displayed in a tree. Closer to home, the Fenian terrorist attacks reached new heights in the early months of 1885 with bombings in Westminster Hall, the Tower of London and – most awkwardly for Sir William Harcourt – the House of Commons. Harcourt still believed that Ireland could only be governed by force, while the Radicals in the Cabinet, and increasingly Gladstone, advocated conciliation and Home Rule.[26] By late May there were 'daily and almost hourly resignations and withdrawals' in the divided Cabinet which acted, Harcourt complained, 'like a man afflicted with epilepsy, one fit succeeds another'.[27]

With the Home Secretary distracted by his own Cabinet's survival, political opponents more interested in the Liberal Party's demise began to see a useful opportunity in Jeremiah. The ex-inspector discovered new allies whose personal ideals and political agendas had also been thwarted by the bullish Harcourt. One such man was the influential and impulsive leader-writer who had abruptly called Rebecca Jarrett to his offices on Whit Monday, 25 May 1885.

*

Having established his own disguise, 'Kennedy' now ordered Jarrett to uncover her life to him in its starkest detail. He was horrified by what he heard.

She was born in Pimlico between 1846 and 1850, her mother's thirteenth child. Her father was said to be a 'well to do' rope merchant, who had once run a shop in Borough.[28] Accounts of Jarrett's life vary: one states her father was a heavy drinker, another that he never touched a drop, but it is clear that he was a womanizer, who eventually left Jarrett's mother to struggle alone.[29] 'Some will say', she wrote, 'what a *bad* mother she must have been but please *don't*, it was my wretched father's doing he left her . . . and lived with other women . . . she took to drink, it was the trouble that drove her to it'.[30] As a child she was 'left a lot to herself' except on Sundays, when her mother would wash her 'very fair hair', 'then if it was fine she [took] me to Cremorne Gardens' from 'only eight or ten years of age'.[31] (Jarrett's recollection of her 'very fair hair' is questionable. In later life, she was noted for having 'almost black' hair – which may have been dyed – but her 'complexion' was also notably 'dark'.)[32] 'You wonder', she explained, 'why so young I got in the way of an impure life why I was brought up in it.'[33] Soon her mother 'got me in the way to look for my share'.[34]

> I was only 12 years of age. My mother was a bit proud of me. I was inclined to be tall, fair . . . blue eyes. I remember [I] had round my neck a string of great blue beads she kept me clean that was my attraction.[35]

Jarrett became a fixture at the Cremorne Gardens, another fresh doxie for hire. Four years on, when her two older brothers returned from sea and learned of the life their younger sister was leading, they turned her into the street. She was sixteen.[36] Jarrett claimed she 'never [saw her] brothers or mother again', but this was untrue. She certainly remained in contact with her mother and may have been using this falsehood to obscure the fact that her mother was soon running a brothel of her own.[37] But Jarrett did depart the family home as an adolescent and plunged into an alcoholic abyss that lasted two decades. Babies were born and lost; she worked as a prostitute and brothel-keeper in London, Manchester and Bristol. Repeating her own early experience, she procured young girls into her trade and sacrificed them to her gentlemen clients.

'These girls,' she told Kennedy, 'were usually about thirteen or fourteen, and . . . they were brought into brothels, were often drugged, and handed over.'[38]

Kennedy was disgusted. 'If all [is] truth,' he told her, 'you must prove it, it [is] too horrible to be believed merely upon the word of a person like [you]'.[39] He demanded that Jarrett purchase more girls 'for him' and thrust £10 on her. She objected, claiming that she felt 'pained' and 'hurt' by opening so much of herself to him and by his bullying tone.[40] After two hours of hard talk she gave in, accepting the money and escaping into the late afternoon. She was to play a 'tool' to yet another man: she would go and find one last girl.[41]

The following morning, Tuesday 26 May 1885, Jarrett bought a jacket to match the 'very light brown stuff dress . . . trimmed with scotch plaid' loaned by a friend for her purpose.[42] She then headed for the epicentre of Outcast London: Whitechapel.[43] Making the same journey, the French journalist Blanchard Jerrold recalled how his hansom's progress soon became 'slow and difficult: angry words are exchanged with the driver; groups of gossiping or quarrelling men and women block the road; the houses are black and grim'.[44]

On the wide, wild Whitechapel Road, Jarrett bought earrings and a brooch, a 'pair of straw-coloured gloves' and a hat to finish her outfit. Whitechapel was the perfect place to find a gay hat, as Montagu Williams would later recall in his own book about London life.

> No one who is a stranger to the East End can have any idea of the kind of female headgear in vogue in that

> locality. The material is cotton velvet, the colour, gaudy, and the size, enormous . . . no matter how shabby or dirty be the rest of the clothing . . . The size and colour of the feathers are points on which there is keen rivalry among the denizens of court and alley.[45]

Jarrett spent £2 putting together her costume.[46] She then walked further east, a flesh-monger returned to her old habitats. 'Whistles, shouts, oaths, growls, and the brazen laughter of tipsy women' filled the air as she turned into Lady Lake Grove, a Whitechapel lair of bawds and old trolls, their bullies and their flashmen.[47] Inside no. 23 she threw down a shilling for a drink, then opened a transaction with a woman inside, who might provide the pure goods Kennedy so desired. Returning a few days later to follow up the deal, Jarrett was taken for a dupe. Having paid out £2 of Kennedy's £10, the promised girl was 'brought in' but promptly 'ran away'.[48]

Swallowing her losses, on Tuesday 2 June, seven days after she first met Kennedy, Jarrett changed tack. This time she decided to try her luck with 'old friends' in the more familiar haunt of Marylebone.[49] At a quarter to eleven that morning she knocked on the door of Nancy Broughton, who lived with her husband 'Bash' (John) in a single room at no. 37 on the dilapidated Charles Street.

The two friends had worked together two years earlier, then Bash and Nancy had allowed 'Becky' Jarrett to share their small room and convalesce when she was 'taken bad with [her] diseased hip' and lost her job at Claridge's Hotel.[50] Returning there, Jarrett reacquainted herself with the pictures of unsmiling popes, the crucifixes and Stations of the Cross that plastered Nancy's walls.[51] Nancy was a Catholic with an ongoing weakness for whisky, which she called her 'lively'.[52] Though she would later deny it, she knew of Jarrett's 'bad' life: that she used to 'carry on' with the male staff in the

Claridge's laundry room over the dinner hour; that she 'had kept gay houses' in the past.[53]

Now Jarrett told Nancy and her young visiting neighbour, Jane Farrer, 'I have a six-roomed house at Wimbledon and I want a little girl to clean around the carpet and the oilcloth, do you know of one?'

Nancy immediately turned to Jane. 'Jane, will you go to place?'

'Yes, Mrs Broughton,' said Jane.

Jarrett turned and looked Jane over. 'She is too big, how old are you?'

'Nineteen.'

'You are too old and too big, I want one younger than you,' said Jarrett. Outside the window, the three saw another girl named Lizzie Stephens walk by. Nancy called her into the room.

'How old are you?' she asked Lizzie.

'Sixteen,' said Lizzie.

'That's too old,' said Jarrett, 'I only want a girl to save me kneeling.'

Lizzie passed news of the position to her younger friends. One of the nearest was Eliza Armstrong, who soon knocked on Nancy's door. A short, sturdy girl, Eliza had 'dark black eyes' and a pouty top lip.[54]

'I should like to go to service,' she said.

'Where is your mother?' asked Nancy.

'Upstairs,' said Eliza (referring to her family's first-floor room on the opposite side of the street).

When Eliza returned with her mother, Mrs Armstrong looked Jarrett over. She saw her seated heavily in her 'stylish' scotch plaid and flash Whitechapel baubles, her inelegant features framed by a racy 'Piccadilly' fringe. She may too have noted the ostentatious hat laid on the bed. She did not like what she saw.

'You will not have my child,' she said, and walked out.

Apparently unperturbed by Mrs Armstrong's brusque departure, Jarrett then turned to Nancy.

'How old is Eliza?' she asked.

'Thirteen,' said Nancy.

'Do you think she is a pure girl?'

'Yes,' said Nancy.

Between seven and seven-thirty that evening Nancy saw Mrs Armstrong in the grey cobbled street. She was clearly the 'worse for drink'.[55] Though Mrs Armstrong claimed to work as a laundress, she had resigned much of her life to the public house.

'I am not going to let my child go for any bloody whore . . . You can go and ***** yourself,' she told Nancy before dissolving back into the evening's creep.

Next morning though, she changed her mind. Wednesday 3 June dawned blue and bright. It was Derby Day, an annual celebration, traditionally spent in drink.[56] When Jarrett limped back to Nancy's lodgings, Mrs Armstrong was watching from her first-floor window and, worried another neighbour's girl might steal Eliza's chance, she followed Jarrett inside, quick as a rat. First she expressed her regret to Nancy for her words the previous evening. She then set about the purpose of her visit.

'Are you still in want of a girl?' she asked.

'Are you willing to let me have Eliza?' said Jarrett.

'Yes, for after you left yesterday Eliza had done nothing but worry me about it,' explained Mrs Armstrong, pretending to the pleasure of indulging her child.[57]

'You must be perfectly willing for her to go, or I will not take her,' said Jarrett, who then turned to Eliza.

'Are you willing to go? You must be willing to go, or I cannot take you,' she said.

'Yes,' replied Eliza, 'I should like to go.'[58]

By three o'clock she was changed out of the dull dress supplied by her mother and into the swell 'rig-out' especially purchased for her by Jarrett, the purple dress and red-feathered hat.[59]

As if to force Mrs Armstrong to heed the feather's warning, Jarrett caught her alone in Nancy's passageway.

'Look at the clothes I have bought for Eliza,' she insisted, holding them up to the mother. 'What do you think of them?'

'Very nice,' replied Mrs Armstrong.

'If she is a pure girl,' said Jarrett, 'I will keep her. If she is not I will return her the same way as I took her.'[60]

Eliza's mother said nothing.

She then disappeared home briefly before returning with a cut and bleeding mouth. Her husband Charles had punched her in his dinner hour because she wanted to attend a funeral in Kilburn that afternoon. The blow appeared only to have increased her determination to go, and she asked Nancy or Jarrett to lend her the sixpence omnibus fare to the cemetery. Having already paid Nancy one sovereign for procuring Eliza and planning more to follow, Jarrett took this as her cue to slip a sovereign into Mrs Armstrong's palm as payment for her child. In the end Jarrett claimed to have paid out £5 for Eliza: £4 to Nancy and £1 to her mother.

'This will do better,' said Mrs Armstrong, who pocketed the money and left. Nancy, Jarrett and even Eliza did not see her again that day.

Mrs Armstrong had not mentioned to her violent husband the imminent hire of Eliza. She took her daughter's discarded clothes home and squirreled them away in a box. She did not even go to the funeral.[61] Instead, she spent Derby Day drinking Jarrett's coin in the local pub, until one of her regular gin furies led to another dry night in a damp police cell.[62]

*

Eliza Armstrong and Rebecca Jarrett were initially destined for Albany Street, to the east of Regent's Park; a long street with a smart cavalry barracks at its northern end. Many of its four-storey townhouses were 'gay', serving as male and female brothels.[63] It was a notorious centre for vice and it was here, at no. 16, that Eliza's true plight began to reveal itself.[64]

That evening she was introduced to the man orchestrating her purchase, Jarrett's acquaintance Kennedy, though he did not tell Eliza his name.

'Do you go to school?' he asked.[65]

'Yes,' said Eliza

'What school?'

'The Board school.'

'Do you go to Sunday school?'

'Yes, to Harrow Road Sunday school at nine in the morning . . . and to the Richmond Street Sunday school on Sunday nights.'

'Do you go to any of the treats [outings] there?'

'Yes once to Epping Forest and twice to Richmond.'

After taking tea with Kennedy and her new mistress, Eliza travelled with Jarrett by hansom cab to a house just off Dorset Square at 3 Milton Street. As with Adelene Tanner, her sale commenced with the authentication of her most valuable possession – her virtue. A Frenchwoman named Madame Louise Mourey occupied the house. She was short and stout with 'a flat sallow face, a turn-up nose [and] beady eyes'.[66] She took Eliza down to a little side room with a bed. Without saying a word she pulled up the girl's clothes and deftly pushed her hands inside Eliza's undergarments, feeling her 'private parts, touching [her] flesh'.[67] In shock Eliza wriggled free and fled the room.

'*She* is a dirty woman,' Eliza complained. Jarrett did not respond.[68]

At around 9.30 p.m., a cabman named Henry Smith was

waiting for his next fare at the stand on Quebec Street, a short walk from Madame Mourey's.[69] Here Charles Kennedy and a tall swarthy gentleman who went by the name of 'Mr Jacques' approached and asked him to drive over the Marylebone Road and up to Milton Street. They ordered Smith to wait just before, but not directly outside the house at no. 3, which was a semi-detached villa with a tree on its vacant side. Kennedy and Mr Jacques hovered close by on the pavement.

When the door of no. 3 opened, a young girl and a lame woman emerged. Having children of his own, Smith caught Eliza's countenance and thought she 'looked rather down'.[70] 'She did not appear to be crying,' Smith thought, 'but she appeared as though she hardly knew what she was up to, nor where she was going'.[71] He noticed Jarrett too, dressed now in a drab black dolman mantle (a tailored cape). Watching her approach, the thought struck Smith that 'a good deal of [Jarrett's] lameness was put on'.[72]

Once inside Smith's cab, Jarrett asked him to take them on to Poland Street in Soho. Now Smith began to suspect 'there was some foul play going on', for Smith 'knew the character of the houses' on Poland Street and was worried for the girl. Still, he obediently followed the order.[73] While Jarrett went into a ham and beef shop on Poland Street to get change from her sovereign for the fare, Smith was startled to spot Kennedy and Mr Jacques again, as he thought they had been left behind on Milton Street. 'They must have got into another cab and drove behind us at a great rate,' he later recalled, 'for I went pretty fast.'[74] He lingered in Poland Street, watching the group with 'a mind to interfere', but Jarrett and the two men outwitted him, moving up the street, out of view. Smith eventually went on his way, but for weeks was troubled by these strange Derby-night scenes.[75]

After she saw that the cabman had safely disappeared,

Jarrett led Eliza back to the ham and beef shop at no. 32. Meats for sale dangled in its brightly lit window. Next to the shop front was a door. Eliza noticed two men enter this door ahead of her but in the darkness, she did not recognize Kennedy.[76] Once inside, Jarrett paid the owner of the brothel £1 for the use of a bedroom. Eliza was taken upstairs. She saw Kennedy and Mr Jacques in a side room drinking brown liquor. They did not acknowledge her or Jarrett as the two passed by.

'Would you go to bed?' asked Jarrett, once they were both inside their room. The bed was shrouded with curtains.

'I don't want to go to bed yet,' Eliza said.[77]

Jarrett gave her a picture book to read, then entreated the child again to go to bed. Eliza undressed and got in between the covers, and Jarrett lay beside her on top of the bed-clothes. Outside, hoarse shouts and screams marked the end of Derby Day and another soused Soho night. Lying quiet in their secluded gloom, Eliza suddenly felt Jarrett 'put a hand-kerchief up to [her] nose'.[78] Disgusted by the 'nasty' smell, Eliza 'threw it away' but Jarrett was insistent. 'Give a good sniff up,' she said.

The kerchief was damp with the cloying sweetness of chloroform. Enclosed in the darkness of the curtains, Eliza then heard the bedroom door open and though she could see nothing beyond the drapes, she immediately understood. A man had come into the room.

Chapter Nine

Oh! What Horrors We Have Seen!

> All those who are squeamish, and all those who are prudish, and all those who prefer to live in a fool's paradise of imaginary innocence and purity . . . will do well not to read the *Pall Mall Gazette* of Monday and the three following days.
>
> William Stead, *Pall Mall Gazette*, 4 July 1885

William Stead was much perturbed by Benjamin Scott's request. Scott was the chair of Dyer's London Committee and had arrived at Stead's office late on Friday 22 May 1885, having headed to the *Pall Mall Gazette* straight from the House of Commons. The white-haired Scott was a generation older than Stead and despite being Chamberlain of the City of London and a wealthy philanthropist had come, 'in great distress', to beg the benevolence of the younger man.[1] 'No one else', Scott insisted, 'can help us.'[2] The third Criminal Law Amendment Bill had just been talked out of Parliament, and Scott and his colleagues on the Committee wanted an explicit national newspaper exposé; something to generate public outrage over the politicians' indifference.

While Stead agreed with the older man that the age of consent law was 'criminally lax', 'every instinct of prudence and self-preservation restrained him' from acquiescing to his caller's entreaties.[3] When it came to the molestation of minors, to the immoral traffic in adolescents and to the sale of young girls in London's streets, a stifling silence was society's preferred response. 'The very horror of the crime', stated Stead, 'was the chief secret of its persistence', indeed, the subject was so 'tabooed by the Press' that even the word 'syphilis' could barely be uttered and was said by one journalist to be barred from *The Times*.[4]

Deep down, Stead wanted to assist. A campaigner for democracy, morality and women's rights, he was a Yorkshire-educated radical who hated the mores of the metropolitan elite and deliberately cast himself as the 'barbarian' of the north.[5] His arts reviewer on the *Pall Mall Gazette*, the Irish playwright George Bernard Shaw, found Stead's lack of social etiquette infuriating but impossible to dislike. 'He was so stupendously ignorant that he never played the game. The truth is that he seldom knew that there was any game to play'.[6] Yet Shaw also admitted that in journalism Stead's ingenuousness was also his greatest asset.[7] He was adept at disarming celebrities, encouraging new writers – both male and female – and bringing a fearless and forthright air to his office. When he became overall editor of the *Gazette* in 1883, at the age of thirty-four, he set about transforming this 'gentleman's magazine redolent of Society and the clubs' into a vehicle for social reform and collective moral renewal.[8] However much he hated London, or 'Babylon' as he christened it, Stead realized he might just use the *Gazette* to gain a 'full slap at' the devil and change society for the better.[9] But he foresaw this would entail trouble, that it would necessitate his own 'plunge into the depths of social hell'.[10]

Two years into his editorship, the time had come. Scott told Stead about Mary Jeffries' maid, Maria Watts. He opened to the editor her confession of the country girl of just thirteen years, subjected to 'a horrible outrage . . . by a wealthy customer of Mrs Jeffries' in her Church Street townhouse. Thanks to Scott, Stead began to understand the interconnectedness of London's iniquity. He saw how 'the Jeffries prosecution and the foreign trade' was linked to the 'violation and entrapping of young girls in London' which in turn was related to the inadequate laws still covering the sex trade and the age of consent.[11]

'All our work,' Scott told Stead, 'will be wasted unless you can rouse up public opinion and compel the Government to take up the Bill . . . If you cannot then we are beaten. Will you try?'

Despite Scott's plea, Stead remained uncertain. To resolve his quandary, he set up an interview with Howard Vincent, the former Director of the CID. The grandly moustachioed Vincent was a barrister, a soldier and a linguist. As head of CID between 1877 and 1884 he had worked closely with Sir William Harcourt, but had recently turned against the Liberal Party and particularly Harcourt after the Home Secretary failed publicly to acknowledge the full achievement of his seven years' work.[12] Harcourt's carelessness had led to the humiliating speculation by some journalists that Vincent was dismissed from the CID for ineptitude, when he had actually resigned to pursue a career in politics.[13] Stead had caught him during a brief break in his career, in which he was free to speak for himself. It was to prove a pivotal conversation.[14]

'Is it or is it not a fact,' asked Stead, 'that if I were to go to the proper houses the keeper would, in return for money down, supply me with a maid . . . a girl who had never been seduced?'

'Certainly,' replied Vincent.

'But are these maids willing or unwilling parties to the transaction?'

Vincent appeared surprised by Stead's question, before replying emphatically, 'Of course they are rarely willing, and as a rule they do not know what they are coming for.'

'Do you mean to tell me,' said Stead, 'that actual rapes, in the legal sense of the word, are constantly being perpetrated in London, on unwilling virgins, procured to rich men by brothel-keepers?'

'There is no doubt of it,' replied Vincent.

'But surely rape is a felony punishable with penal servitude.'

'Whom is she to prosecute? Who would believe her? A woman who has lost her chastity is always a discredited witness.'

'Why,' Stead mused, 'the very thought is enough to raise hell.'

'It is true,' said Vincent, 'and although it ought to raise hell, it does not even rouse the neighbours.'[15]

Stead's decision was made. He planned a series of revelatory newspaper articles that would reveal the extent of criminal vice in London and beyond. He would shock the nation into demanding legislative change by proving once and for all that a vile and abusive sex industry flourished – unchecked and un-policed – at the very centre of the British Empire. His series of articles was to be titled *The Maiden Tribute of Modern Babylon*.

*

First Stead called to the *Gazette* offices a group of 'zealous helpers, ex-officials, jail chaplains' and newspaper reporters. Together they formed an investigative team Stead labelled the 'Secret Commission', of which he was 'Chief Director'. Included in the Commission were members of Scott and Dyer's London Committee; William Bramwell Booth, Chief of Staff at the Salvation Army; Josephine Butler and her son George; the pamphleteering Reverend Andrew Mearns and a host of protection societies, moral reformers and rescue workers.[16] The Secret Commission also embraced Jeremiah Minahan, who could supply information on the business of vice and the culture of the London police force.

Stead determined that the *Maiden Tribute* articles would tell a 'simple tale that the common people could read and understand'.[17] To achieve this he introduced an innovative writing style to the *Gazette* termed the 'New Journalism', which presented news stories in an accessible way, via the introduction of 'novelty, variety, sensation [and] sympathy'.[18] Through verbatim interviews, article headlines and illustrations – tactics already employed by the cheap scandal sheets – Stead sought to draw his readers closer to the issues he reported.

The Secret Commission began by conducting extensive interviews, from the Conservative MP George Cavendish-Bentinck, who was 'disappointing', to the 'very communicative' Mary Jeffries, who spent several hours with one of Stead's reporters bad-mouthing her business rivals, while pleading she was merely the victim of 'the irony of destiny'.[19] Cautious about stringent libel laws and unwilling to 'hold up individuals to popular execration', Stead did not identify Jeffries' clientele, though thanks to Jeremiah Minahan he was now aware of their eminence.[20] Others involved in his Secret Commission were not so coy.

*

On 28 May 1885, the intrepid *Christian Commonwealth* published an interview with the purity preacher James B. Wookey. 'Have you any reason to believe that men of high rank in England are patrons of procuresses of the Mrs Jeffries stamp?' asked the *Commonwealth* reporter.

'Yes,' replied Wookey, 'men who profess to have royal blood in their veins. Members of both houses of Parliament have been watched visiting aristocratic houses of bad character.'

'Is there any probability of the names of these men coming out before the public?'

'Yes,' said Wookey.

Wookey had, in fact, already fulfilled this promise – though not in print. On 26 April 1885, during a Sabbath meeting of working men at the gabled Corn Exchange in Luton, he had made several startling disclosures. Standing on the narrow platform inside the crowded hall, Wookey declared that the Jeffries' police court hearing of that same month had proved the brothel-keeper's 'human slaughter-houses' were 'used exclusively by the aristocracy'.[21] Having had 'the painful privilege of looking through [the] immense quantity of evidence' against Jeffries – gathered largely by the ex-inspector Minahan – Wookey assured his listeners that 'amongst the crowd of male debauchees . . . not a few of exalted rank' had been observed sneaking into Church Street.[22] He then publicly named a number – but not all – of the powerful and wealthy men that Jeremiah had held close to his heart for many months.

Wookey's list included 'four noblemen, one baronet, colonels, captains, consuls and that of a conspicuous member of the English royal family'.[23] Only Alfred Dyer's newspaper, the *Sentinel*, was sure enough of its facts to risk printing Wookey's speech in full. In June 1885, it boldly named nine of Jeffries' clients. The list included Lord Henry Lennox, a Conservative politician who had opposed the repeal of the Contagious Diseases Acts and accused Butler and her campaigners of releasing pamphlets 'couched in the most filthy language and containing the most indecent details'.[24] Also Lord Aylesford, a great friend to Prince Edward who, according to his brother-in-law Owen Williams, trailed a most 'unsavoury' reputation.[25] The Hon. Tyrwhitt Wilson, Grenadier Guard and equerry to Prince Edward, was also listed, as was, most sensationally, the Prince of Wales himself: a man referred to in less reputable quarters as 'Dirty Bertie'.

It had been known for years that the Prince of Wales was

a notorious philanderer. His rakish reputation stretched as far as Paris, where in his naturalistic novel on the Parisian *demi-monde*, *Nana* (1880), Émile Zola described a contemporary English prince admiring the 'swelling bosom' of a high-class cocotte 'with the air of a connoisseur'.[26] Zola barely bothered to disguise that his Prince was the future Edward VII, referring to him as the 'Prince of Scotland'. Though it was rare for the Prince of Wales' peccadilloes to be placed unequivocally in the public sphere, it was an open secret that he spent much of his time with a group of aristocrats who pursued 'fast' lifestyles more akin to eighteenth-century libertinism than the principles of the respectable middle classes. When Edward's adulterous affairs did lead him into the unambiguous territory of the courtroom – he was embroiled in two high-profile divorce scandals – his aristocratic coterie, political peers and often his mother could be relied upon to cover over his transgressions.[27] In 1871, a representative of the Prince had paid off the brother of an Italian courtesan for the return of some incriminating letters the Prince did not want to 'get about'.[28] And newspaper editors could be silenced with a libel suit if they went too far.[29] This fear, together with deference and an ongoing squeamishness about the subject matter, meant that Wookey and Dyer's revelations in May and June of 1885 were greeted with an eerie silence by the rest of the national press, as well as by the gentlemen accused.

*

In order to unveil the workings of London's netherworld beyond all doubt, Stead and his Secret Commission went undercover. Armed with false names, fake moustaches and the guiding light of their moral virtue, they made for the depths of the dreaded 'inferno'.[30] 'We have had to buy children,' wrote Josephine Butler to a friend on 5 June 1885,

' . . . and my dear son [George] volunteered to go in disguise into one of the high-class dens with *padded rooms*'.[31] Stead himself – a teetotal Nonconformist – took to quaffing champagne and puffing cigars in the masquerade of a dissolute voyeur. He questioned brothel-keepers and procuresses all over the metropolis and filled his reports with their detailed responses. Under salacious headlines like 'Virgins Willing and Unwilling' and 'Strapping Girls Down' he explained in stark terms to the readers of the *Pall Mall Gazette* exactly how new girls or 'marks' were preyed upon in London and the countryside. 'Pretty girls who are poor, and who have either no parents or are away from home, are easiest picked up', explained one procurer, whose chosen quarries were then hoodwinked into missing their train home and kept overnight in London for seduction. 'To tell the truth, she was drugged,' continued another casually, ' . . . sometimes chloroform . . . but I always used laudanum'. Some spoke of prostitutes' daughters, nurtured to be sold. Others said many girls who entered their bawdy houses were willing – at least until 'the man comes'. 'Once she is in my house,' boasted a bawd, 'she does not go out till the job is done'. One fourteen-year-old was tied to a bed. Others were locked up. Some girls were ensnared by the ruse of the 'dress houses', which rigged recruits in gay clothes, then insisted their tailor's 'debt' be paid off through brothel work.[32]

In a bawdy house in Wanstead, East London, a member of Stead's Secret Commission – a young unnamed Salvation Army girl – became trapped when she posed undercover as a prostitute. Under the guise of a client, Stead visited her regularly and was informed that she was soon to be trafficked to the Continent. Before he had time to orchestrate her escape, the suspicious brothel-owner searched the girl's possessions and found a Salvation Army badge in the lining of her coat. Her disguise foiled, the girl tried to flee her keeper's wrath by jumping from the window. Her Army cohorts, sent to her rescue, found her lying in the garden with a broken ankle.[33] Stead did not mention this episode in his subsequent articles.

Instead he dwelt more on his own heroic adventures. In a restaurant off Leicester Square with rooms for hire upstairs, Stead spent one June evening with a fifteen-year-old girl named Annie who had been 'decoyed' into immorality by a friend called Jane. Annie explained how Jane asked her to go for a walk one evening to have an ice cream.[34]

'It is such a famous shop for ices,' Jane enthused, 'and perhaps we shall see my uncle.'

'Afterwards,' Annie told Stead, '[I found out] he was no more her uncle than I was.'

Jane's 'uncle' plied Annie with four glasses of wine, until 'her head was queer [and she] did not care what [she] did.'

Then Jane said, 'Annie, you must come upstairs now.'

'What for?' asked Annie.

'Never mind what for,' said Jane, 'you will get lots of money.'

Annie remembered thinking that 'it was after no good this going upstairs', but Jane insisted. The man followed. Annie remembered struggling when Jane tried to undress her, then 'everything went dizzy' and she woke up with the 'uncle' in bed beside her. She screamed and 'begged him to go away' but he paid no heed.

Afterwards he gave Jane £4. She allowed Annie half and kept the rest 'as her pay for getting me seduced'. Considering herself one of the 'fallen' now, Annie had since joined the thousands of other casual prostitutes in London, bolstering her weekly wage with brothel gold.[35]

Stead next encountered the more 'systemized business' of recruiting maids in the stance of 'Mesdames X and Z'.[36] This was a London firm 'not to be found in "The Post Office Directory"' – but of equal efficiency. Seduced in the same manner as Annie when she was sixteen years old, Madam X chose to turn her misfortune into a thriving business. Her ambition was to rival the great Mary Jeffries, whose remarkable achievements were much admired in the trade. After two years, Madam X was busy enough to take on a partner: Madam Z, aged twenty. Both regularly scouted new marks and told Stead that 'nurse girls' (nannies) were the best: 'there are any number in [the parks] every morning and all are virgins'. Selling maidenhoods was their speciality. 'Our gentlemen want maids,' they said, 'not damaged articles.'

In a 'vein of bravado' and champagne fumes, Stead then risked his own request. 'Come,' he said to the mesdames, 'what do you say to delivering me five [girls] on Saturday next? . . . Could you deliver me a parcel of maids, for me to distribute among my friends?'

Within a fortnight, the Mesdames had supplied Stead with seven girls between the ages of fourteen and eighteen. All signed a contract allowing that they may 'be seduced by anyone when and where [Stead] please, provided only . . . [he] give two days notice'. Four had doctor's certificates attesting to their virginity. The cost of Stead's adolescent harem, prepped for seduction, was around £5 per girl.

He recorded an interview with one of them, a sixteen-year-old milliner's apprentice who was pretty, 'simple and affectionate' and who bit her lip nervously. Her father, she told Stead, was 'afflicted – that is touched in his wits' and her 'mother a charwoman'.[37] At the milliner's she received 5s a week. In exchange for her virtue she would receive £2 – the equivalent of two months' wages. Stead warned her of the risk she would be taking to her reputation and of the possibility of pregnancy.

'But having a baby doesn't come from being seduced, does it?' she said. 'I had no idea of that.'

He offered her £1 to retain her maidenhood, to which she

replied without hesitation, 'Please sir,' she said, 'I will be seduced.'

'And face the pain and the shame all for the difference of one pound?' said Stead.

'Yes sir,' she said, bursting into tears, 'we are so poor.'[38]

Stead's experiences with such hopelessness left him feeling spent. Despite his nocturnal adventures, he continued editing the *Gazette* by day and was becoming increasingly exhausted and even slightly unhinged. His workload was further increased by the unanimous resignation on 8 June 1885 of Gladstone, Harcourt and their entire disarrayed Cabinet after they were defeated in the Commons by an alliance of Irish and Conservative MPs over a vote to increase alcohol duty.[39] Stead admitted the great strain of this period: that he became 'intensely nervous . . . owing to the political crisis [and] the complete change in manner of my life'.[40] During the few dawn hours that remained between running the *Gazette* and 'threading [his] way through those miserable haunts', Stead would bed down on his office floor to sleep.[41] Josephine Butler recalled returning with him to the *Gazette*'s office one midsummer midnight.

> The lights were out not a soul was there. I scarcely recognized the haggard face before me as that of Mr. Stead. He threw himself across his desk with a cry . . . and sobbed out the words: "Oh Mrs Butler, let me weep or my heart will break."[42]

Stead's histrionics before the saintly Mrs Butler revealed not only his fatigue but also perhaps a tinge of guilt. A married man, he had just spent hours in 'fashionable West End brothels' with 'little tender girls' on his knee.[43] The netherworld was creeping under Stead's skin, testing his humanity, just as Hyde had tormented Jekyll.

*

An 1885 Home Office file contains several police statements recounting the odd tale of William Stead and a prostitute named Sarah MacFarlane, who lived in Fitzrovia, north of Oxford Street. In July, Sarah MacFarlane and her twelve-year-old daughter were persuaded by a French acquaintance named Madame Vignon to attend her lodgings at 1 Silver Place in Soho. In a room on the first floor, Sarah – who was drunk – was introduced to a stranger she remembered as being 'tall, very fair, [with] full whiskers'. Though she did not know his real name, she was meeting Stead.[44]

'How do you do?' he opened. 'Madame [Vignon] has told me all about you and I want to assist you by placing your children in a school if you are willing for them to go.'

'If it is really a school and my husband is willing,' Sarah replied, 'I shall not object.'[45]

Stead then tried to speak to Sarah alone, but was thwarted by Madame Vignon's children, who kept running in and out of the room. He promised instead to write to her later and left a seven-shilling tip. There then followed an argument between Sarah MacFarlane and Madame Vignon over Stead's sweetener.

'Give me some money,' Vignon demanded.

'I have not received any money,' lied Sarah.

In the 'high words' that followed, Sarah complained Madame Vignon had wanted her 'to sell my little girl for £5 to the gentleman and sign a paper, £4 for me and £1 to you for commission'.[46]

Although the Scotland Yard detectives who recorded these claims were doubtful as to their veracity, it was true that Stead wanted to write about a mother desperate enough to sell her own daughter for seduction. Sarah MacFarlane also claimed that Stead did write to her and met her again. This time, however, the two went alone 'to a private house in Fitzroy Court where [they] engaged a room for a short time and whilst there [Stead] . . . kissed me and said he had taken a great fancy to me', though Sarah insisted 'nothing further happened'.[47] Whether she was telling a tall tale or not, Stead had certainly and for some weeks been exploring the perilous border between right and wrong.

*

Wanting to know more about the traffickers, Stead interviewed the Belgian *placeur*, John Sallecartes, in a restaurant on the Strand, most likely Gatti's, opposite Charing Cross railway station. Stead often met new writers at Gatti's and had also taken a young German prostitute working in London for dinner there as part of his investigations. Catering to all classes, Gatti's was famous for its ices, its new-fangled filter coffee and as a rendezvous for London's finest chess players. It was also one of the first to incorporate electric lights into its interior, enabling Stead and Sallecartes to examine each other in the starkest detail.[48] Having been moved by the plight of Adelene Tanner and the other trafficked girls in 1880, Stead expected to be awed by Sallecartes, a villain of such 'high reputation amongst the exporters of English girls'. Instead he encountered a 'broken down', greying old man in need of good food and care.[49]

The prospect of a good dinner seems to have enticed Sallecartes into being a forthright interviewee. He told Stead that twenty young girls were still traded to the brothels of Belgium and Northern France each month, around two hundred and fifty per year. He estimated there were 'a hundred English girls in Belgian houses of ill fame at the moment', but also explained how the system was fluid, how it vanished its victims and defied all certainties:

> Girls do not as a rule stay very long in one house. They are constantly being exchanged and passed on from

> brothel to brothel, so that there is no knowing how far into the interior of the Continent they may ultimately make their way.[50]

Though Sallecartes claimed he had renounced his villainy, Stead did not query him about any feelings of remorse. Some girls had died as a result of his industry, while Adelene Tanner continued to exist in a fraught, damaged twilight.

'It is a regular business,' Sallecartes told Stead crisply, who likewise had his own commerce to consider.[51]

The eventual publication of *The Maiden Tribute of Modern Babylon* in the *Pall Mall Gazette* from Monday 6 until Friday 10 July 1885 was to prove one of the most explosive, controversial and shocking pieces of journalism England had ever seen. Its impact on the public was unprecedented. 'The sensation', remembered Stead, 'was instantaneous and worldwide. [The articles] set London and the whole country in a blaze of indignation'.[52]

Stead had maximized this outrage by revealing the most appalling of his Secret Commission findings on the very first day of publication. Under the startling headline, 'A CHILD OF 13 SOLD FOR £5', he sketched out his discovery of a slum dwelling mother, feckless and desperate enough to sell her own daughter into iniquity. The child's name was 'Lily':

> At the beginning of Derby week, a woman, an old hand in the work of procuration . . . opened negotiations for the purchase of a maid . . . The maid was wanted, it was said, to start a house [brothel] with, and there was no disguise on either side that the sale was to be effected for immoral purposes. While the negotiations were going on, a drunken neighbour came into the house . . . and speedily became aware of the nature of the transaction. So far from being horrified at the proposed sale of the girl, she whispered eagerly to the seller, 'Don't you think she

> would take our Lily? I think she would suit.' Lily was her own daughter, a bright, fresh-looking little girl, who was thirteen years old . . . The brothel-keeper offered her a sovereign for her daughter. The woman was poor, dissolute, and indifferent to everything but drink. The father, who was also a drunken man . . . received the news without even inquiring where she was going to. The brothel-keeper having thus secured possession of the child, then sold her to the procuress for . . . £5 – £3 paid down and the remaining £2 after her virginity had been professionally certified . . . Lily was a little cockney child . . . She had been at school, could read and write, and . . . [had attended] two school trips to Richmond and one to Epping Forest.
>
> . . . The first thing to be done after the child was severed from home was to secure the certificate of virginity . . . In order to avoid trouble she was taken in a cab to the house of a midwife, whose skill in pronouncing upon the physical evidences of virginity is generally recognized in the profession.
>
> . . . From the midwife's the innocent girl was taken to a house of ill fame, No. –, P—— street, where, notwithstanding her extreme youth, she was admitted without question. She was taken upstairs, undressed, and put to bed, the woman who bought her putting her to sleep. She was rather restless, but under the influence of chloroform she soon went over. Then the woman withdrew. All was quiet and still. A few moments later the door opened, and the purchaser entered the bedroom. He closed and locked the door. There was a brief silence. And then there rose a wild and piteous cry . . . 'There's a man in the room! Take me home; oh, take me home!'[53]

On the second day, Tuesday 7 July, letters reacting to Monday's report were already pouring into the *Gazette*'s office; while outside in the shaded, mean-looking street a crowd gathered in the heat in anticipation of the next evening's edition. When W. H. Smith's announced the same day that it had banned the *Gazette* from its railway stands for the duration of Stead's obscene exposé, the heated mob swelled with chancers keen to sell copies at a profit.

Up until this moment, the *Gazette* had maintained a respectable daily readership of twelve thousand. During the *Maiden Tribute* campaign, unauthorized reprints alone were said to have surpassed one and a half million.[54] By noon on Wednesday 8 July the police had to be called to guard against the 'gaunt, hollow-faced men and women' assembling once more outside the newspaper offices and at one o'clock the surging, 'resistless tide' smashed several windows on the ground floor.[55] More police were sent for by a half-panicked, half-delighted Stead, and at eight o'clock that same evening all supplies were exhausted.

For some, Stead's revelations were heroic, manly and wholly justified. To others they were disgusting, filthy and obscene. In the wake of his industry coup, all his rival news editors maintained a tight 'conspiracy of silence', with the exception of the upper-class *St. James Gazette*, which was furious.[56] Referring to *The Maiden Tribute* as 'the vilest parcel of obscenity that has ever issued from the public press', it condemned Stead as a 'louting literary blackguard' who 'on behalf of the working man . . . has followed vice to its most loathsome haunts'.[57]

Most irksome to the *St. James* was Stead's sweeping accusations that at the heart of London's vice problem were 'the princes and dukes, and ministers and judges, and the rich of all classes' who purchased the 'daughters of the poor'.[58]

Even more alarming to the patrician elite was Stead's warning that such abuses 'may hereafter be the virus of a social revolution'.[59] 'The future', he insisted, 'belongs to the combined forces of Democracy and Socialism, which when united are irresistible [and will] combine in protesting against . . . the vices of the rich'.[60]

Inside the House of Commons, Cavendish-Bentinck accused Stead of appropriating the Criminal Law Amendment Bill as an instrument in 'class warfare'.[61] Charles Warton MP, a diehard chauvinist said to favour keeping the age of consent below the age of ten, complained 'there was nothing more congenial to the ill-conditioned Democrat than to cast foul slanders and aspersions on the higher orders of society'.[62] Nonetheless Stead had successfully embarrassed England's ruling class on a national scale. Worse still, new technology in the form of the telegraph meant Stead's accusations reverberated throughout Europe, the Empire and America. 'England was stripped naked and shamed before the world,' remembered the socialist Lord Snell, 'and she did not like it'.[63] The 'rulers of Empire' would neither forget nor forgive their humiliation at the hands of this northern 'barbarian', but for now, having heard of the riots outside the *Gazette* and fearing, perhaps, further unrest on London's simmering streets, Parliament was rattled enough to acquiesce to Stead's demands.

At the centre of the *Maiden Tribute* storm, on Thursday 9 July 1885 the newly returned Conservative Home Secretary, Sir Richard Assheton Cross, reintroduced the Criminal Law Amendment Bill to the Commons, warning that he did not 'believe that public opinion would be satisfied unless the Bill is not only read a second time, but . . . passed'.[64]

*

The return of this legislation – which only a few weeks earlier was thought dead and gone – was as huge a triumph for Dyer, Scott and Butler as it was for William Stead, who had ably demonstrated that shame and scandal were a potent, electric force in modern journalism. At the very centre of the tumultuous 1880s, while the British government floundered, public opinion – led by a single newspaper – had demonstrated its formidable strength. Over the heady summer of 1885, radicals and reformers alike enjoyed a short-lived reckoning. But waiting still in the shadows was the ex-inspector Jeremiah Minahan, and his thirst for vendetta had yet to be quenched.

Chapter Ten

It is Excellent to Have a Giant's Strength but Tyrannous to Use it

> There are guilty men on the Treasury Bench who now begin to be most uneasy.
>
> Josephine Butler, 5 June 1885[1]

Flush by the Holborn Viaduct on the dusty Farringdon Road stood the Congregationalist Memorial Hall. It was here on 22 July 1885 that the elite of London's Nonconformist reformers gathered to thank Jeremiah Minahan for his courage in the prosecution of Mary Jeffries. Throughout the months of May and June, the *Sentinel*, the *Christian* and the *Christian Commonwealth* newspapers had corralled the pennies and pounds of their readers on Jeremiah's behalf to compensate his loss of position and pension. In the absence of Alfred Dyer, who was unwell, it fell to James B. Wookey to present Jeremiah with the substantial sum of £120 3s 3d. One of Jeremiah's biggest benefactors was Dr Elizabeth Blackwell of Hastings. Others included Josephine Butler and Miss A. E. N. Bewicke, a writer and minor celebrity, famous for her witty, dark-edged novels, which explored the subjugation of women and derided upper-class gentlemen.[2] A small brown-haired talkative woman of a nervous disposition, she stepped forward to loudly offer the handsome Mr Minahan the 'tribute of gratitude from thousands of women of England'.[3] Without Jeremiah's stand against the malpractice of the police at

Chelsea and the events that he had set in motion, the reformers roundly believed that the Criminal Law Amendment Bill would have long ago been forgotten by Parliament. Yet while those crowded into the Memorial Hall's boardroom held the ex-inspector a hero in their hearts, Jeremiah could only nurse vengeance in his.

Upon the receipt of his tribute he gratefully acknowledged the kindness shown him by all his benefactors and supporters. He also spoke of Stead's revelations in the *Pall Mall Gazette*, which had played an equal role in motivating reform and 'although new to some people' were 'not new to him' or to any of the 'police of London'.[4] And while Jeremiah 'sincerely hoped' the forthcoming Criminal Law Amendment Act would give 'better protection to young girls', he warned that until the current 'state of the police force' was thoroughly and impartially investigated, any new law 'would be of little avail if the police neglected to put [it] in motion'.[5]

Later, the Chamberlain of the City of London, Benjamin Scott, took the floor. As a rich man of seventy-one years, he had little to lose by speaking his mind. His sharp polemic was given prominence in the *Pall Mall Gazette*:

EX INSPECTOR MINAHAN'S TESTIMONIAL

> Mr Benjamin Scott proposed a resolution demanding of the Government an independent inquiry into Mr. Minahan's case, including his allegations of collusion between superior police officials and notorious lawbreakers, particularly with reference to the Jeffries prosecution . . . [He] expressed himself in strong terms of disapproval the course which Sir William Harcourt had taken in regard to Mr. Minahan's case. He was very sorry as a Liberal to speak in condemnation of Sir William Harcourt, but all throughout this business and in similar matters the late

Home Secretary seemed not to have done his duty as a gentleman and a Liberal statesman. (Hear! Hear!)[6]

Four days after Scott's words were reported, George Cavendish-Bentinck MP stood up in the Commons to defend Harcourt. Though Harcourt was Cavendish-Bentinck's political opponent, he was – more importantly – his social equal and intimate. Harcourt and his son Loulou (Lewis), who served as his father's private secretary, attended parties at George Cavendish-Bentinck's home hosted by his wife, a celebrated socialite known as 'Britannia'.[7] The two men were also London neighbours, with the Harcourts living at 7 Grafton Street, Mayfair, and the Cavendish-Bentincks at no. 3. And so the squat, red-faced Conservative MP pushed his cushiony jowls into a question addressed to the new Home Secretary, Sir Richard Assheton Cross, asking whether there was 'any foundation' for Mr Scott's 'serious charges' against Harcourt or the Metropolitan Police and 'whether any, and what, proceedings should be taken in respect of either accusation?'[8] In effect, he was dangling the possibility of slander over Benjamin Scott. Cross's response was equally suggestive. 'I cannot,' he said, 'endorse the statement of the Chamberlain [Scott] . . . With regard to the police . . . any vague and general accusations are, to my mind, most unfair'.[9] As to Harcourt, however, Cross suggested he could 'answer the charges for himself'.[10] Harcourt chose to remain silent, which did nothing to keep further awkward questions or scurrilous rumouring at bay. Particularly as Jeremiah Minahan had now discovered an entire party of political allies who shared his increasingly obsessive desire to hound Harcourt.

*

At two o'clock in the morning on Saturday 1 August 1885, during a prolonged debate over the extension of police powers necessitated by the Criminal Law Amendment Bill, Edmund Gray, the Irish MP for County Carlow and a prominent member of Charles Parnell's Irish Parliamentary Party (Irish Party), stood up in the Commons. As Westminster's third party, the Irish Party held sway over both the flailing Liberal Party and the Conservatives, a position made more acute during the political crisis that summer, which had resulted in a Conservative minority government. Under Parnell, the Irish Party aligned themselves to those that might further their objective of Irish self-governance, while obstructing those that did not.[11] Though Gray was more moderate than his party leader, who was said to 'hate England', as a fellow Irishman from a Protestant, well-to-do background, he may nonetheless have related to the experiences of Parnell, who was 'looked down on as an Irishman in Cambridge; [and his] Irish Party looked down on, as a thing of naught, in the English Parliament'.[12] Gray's family also owned the oldest Nationalist newspaper in Ireland, the *Freeman's Journal*.

During his tenure as Home Secretary, Harcourt had attracted a number of adversaries in the Irish Party. He had introduced oppressive measures to tackle Irish dissidence, including the Explosive Substances Act (1883); and the Prevention of Crimes (Ireland) Act (1882), which ended trial by jury in 'special' cases, increased police powers and allowed government supervision of newspapers in Ireland. The coercion of Ireland, Harcourt had informed his Cabinet in 1880, was like 'caviare: unpleasant at first to the palate, it becomes agreeable with use'.[13]

In February 1880, Harcourt had been caught secretly opening the private correspondence of the Irish Members in Parliament, a transgression he attempted blankly to deny.[14] Later that month, Parnell complained to the Commons that men from the British Embassy had been following him during a trip to Paris. The Foreign Office denied all knowledge of any such arrangement; it was in fact Harcourt who had ordered Parnell and other 'Irish leaders' to be spied upon by his secret-police agents.[15] Harcourt's underhand manoeuvres also meant that he was aware of Parnell's adulterous affair with a woman named Katherine O'Shea, months before anyone else.[16] When the affair became public in 1889–90, Parnell's political career was destroyed and Harcourt was gratified, describing to his wife the satisfaction he felt 'in remembering that I have never shaken hands with him'.[17]

Within this atmosphere of animosity, it was unsurprising that Parnell's supporters were interested in using Jeremiah's cause to rile their enemy. Jeremiah himself may have found comfort in the company of men who – though from a different class – shared his accent, his memories of home and his ill-usage at the hands of the English Establishment. While Harcourt resented the fact that with the Liberals in disarray and the Conservatives in a minority, a 'double-faced scoundrel and double-dyed liar' like Parnell was more influential than ever, for Jeremiah, this meant that a number of powerful men kept up the political interest in his predicament.[18]

In querying how the '6,000 to 10,000 disorderly houses in London' were to be policed by the new Bill, Edmund Gray returned the former Home Secretary yet again to his actions over Jeremiah Minahan and the 'notorious Jeffries prosecution'. As it had been proven that 'Minahan was right, and his superior officers were wrong and corrupt', stated Gray, did it not follow that the police, from the constables up to the Commissioners could no longer be trusted? And that both the police and the judiciary would now 'simply perpetuate the "Jeffries rule" ', which was that any brothel-keeper who pleaded guilty and protected her clientele would 'get off with a fine', while those who did not would be sent to prison?[19]

This was Harcourt's reply:

> Minahan was not dismissed from the Force in connection with the Jeffries case. The charge against Minahan was that of general insubordination. ["Oh, oh!"] . . . [His] charges against his superior officers . . . were found to be entirely untrue from first to last . . . It was after he had left the Police Force, and as a means, I believe, of forcing his way back again, that he took up the Jeffries case. ["Oh, oh!"] . . . If the police were to be discredited on the authority of a discharged officer, who was going round collecting subscriptions for himself . . . against the testimony of the whole body of the police, the magistrates, and the Secretary of State, they would believe anything.[20]

The following few days saw several responses to this late-night spat. While the *Leeds Mercury* condemned the Irish MP for his 'scandalous attack' on Harcourt, the *Freeman's Journal* reiterated Gray's allegation that Harcourt was 'strongly suspected of not having played too creditable a part in dealing' with the Jeffries case.[21] More significantly, Jeremiah Minahan responded directly to Harcourt's affronts in a letter, published by the *Pall Mall Gazette* on Monday 3 August 1885:

> THE JEFFRIES CASE AND MR. MINAHAN.
>
> Mr. Minahan writes to us as follows:-
>
> With reference to Sir William Harcourt's speech in the House of Commons last night, will you permit me through your columns to answer his *untruthful attack upon me* [author's italics]. It is scarcely necessary to say that I did not 'take up the Jeffries case' as I had neither the means nor the power to do so. The case was taken up by a committee of gentlemen. I was employed as their servant. I was degraded [from the police force] for describing

> Mrs. Jeffries' houses in my report as 'brothels for the nobility'. When I asked Colonel Labalmondiere (Assistant Commissioner) what his grounds were for suspending me, he replied, 'I suspend you on your report.' He then read out to me the words 'brothels for the nobility' and said, 'That is highly improper'. He gave no other reason.[22]

Jeremiah's choice of words, '*attack upon me*', suggests that he really was taking Harcourt's insults to heart. Since January of the year before, Harcourt had consistently refused Jeremiah an independent inquiry into his treatment by the Metropolitan Police, and in April 1885 he had stated that all Jeremiah's allegations about Mary Jeffries' brothels were 'untrue'. When, in May 1885, Mary Jeffries contradicted this at the Middlesex Sessions House, Harcourt changed tack by insisting instead that Jeremiah was an officious fabricator, a man who had made 'unfounded charges' against his fellow officers, despite the fact that Harcourt had never allowed these 'charges' to be adequately investigated.

Now, Jeremiah joined forces with another Irishman, a rash character named Philip Callan, who was MP for County Louth. 'Phil' Callan was broad-shouldered, well-built and 'manly'; he was also a mischievous bon-vivant with a loose tongue and a trouble-prone temperament that entailed he was often caught up in ill-considered fall-outs and libel actions.[23] As far as Harcourt was concerned, Callan was a man to be feared.

On the same day Jeremiah's letter appeared, Callan asked Harcourt in the House of Commons why he claimed to know 'nothing of the prosecution of the Jeffries' case' when during its third pre-trial hearing ' . . . a representative of the Home Office [had attended] the police court and [made] a report to his superiors?'[24] Callan was referring to Mr Batchelor, the mysterious civil servant from the Solicitor's Department of the Treasury, which reported directly to the Home Secretary. Callan then asked whether Harcourt had also read Minahan's letter in that evening's *Pall Mall Gazette* stating that Jeremiah 'was dismissed for describing Mrs Jeffries' house as a "brothel for the nobility" '.[25] Without stopping to query Harcourt's responses, Callan then moved straight to his real point, which was to inform the House of Commons of his intention to demand a formal investigation into 'the conduct of the late Home Secretary with reference to the Jeffries case'.[26] Callan also made it clear that he was acting on new intelligence he had uncovered as to the true nature of Harcourt's agenda, that he knew the *real* reason why Harcourt appeared so keen to protect Jeffries and to paint Jeremiah Minahan the villain.

'Mr. Callan', explained the political correspondent for the *Liverpool Mercury*, 'has taken the Jeffries case in hand and has been holding a small secret commission of his own. He has unearthed what he believes to be a great scandal but, indiscreet of speech as he is, he will scarcely dare to ventilate it . . . until he is sure of his facts'.[27] But Callan was assured of the provision of 'his facts', for seated upstairs in the Commons public gallery with his eyes trained on Harcourt, breathing his air, observing his discomfort under Callan's menace, sat the ex-inspector.[28]

Chapter Eleven

A Special Correspondent

> I cannot tell whether the woman is really anxious to have the child back, or whether she is being made the tool of others.
>
> Letter from William Bramwell Booth, Salvation Army, 7 August 1885[1]

Like the squally showers that dominated England's skies during the second week of August 1885, yet more reprisals soon dampened the political atmosphere. On Tuesday 11 August, George Cavendish-Bentinck next wondered aloud in the Commons whether the attention of Sir Richard Assheton Cross had been drawn to an article published two days earlier in Sunday's *Lloyd's Weekly*. The article, he said, referred to the vanishing 'of a girl under fourteen years of age' whose name, he informed the House, was 'Eliza Armstrong'. Headed 'A Mother's Search For Her Child', the report had been written by the newspaper's special correspondent: Henry Hales.

*

By the heated week of Stead's *Pall Mall Gazette* sensation, free local schooling had been available to Charles Street residents for more than thirty-six years.[2] A generation of locals had thus daily learnt a little reading, writing and arithmetic, including Mrs Stollard and Mrs Mudd – neighbours to young Eliza's smart-mouthed mother – who had read the *Gazette*'s

6 July report about a 'Child sold for £5', and duly drawn the same unholy conclusion.

Having left Charles Street on Derby Day, Wednesday 3 June, Eliza had been missing for over a month by the time of the *Maiden Tribute*'s publication. Though she had promised to write home regularly, no letters had found their way to 32 Charles Street. Nancy Broughton, however, had been blessed with one missive a week after Eliza disappeared, sent from Hope Cottage in Winchester and containing a second sovereign.

> Dear Nancy,
>
> I dare say you are looking for this letter from me, but I am so happy to tell you that Eliza is all right and doing well with me. I have bought her a lot more clothes. She looks quite happy. She sends her love to her mother and father and to you. I am on a visit, and she is with me stopping for a week, but we go home next week . . . I shall soon come and see you again, if you will let me.
>
> REBECCA[3]

When Nancy showed the letter to Mrs Armstrong, Eliza's mother was struck by Rebecca Jarrett's phrase, 'if you will let me'. 'A very funny remark', she thought.[4] Yet if she harboured any foreboding then, it became overwhelming when the Mesdames Mudd and Stollard approached her three weeks later, the *Maiden Tribute* in mind. 'It looks,' they said, 'as if you might have sold your child'.[5]

Mrs Armstrong read the report. She absorbed details of 'Lily's' sale in 'Derby week'; of a 'drunken' mother who exchanged her girl for a 'sovereign' and of the much larger profit – £5 according to the *Gazette* – pocketed by a 'brothel-keeper' neighbour. She then marched straight across to Bash and Nancy's room, where she found the couple sitting beneath Christ's torment, eating their tea.

'What a dreadful thing that is in the *Gazette*,' said Mrs Armstrong.

'Yes,' said Nancy, 'I am all of a tremble.'

'I cannot be easy,' said Mrs Armstrong, 'I will go to the magistrate tomorrow.'

'Perhaps she [Eliza] will come home on Monday,' said Bash.

'No,' said Mrs Armstrong, 'I have read the *Pall Mall Gazette* and something strikes me that "Lily" is my child.'

'Becky [Rebecca Jarrett] would not do such a thing to your child,' said Bash.[6]

But Mrs Armstrong's neighbours had already taken to hurling shouts of '*Gazette! Gazette! Gazette!*' around Charles Street's weeping walls. Talk of the Armstrongs' shame was spreading like a fever. It travelled through broken window-panes, up dark, mean stairwells and into close and crowded rooms. Angry accusations ensued as Mrs Armstrong sought to defend herself from the terrifying possibility that it really was *she* who stood centre-stage in Stead's awful report: the 'dissolute, indifferent' mother who had sold her child for one pound.[7]

Her husband, who Mrs Armstrong had kept largely in the dark about her dealings with Nancy and Jarrett, suffered the same. A well-built man with a dark moustache and a bitten expression, Charlie Armstrong may have been known to be handy with his fists, but that did not counter the fact that 'every day . . . it was in everybody's mouth that my wife had sold the child and they blamed me as well for it'.[8] It was soon revealed to him that Nancy Broughton had been spied with at least one sovereign on the day Rebecca Jarrett took Eliza away, and his wife certainly knew of a second sent through the post. Charles Street 'smelt a rat' and looked now to Nancy as the likely 'brothel-keeper', reported to have orchestrated the deal between mother and procuress. 'People', Charlie reflected, 'do not give away sovereigns for nothing'.[9]

Mrs Armstrong's fecklessness and Eliza's disappearance were not the only concerns burdening the residents of Charles Street. Thanks to the disclosures in the *Pall Mall Gazette*, both the Armstrongs and Nancy Broughton had committed the secondary, social crime of bringing notoriety upon the entire community. Since the emphasis in working-class areas was not so much on the home but on the collective life outside: the extended family, the pub, the open-air market and the street corner, outward appearances were paramount.[10] So it was inevitable that Mrs Armstrong felt a need to assuage the charges of the *Pall Mall Gazette*. She had to repair Charles Street's reputation by first clearing her own – 'I have had the scandal of the neighbours in the street,' she explained, 'that I sold my child for £5 for improper purposes' – and the first method she chose was to state her innocence loudly and in public.[11]

At the end of the week she sought a second word with Nancy Broughton. Rather than retiring to the privacy of Nancy's room, this time she caught her by her front door in full view of the street. The heat of the day, which was to break eighty degrees, was already rising. The stink of rotting rubbish pressed upon Nancy and Mrs Armstrong with the breath of an expectant Charles Street crowd.

Before this gathered audience of 'every one', Mrs Armstrong then unleashed upon Nancy the burden of her embarrassments. She denounced Nancy as a 'whore', a 'prostitute' and a 'drunken brothel-keeper' who had 'sold her child [Eliza] for £5'. She then insisted that she 'would have [Nancy] up, the same as she would have Jarrett up' and that she was going to the local police court to do just that. Nancy did not answer. Fearful of the crowd and Mrs Armstrong's exuberance, she did not speak a word: 'good, bad or indifferent'.

Undeterred by her silence, Mrs Armstrong stormed off south, flashing through the traffic and sudden sunshine of the great Marylebone Road, before dipping back into the cooler shadows of Seymour Street. At no. 2 she turned a sharp right into the Marylebone police court. She needed official assistance now, to bring Eliza home and 'prove [she] never sold her'.[12] Passing through the tall doors and into the narrow waiting room beyond, she waited with the pugilists and disputers, the cats and the coves biding their instant before the Marylebone beak.

When the editor of *Lloyd's Weekly*, a sharp-faced, self-made man named Thomas Catling, read the court reporter's account of Mrs Armstrong's appearance before the Marylebone magistrate on Saturday 11 July, he immediately intuited scandal in the story of Eliza's disappearance, the kind of scandal that would push his sales well beyond those of his rivals, the *News of the World* and *Reynolds's Weekly*. Catling also suspected that the circumstances surrounding the tale required an able correspondent's biting hold. So he put one of his best men on the job, instructing him to travel direct to Lisson Grove and investigate. Within hours of her exchange with the magistrate – whose name was William Cooke – Mrs Armstrong returned home to Charles Street, to find Henry Hales waiting for her.

*

Hales came from a faster, brasher place than London, a place then perceived to be one of the most radical and classless in England.[13] For centuries Birmingham – whose city motto was 'Forward' – had been both a Nonconformist stronghold and a flourishing centre of skilled industry; it was a city of upstarts, self-made and self-educated, proud and pioneering.[14] By the nineteenth century its 'handiwork' could be detected in any Victorian dwelling: 'doors and windows, stoves and cupboards, staircase and closet . . . the bed we lie on, the very clothes we wear – all testify to [Birmingham's] busy craftsmanship' stated *Leisure Hour* in 1865.[15] The skill and entrepreneurialism of the city's workforce protected them, at least initially, from industrial mechanization and located them in smaller workshops where masters were largely recruited from the workforce. Businessmen and workmen in Birmingham were not divided by 'tall walls of social privilege'; they knew each other, shared the same social conscience and tried to create a civic landscape both unique and progressive.[16] 'As [with] the sea', stated the Quaker politician John Bright, 'wherever you dip a cup into it, will be found salt, so the constituency of Birmingham, wherever you test it will be found to be a Radical.'[17]

Hales' father worked first as a hosier before turning his hand to the craft of making tortoiseshell handbags, and aged twenty-one, Henry joined him in the same trade.[18] His fifteen-year-old brother was a 'Japanner' – a lacquer-worker.[19] His father's skill enabled the seven-strong family to live in a new-built brick terraced house in John Street, Lozells, close by the old grounds of a country house named Aston Villa. The Hales formed part of the respectable working class in Birmingham, the group that benefited most from the city's pioneering educational institutes, libraries, lecture halls and self-improvement schemes. On 6 January 1853, when Hales was on the threshold of adulthood, Charles Dickens gave a speech in Birmingham praising the city's grammar school, its schools for women and girls, its polytechnic institute, its schools of design and medicine: 'I have seen their results', Dickens said, 'in the demeanour of your working people, excellently balanced by a nice instinct, as free from servility on the one hand, as from self-conceit on the other'.[20] Henry Hales went on to seek his black-coated, professional career in the national newspapers. In his thirties he moved to London and took up a job in the advertising department of the *Morning Star*. Thanks to his break with Professor Risley's predatory meanderings, Hales then moved solely into editorial work, and during the next sixteen years established himself as an investigative journalist adept at exposing corruption and embarrassing public figures.[21]

Though Cavendish-Bentinck had referred in the Commons to Hales' article of Sunday 9 August, about the missing Eliza Armstrong, the *Lloyd's* reporter had first written on the case almost one month earlier, on Sunday 12 July, the day after Mrs Armstrong visited the police court. In this, his first of a series of influential articles that were to untangle what really happened to the missing girl, Hales recorded his original interview with Eliza's mother. First Mrs Armstrong had informed Hales that Nancy Broughton was the 'neighbour' who had suggested the place for Eliza; next she implied that Rebecca Jarrett was not a complete stranger; finally she tried to swerve Hales into seeing Nancy as the arch-doxie, saying that it was 'very strange such a rough-looking woman as the mistress . . . should give Mrs Broughton a sovereign for her trouble, and the girl an entire new outfit of clothing'.[22] All of which begged the question why she had permitted her child to depart under such suspicious circumstances; but if he wanted to pocket the story, Hales needed to keep Mrs Armstrong snug, so he kept such thoughts to himself.

Wary perhaps of the fact that the magistrate William Cooke had instructed the Marylebone constabulary to carry out further investigations, Hales decided to act immediately on the one lead that Nancy Broughton offered him, which was that 'the first house the girl was taken to was in Albany Street, near to the Albany Barracks'.[23] Hoping perhaps for a sensational denouement between Eliza's vinegary mother and an equally soaked bawd, Hales decided to take Mrs Armstrong with him. They found no trace of Jarrett or Eliza, but the queer couple's calls at Albany Street will have dispelled any doubts in Mrs Armstrong's mind as to the nature of the street; a tenacious reporter, Hales must have knocked on a number of brothel doors before admitting defeat. Yet this did not spell the end of their partnership. The pairing of the intemperate mother and the experienced newsmonger was to flourish over the following weeks, bringing dividends to both. First though, one Inspector Edward Borner of Scotland Yard would briefly interrupt their burgeoning acquaintance.

On Tuesday 14 July, two days after Hales published his first report on the disappearance of Eliza and eight days after Stead's revelations, Inspector Borner, acting under instructions instigated by William Cooke, made his own deliberate way to Charles Street to investigate. He too visited the girl's mother and Nancy Broughton, who produced again the letter written by Rebecca Jarrett from Hope Cottage in Winchester. Crucially, neither woman mentioned to Inspector Borner their suspicion that there might be some connection between 'Lily' as reported in Stead's *Maiden Tribute* and Eliza. Whether through guilt or the fear of self-incrimination, neither did they tell the policeman that Eliza had been taken in the first instance to Albany Street.[24]

Borner's only lead was the address – Hope Cottage, Winchester – provided by Jarrett in her letter to Nancy. The following day, Wednesday 15th, he travelled the sixty-odd miles to Winchester to see for himself whether Eliza or Jarrett were to be found there, but he arrived too late. Hope Cottage was 'closed' up.[25] His enquiries next led him to Mrs Josephine Butler, who also lived in Winchester and was known to have some connection with the doings at Hope Cottage. Borner found Mrs Butler at home in the Close, a peaceful, verdant enclave of Winchester Cathedral, where her husband, George, served as a canon.

Bruised by her experience of partial policing during her

Contagious Diseases Acts campaign, Mrs Butler was, however, unwilling to help. She refused on principle ever to answer any policeman's questions, though when the inspector attempted to check her recalcitrance by informing her that Eliza's mother 'had applied to the Magistrate for her child' she allowed him one new thread to follow.[26] He should, she suggested, try communicating with William Bramwell Booth, Chief of Staff of the Salvation Army, on his return to London.

Next morning, Thursday 16th, Borner returned to the city and made his way directly to Booth's offices at 101 Victoria Street, Westminster. The international headquarters of the Salvation Army was imposing: half-a-dozen shop-fronts wide and several storeys tall, it housed the leaders of a Christian movement that had, since its origination in London's East End two decades earlier, become a runaway success. The Army's crimson flag flew high, with its yellow central star and its singular evangelical message: 'Blood and Fire'. Highly conspicuous in their uniforms and marching bands, Salvation Army officers were regularly scoffed at and even physically attacked in the streets for their earnestness, but within three years of Borner's visit the offices at Victoria Street oversaw 7,107 officers, 2,587 corps and 653 outposts in thirty-three different countries worldwide.[27] Under the scrutiny of the social investigator Charles Booth, the Army was found to 'hold in single faith, and with a very passionate conviction, [a] desire that all men should be forced to hear of Salvation'.[28] Theirs was an Army of religious converts, who used 'vivid language' to proselytize their godly vision to anyone curious enough to listen.[29] But Charles Booth was sceptical as to their effect in the long term. Even those 'touched' briefly by the Army zealots, Booth wrote, were unlikely to be 'permanently affected by the heightened emotions and excitement so unsparingly used'.[30]

Inside the Army's Chief of Staff's office, Inspector Borner found a jumpy twenty-nine-year-old: William Bramwell Booth, the son of General Booth, an evangelical street preacher who founded the Salvation Army in 1865. William's dark curly beard reached down to his chest and he held a trumpet-shaped hearing device to his ear. He could be a cheerful, kind and jocular man but his midday charms disguised a midnight temperament. According to Edward Begbie, a journalist and author once involved in the Salvation Army, behind Booth's friendly exterior was a man who held 'violence in his mind and violence in his religion'.[31] Begbie was 'convinced' that 'at the back of everything [was] the cold and commanding intensity of a really great fanatic'.[32]

Borner made straight for his point. 'I am Inspector Borner,' he said, 'I have come to see you . . . about a girl named Eliza Armstrong; I have been referred to you by Mrs Josephine Butler, of Winchester'.[33]

'I know something of the case, but I cannot tell you exactly where the child is at present,' Booth said, 'but if you like I will have inquiries made during the day and let you know.'[34]

Satisfied by the promise of such a pious man, Borner returned to Scotland Yard to await Booth's correspondence. He was to wait a long time.

When Hales returned to Charles Street on Saturday 18 July, to update the story for his next edition of *Lloyd's*, he discovered that Inspector Borner had also been back to let Eliza's mother know that 'her child was quite well and that she had now better let the matter drop'.[35] Borner's words reflected the view shared by Booth, that young Eliza was better off in the hands of well-to-do Christian Salvationists – however fanatical – than in the care of her dubious, slum-dwelling mother. Next day, under the headline 'A LOST DAUGHTER TRACED', Hales could only muster one paragraph for *Lloyd's* about Eliza. First he reiterated Borner's belief that

Eliza appeared to have been 'found', then reported how officers had warned Mrs Armstrong to 'refuse information to the Press'. Shut out from his own scoop, Hales was furious: 'The police', he wrote, had shown 'a foolish dread of the publicity which is their best aid in all such cases'.[36]

Given the impasse between a policeman inclined to wait and a pressman obstructed from his pursuit, Eliza stayed missing. By the end of July, there was still no information on her whereabouts, and until she was bodily returned and paraded through Charles Street, Mrs Armstrong was unable to rest. So she went again to see William Cooke. This time the magistrate advised that Mrs Armstrong and Inspector Borner should return together to the Salvation Army's headquarters to ask William Bramwell Booth outright: where was Eliza?

At eleven o'clock on Saturday 1 August, the dark-eyed mother of the missing child did just that. On the office wall behind William Bramwell Booth's head was a portrait of his own preacher mother, Catherine, whose clean-scrubbed countenance and clement eyes looked down with godly contentment upon Mrs Armstrong's vexation. It was an expression that found its echo in her child. Edward Begbie recalled how their two faces were 'hauntingly identical; so much so that one comes to regard the coachman-like whiskers clapped to [William's] cheeks as in the nature of a disguise, thinking of him as his mother's eldest daughter rather than as his father's eldest son'.[37]

With the eyes of mother and son upon them both, Inspector Borner opened the proceedings with his inimitable directness.[38]

'This is Mr. Booth,' he told Mrs Armstrong, 'now speak to him.'

'I have come to speak to you about my child, I want her back,' she said.

'You cannot have her,' replied Booth, 'for she is in the

South of France with a lady, being well brought up and educated.'

'Why cannot I have her back?'

'Because I have been put to great expense; have you £100?'

'No, sir, I am only a poor woman.'

'Well, that is about what it cost me; why don't you let her remain? I will pay you her wages monthly, or how you like, and I will give you her address, and you can communicate with her, and when she comes to England you can see her.'

Booth then turned to Inspector Borner. 'What do you think,' he asked, 'two or three shillings a week?'

'That is a question which I cannot interfere in,' said Borner, 'it is for the parents.'

'No, sir,' interrupted Mrs Armstrong, 'I want my child back.'

'Why don't you let her remain?' Booth asked Mrs Armstrong.

'Because,' explained Mrs Armstrong, 'I want her back to take before a magistrate to prove that I never sold her.'

According to his own recollection, Booth then got up from his seat and moved closer to Mrs Armstrong.

'Did you not know something of Rebecca [Jarrett] before?' he asked her suddenly.

'Yes, I did,' she replied.

'Do you know what sort of woman she was?'

'Yes,' she said.

'Was it not,' he asked, 'a very extraordinary thing that you should let your little child go with such a woman?'[39]

Mrs Armstrong did not reply. Booth then crossed to another desk in the room and took up a piece of paper.

'If you are determined to have her back, there, this is her address, that is all I can do for you,' he said.

On the paper were the following words: 'Eliza Armstrong care of Monsieur T.H. Berard, Loriol, Drome, France'.

Booth offered no explanation as to how Eliza had made her way out of the country and down to the south of France, nor who had taken her there. He did not refer to 'Rebecca' again and Inspector Borner did not trouble him with further enquiry, apparently returning to his previous belief, that as the Salvation Army had made it clear they had somehow saved the child – though from what or whom remained uncertain – she could no longer be presumed missing. It was simply up to Mrs Armstrong now to decide whether Eliza was better off with a 'lady' in France or whether she should return to Charles Street. Raised in poverty and its accompanying deference, she politely thanked Booth for the information he had thrown at her.

'You had better,' he finished, 'consult your husband, and let me know if you determine to let the child remain.'[40]

The next day was Sunday 2 August, which marked the commencement of Inspector Borner's summer holiday in Wisbech, a quaint market town on the River Nene in Cambridgeshire. Borner would absent himself from London for almost three weeks, slowing still further the lackadaisical endeavours of Scotland Yard to actually unearth young Eliza or those who had initiated her vanishing. His absence left the door of opportunity open a crack for a 'fly' reporter like Henry Hales, who immediately swooped back to Charles Street and reclaimed his story.

Mrs Armstrong found herself rather in need of the fellow-feeling offered by Hales. Having learned of William Bramwell Booth's 'high tone' and his unwillingness to explain precisely 'how the child got into the possession of the Salvation Army people', Hales offered Eliza's mother a revelatory and far less servile point of view: the radical notion that it was actually *she* who was the true victim in this singular case.[41] Booth might be a middle-class 'religionist' but he had no jurisdiction over her family and appeared to have been involved in a meddlesome outrage upon the Armstrongs' home, indeed upon Mrs Armstrong's own daughter, the true nature of which was yet to be fully understood.[42] Until Eliza was physically returned, Hales would assist Mrs Armstrong in finding out how Booth had come to attain the girl from Rebecca Jarrett and what exactly Jarrett had allowed Eliza to lose before the Salvationists came to the 'rescue'.

With the anxious Mrs Armstrong comfortably in his ink-stained grasp, on Thursday 6 August, Hales next took her to Winchester. They too found Hope Cottage – 'a two-storey' house 'with six rooms' – shut up with no sign of the woman or girl. When Hales badgered Jarrett's neighbours they informed him that Hope Cottage was 'generally known as "the farm for fallen women" ' and was used by some of the 'Salvation Army people to keep fallen women and girls'. Rebecca Jarrett worked as its matron. They were a 'rummy lot', said one local. When Hales asked why, 'They replied – Because they fetched bad women, and nice little girls from where they could get them and shut them up together for days and nights unattended . . . without any one to mind them'. Quite why the matron of a Magdalene refuge 'should have been employed in decoying a child from home', wrote Hales in purported bafflement, 'is at present a matter for the public to form their own opinion on'.[43]

Hales then established that on 'Wednesday last' the Pickford's removal company had taken the furniture from Hope Cottage and all remaining inmates had been sent away. He traced both the removed goods and a gaggle of Jarrett's disgraced girls to another Home of Rest on Canon Street, a narrow stretch of Georgian, double-fronted cottages in the shade of the cathedral. Mrs Armstrong and Hales had barely set foot inside the home when 'an elderly ladylike person observed' to them: 'I know what you have come for . . . You have come thinking to see that lost girl from London here'.

She then asserted – rather suspiciously – that Eliza Armstrong 'was not there and she knew nothing at all about her', but Hales stubbornly refused to depart. They were eventually shepherded into a reception room by the home's matron, Mrs Hillier, where Hales set about an earnest appeal 'that in the interests of truth, justice and of humanity they should tell all they knew in reference to . . . Rebecca Jarrett'.[44]

First Mrs Hillier expressed her 'deep sympathy' with Mrs Armstrong 'in the loss of her child', then issued a warning: 'I am going to speak to you in very plain language because I feel that the case needs it. [Rebecca Jarrett] confessed [to us] that she had for a long time been a brothel-keeper and one of the worst procuresses in London. She told of crimes almost incredible'.[45]

According to Mrs Hillier, when Jarrett had first arrived at the Home of Rest, she 'was suffering from a diseased hip' and 'believed herself upon her dying bed. We did not expect she would recover, and she became a converted woman in this house'.

'Pardon me, Madam,' interposed Hales – who already nursed reservations as to Jarrett's veracity – 'are you aware that she has been in other homes at Ramsgate and various places . . . and that she had professed conversion there?'

'I am aware,' replied Mrs Hillier, 'that she has been in other homes but not so near death . . . As she prayed for life she made a vow that if God would only restore her she would devote herself to rescue work.'

'I will not ask you,' said Hales, 'as to the purpose for which this child Armstrong was got away, but we have arrived at this fact: That she was decoyed from her parents by a professedly religious woman and that woman the acknowledged matron of the Winchester home [Hope Cottage]?'

'Yes,' said Mrs Hillier.

'Do you think that . . . anybody from the religionists have the right to decoy a child from its mother?'

'No.'

'Do you consider it a religious or justifiable act for Mr. Bramwell Booth . . . when he knows that this poor woman is hunting for her lost child, to cause her to run from place to place, and at last get the child out of the country?'

'No; and I think the mother is perfectly justified in doing all she can to get her child back.'[46]

But Mrs Armstrong was no closer to finding Jarrett or understanding what had happened to her daughter before she fell to the shelter of the Salvation Army. The trip had merely confirmed that her earliest suspicions about Jarrett were correct: Nancy Broughton's double-faced friend was at once a brothel-keeper and a rescue worker, an angel and a whore. Which side of herself she had presented to young Eliza had yet to be revealed.

*

Henry Hales' report outlining their adventures in Winchester was the one published in *Lloyd's Weekly* on Sunday 9 August. His article made clear that there was an unexplained link between the Salvation Army, Rebecca Jarrett and the missing girl; a link that Booth had still failed to elucidate. 'Surely', goaded Hales, 'the public will expect . . . the Salvation Army to be called upon to say *what has become of the missing girl*'.[47] George Cavendish-Bentinck MP agreed. It was this *Lloyd's* article that he referred the Home Secretary to in the House of Commons on Tuesday 11 August.

'My attention,' Richard Assheton Cross replied to him, 'has been called to [this] case and I have made considerable inquiries about it, and the result is that I have thought it my duty to lay the evidence before the Attorney General.'[48]

Thanks to the *St. James Gazette*, which had referred its

upper-class readers to Hales' revelations and twice suggested the Salvation Army was responsible for the missing girl, London's political elite were rumouring about the Eliza Armstrong case just as much as the near-million readers of *Lloyd's*.[49] Cross was one of the few men in England with the agency to sift out the true tale. On Friday 14 August, he wrote to the Solicitor of the Treasury (Director of Public Prosecutions) requesting that he 'thoroughly investigate the case of Eliza Armstrong [and] take the statements of Mrs. Armstrong, Mrs. Broughton, Mrs. Butler and any other witnesses whose evidence can . . . shew under what circumstances the child was taken from her mother'.[50]

Within days, Mrs Armstrong would be called to Scotland Yard and Inspector Borner would be returned from his sojourn in the Fens, but neither Hales nor his editor, Thomas Catling, had any intention of allowing the attorney-general to scupper their scoop. 'What course of action [the attorney-general] will advise remains to be seen,' ran the *Lloyd's* report, 'but meanwhile we have thought it our duty to leave no stone unturned to assist the mother in her search.'[51]

In the hours and days following Cavendish-Bentinck's question in the Commons, Hales renewed his dogged inquiries, and just in time for his next report he was rewarded with a sensational breakthrough. Hales had succeeded where 'the police and detective force had failed', and had unearthed a French *accoucheuse* of questionable character who dwelt at 3 Milton Street on the wealthy side of Lisson Grove.[52] Her name was Madame Louise Mourey.

Determining to take Eliza's mother to call upon her, but also cautious, Hales opted this time to take Charles Armstrong with them too. Posting him outside the house but 'near at hand', he sent Mrs Armstrong ahead to knock at the door, knowing a woman would be a more common caller at the midwife's home. Before Mourey's servant could shut the front door behind Mrs Armstrong, Hales joined her in the hallway.[53]

'You cannot see Madame without an introduction,' insisted the servant.

'Then I will introduce myself,' offered Hales.

Startled by his sauce, the servant ran off down a flight of stairs and into what appeared to be a small consulting room, with a narrow bed. Mrs Armstrong and Hales followed.

'There's a man in the house, there's a man in the house,' the servant exclaimed, 'and he's down in the room.'

Suddenly an angry Frenchman appeared and started gesticulating violently, while outside in the yard a large Newfoundland dog panted and barked, pulling hard on his chain. Seemingly unruffled, Hales stayed put, insisting he only wanted to ask Madame a few questions. Eventually Mourey appeared. In the first instance, she tried to deny all knowledge of young Eliza, but she was no match for an artful fox like Hales.

'Don't you remember,' he asked, 'a woman bringing a little girl here on the Derby night?'

Mourey hesitated and shook her head. Then she said, 'Do you mean a good many weeks ago?'

'Yes, some weeks ago.'

'Do you mean a nice little girl that was brought by a big woman?'

'Yes.'

'And the woman walked lame with a stick?'

'Yes,' said Hales, 'this person is that little girl's mother; and we want to know what you know about her.'

'I know nothing about her, I only did my business.'

'Well what was she brought here for?'

'For me to examine her.'

'And did you examine the girl?'

'Yes.'

'But why was she examined?'

'A gentleman wished it.'

'Yours was a beautiful little child,' she told Mrs Armstrong, attempting to divert Hales from his raw line of questioning.

'I know that,' Eliza's mother snapped back.

'Who was the man?' demanded Hales.

'I don't know,' said Mourey, 'I never saw him before.'

Hales next pushed too far, igniting another angry scuffle with the Frenchman. Fearful her new friend was about to be attacked, Mrs Armstrong ran for the front door. 'Charlie, Charlie,' she cried, 'come in!' Into the house strode her tall and powerful husband, black with soot from head to foot. Seeing this apparition bearing down on them, 'the female servants ran back' in horror, the Frenchman 'seemed paralysed' and Madame Mourey 'threw up her hands'. There was a momentary pause.

'Why, you are all as white as turnips,' Charlie told the group. 'What is the matter?'

When Mrs Armstrong explained in vengeful terms how the Frenchwoman had interfered with their daughter, Hales took his cue to usher Eliza's parents 'quickly and quietly' out of the house.[54]

On the following Sunday, 16 August, Hales' report in *Lloyd's* included both a description of the Armstrongs' visit to Madame Mourey and a revelatory 'explanation' from William Bramwell Booth in which he openly admitted his part in Eliza's disappearance.

As Hales had edged nearer to the truth of Eliza's experiences beyond Charles Street, Booth had been acting more and more like a man with something to hide. According to Thomas Catling, Booth had already tried to 'silence *Lloyd's* through the intervention of a friend' and when this failed, he called in person 'one Saturday at the [*Lloyd's*] office and waited over half an hour to see [Catling] making plain that the case was deemed important'.[55] Booth then wrote a note telling Catling: 'I cannot help regretting that you have allowed the matter to assume the direction it has taken in your columns'.[56] Catling responded by sending an office messenger to visit Booth's house in Stamford Hill to ask what the Salvation Army would prefer him to convey in his newspaper. While the messenger awaited a response, 'several Salvationists gathered round him and plumping down on their knees held a prayer meeting for the "young man from *Lloyd's*" '.[57] These are the words he eventually came away with:

MR BOOTH'S EXPLANATIONS

> The child Eliza Armstrong was entrusted to our care by some persons who wished to save her from the demoralizing surroundings in which she was placed. I have the little girl in safe keeping now . . . As to the adventures which Eliza Armstrong may have had before she came into my hands, I have nothing to do with [sic] . . . The woman Jarrett was not at the time of these occurrences connected with the Salvation Army.[58]

Booth finally clarified that he took Eliza into his care the day after Derby Day, Thursday 4 June 1885, but he still deliberately distanced himself from the 'adventures' that 'Eliza may have had before' this, leaving one lost night when the child was with Jarrett and other persons unknown. During these missing hours, Hales had proved that Eliza was intimately 'examined' by Madame Mourey; he had also discovered that Jarrett next took the child to a brothel in Soho: information that had come courtesy of a witness who noted the strange behaviour of Jarrett and two male accomplices on Derby night. The witness was Henry Smith, the cabman who noticed Eliza's discomfited state after leaving Madame Mourey and who had then reluctantly delivered her to Poland

Street. More sensationally, Smith had described to Hales the two gentlemen who first summoned his cab on Quebec Street then waited suspiciously for Eliza at Milton Street and again on Poland Street. Though Jarrett may have referred to one of these two miscreants as 'Charles Kennedy', the wiry, energetic man Smith described was much better known to Hales by his real name: William Thomas Stead. Charles Kennedy was Stead's *Maiden Tribute* pseudonym, the identity he had adopted during his undercover exploration of London's iniquity.

Though he had not yet made it public, Hales had just discovered that it was the righteous editor of the *Pall Mall Gazette* – the man who only recently had chastised the entire London Establishment for its improbity – who had set up the molestation of the innocent Eliza, then installed her inside a low brothel. And if Eliza really was the *Pall Mall Gazette*'s 'Lily', as Mrs Armstrong feared, Stead had also overseen Jarrett's dosing of the child with chloroform and was most likely the selfsame 'man in the room!' – the lusty roué who had entered the brothel bedroom where Mrs Armstrong's girl lay alone in the dark. *Lloyd's*' special correspondent Henry Hales was thus the first to establish that in trying to redraw the nation's moral boundaries, William Stead had utterly failed to police his own.

Chapter Twelve

It Will Be A Fearful Business If All This Appears

Oh how wide is the diapason of my mind! From what a height to what a depth!

Richard Monckton Milnes,
esteemed friend of Sir William Harcourt, n.d.[1]

On the morning of Thursday 6 August 1885, the *Sunbeam* – an elegant three-masted schooner – prepared to get under way. From the Cowes esplanade with its bunting and flags, the steam-assisted yacht was to sail north from the Isle of Wight across to Portsmouth Harbour. The cool August morning refreshed those still reeling from the drunken party and firework display of the previous night, marking the end of the Cowes Regatta – a key social event of the Season.[2] At the *Sunbeam*'s helm was the Liberal MP Sir Thomas Brassey. Known as 'the dean' of British yachtsmen, Brassey had famously circumnavigated the world in the *Sunbeam* with his five children, two dogs, three birds, a kitten and his intrepid buck-toothed wife, Annie.[3] The Brasseys were honoured on board by the presence of Prince Edward and the twenty-two-year-old 'Loulou' Harcourt, son and private secretary to Sir William Harcourt. Though Sir William himself was a keen yachtsman who had once owned a small schooner – christened *Loulou* after his son – he appears to have been kept from Cowes on parliamentary business in London. The controversies surrounding the Criminal Law Amendment Bill were still ongoing, as were the insinuations of certain Irish Party members.

The Brasseys' sumptuous yacht was stuffed with easy chairs and sofas, curtains, candelabra and amusing ethnographic objects from around the globe, but the group's pleasures were soon punctured by the arrival of a telegram:

> I want you to come up to see me in London this afternoon on a matter of urgent importance. Do not fail and bring your things with you.[4]

The curt message was from Harcourt to Loulou and betrayed an unusual panic. Loulou knew he must return home immediately. The Brasseys suggested his fastest route would be to cross the Solent with them on the *Sunbeam* and take the 5.45 p.m. train to London from Portsmouth Harbour. The telegram had 'upset [Loulou] very much as [he] thought someone was ill'; he would need to travel a hundred miles before he could find out who – or what – had so vexed his father. This 'not knowing' condemned him to suffer the day in a fearful 'agony'.[5]

*

Loulou was a tall and reedy young man who had inherited his father's prominent nose, and cultivated a modern brush moustache. His eyes were cool and indifferent, even reptilian. The Harcourts' biographer, Patrick Jackson, describes him as 'cold-blooded and calculating'.[6] Unlike his bombastic, impulsive father, Loulou was controlled, smooth and watchful. Despite their opposing temperaments, the two had always shared a famously close bond: since Loulou was a child, they had been steadfast companions and would remain so until Harcourt's death in 1904. At the age of thirteen, Loulou had even accompanied Harcourt on his honeymoon to Paris following his second marriage. Prior to her wedding, Loulou's new stepmother, an American widow named Elizabeth Cabot Ives, had been warned by her future husband that Loulou was 'always to be the *first* object' in their marriage, or else their union would be 'impossible'.[7] It was Loulou who was Harcourt's partner in life. No one could assume to come between them.

At eighteen, Loulou came down from Eton and eschewed university to return to his father's side. Upon taking up the post in Parliament as his father's private secretary, he quickly became his most indispensable adviser, goading his father's ambition and drowning him in filial adulation.

Loulou (officially Lewis) Harcourt was born at Pont Street, Knightsbridge, on 31 January 1863. His mother, Thérèse, was the daughter of the writer Thomas Henry Lister and his wife, Lady Maria, a Regency beauty with a delicate heart-shaped face.[8] When Harcourt first announced his engagement to Thérèse in the summer of 1859, his old friend Lady Minto wrote to him describing his fiancée as 'more *simpatica* . . . than any other young lady of the London world'.[9] Another great friend and mentor to Harcourt, Richard Monckton Milnes (later Lord Houghton), wrote in a rather less gushing vein:

> I never forget what the phrenologist said about your mixture of benevolence and combativeness – but I find it difficult to get others to believe it. You are lucky to have found one person who does – May you be as happy as is good for you![10]

Thérèse Lister and 'Willie' Harcourt were married at All Saints Church in Kensington on 5 November 1859. In the happy months that followed, Harcourt was aware that not only had he caught himself an amenable, attractive bride, but that he had also made an astute career move. For as Milnes had also pointed out at the time of their engagement, 'you are going into a very distinguished family and will be connected with the only man in England I look on as certain to be Prime Minister, so you will probably not be overlooked'.[11] Harcourt's new father-in-law (and Thérèse's stepfather) was Sir George Cornewall Lewis, who was serving as Home Secretary to the Prime Minister, Palmerston, and the Chancellor, William Gladstone, in their newly formed Liberal Party. As well as being perfectly placed to assist in Harcourt's future political career, Lewis also proved a calm guide to his volatile son-in-law, who named his second son Loulou after him.

Such an advantageous marriage was not entirely the result of Harcourt's own irresistible graces. For this, as with many more of his career successes and personal triumphs, he was indebted to the orchestrations of his energetic aunt, Lady Waldegrave. Harcourt's aunt was not only a legendary match-maker but also – conveniently for him – one of the most influential political hostesses of the nineteenth century. In February 1898, a journalist in the *Graphic* described her salon:

> Around her sofa throne crowded the men and women who were making the history of the time . . . Political programmes were discussed and decided upon . . . promising postulants were examined, and were accepted or rejected according to judgement passed upon them by Lady Waldegrave . . . This one craved for place, Lady Waldegrave procured it for him . . . another yearned for social recognition, in an instant every door in Mayfair flew open to receive him. It was a special honour for a young man to be invited to visit Strawberry Hill [Waldegrave's estate], for it meant his elders perceived he possessed qualities which if properly cultivated, might be useful to the State or to the party.[12]

Despite being just six years older than Harcourt, Lady Waldegrave took her nephew on as her protégé after he came down from Cambridge in the spring of 1851. Over the following two decades she played a major role in moulding the huffish, tactless Willie Harcourt into a political and social success.

Just as clever and driven as her nephew, Lady Waldegrave had married Harcourt's uncle, George Granville Harcourt, when she was just twenty-six years old and he was sixty-two, desiring the latter's entrée into the most exclusive enclaves of polite society, and to cross a threshold previously barred to her by both her background and the perceived indiscretions of her youth. As the commoner daughter of a famous Jewish opera singer, Waldegrave's questionable beginnings were muddied still further by her two youthful marriages to first one then another of the drunken and dissolute sons of the sixth Earl Waldegrave, both of whom died young. In return for George Harcourt's unimpeachable social credentials, 'the Jewess' – as her miserable new mother-in-law labelled her – at least brought into the Harcourt fold the vast inheritance left to her by her first two amours, which constituted an annual income of £20,000.[13]

Now superbly connected as well as fabulously wealthy, Lady Waldegrave dedicated each of her fourteen summers with George to lavishly and selectively entertaining at both the Harcourt family seat, Nuneham House in Oxfordshire, and at her own Strawberry Hill, a Gothic revival mansion in Twickenham. As well as Willie Harcourt and his great friend Richard Monckton Milnes, guests to be found sipping sherry and champagne at these famous 'Friday to Monday' parties would usually include one or two parliamentary grandees such as Sir Robert Peel or Gladstone, a small smattering of exiled French royals, one or two European ambassadors and ministers, certain favoured members of the English aristocracy (including of course Prince Edward), and artists, writers and dramatists.[14] Lady Waldegrave's salons became a citadel for the rising Liberal Party elite, and she positioned herself as hostess and confidante to some of the most powerful men of the Victorian era. In a climate where politicians often switched allegiances, or still voted according to principle or advancement rather than adhere to the party whip, women like Lady Waldegrave played an invaluable role in providing – amidst good food and pleasant surroundings – an extra-parliamentary opportunity for political persuasion.[15] It was a role Willie Harcourt's aunt ministered so skilfully that Benjamin Disraeli insisted she would have made a 'brilliant' Prime Minister.[16]

Much to the irritation of his uncle George, Harcourt attended his aunt's salons practically every weekend. While George found his nephew infuriatingly churlish, immature and intolerant, his wife was far cleverer at managing the young Harcourt's arrogance and unafraid to put him in his place – which Harcourt respected and rather enjoyed. Lady Waldegrave's biographer Osbert Wyndham Hewett recounts one sullen dinner party during which Willie Harcourt 'being put out about something, was doing tremendous tragic business, folding his arms and looking like Hamlet'. To break the atmosphere Lady Waldegrave asked aloud, in front of her guests, what the sulking Harcourt was thinking about. 'Looking up from his plate with [his] usual mixture of hauteur and insolence', Harcourt petulantly replied: 'Beef.'

'Overdone!' Lady Waldegrave snapped back, to everyone's amusement.[17]

When Harcourt first set his sights on Thérèse Lister, her mother insisted she found him 'odious' and was firmly against any match, writing to her brother that 'if [Harcourt] could not hope to obtain your goodwill, which he had left in Lady Waldegrave's hands to try and obtain, he could not expect that I should allow him to speak to Thérèse'.[18] She had good reason to be wary of Harcourt in 1859, for it was well known that Thérèse was not her unwelcome suitor's first love.

Seven years earlier, in his early twenties, Harcourt had fallen for a pretty, dark-haired woman with a long nose and a rosebud mouth named Mary Bulteel, whom he had met at a reception in London. Her mother was Lady Elizabeth Bulteel, the daughter of the former Whig Prime Minister, Lord Grey. Mary was intensely religious but also serious, intelligent and of a progressive, liberal outlook; Queen Victoria rightly suspected her of 'cleverness' and of having rather 'advanced views'.[19] In Harcourt, Mary first saw a tall, assuming but handsome young man soon to be called to the Bar and still full of the awkward pride and romantic ideals of a young graduate. The two exchanged poetry, letters and promises of love that soon alchemized into an engagement. Harcourt was effusive about his forthcoming nuptials in a letter to Richard Monckton Milnes: 'Our marriage', he wrote, 'can't take place till I make something for us to live on; but . . . this will make me work 100 horse power at law which I really like as nothing agrees with me so well as hard work, except being in love'.[20] That Harcourt had to work so hard to earn Mary's hand must have grated on his social insecurities, but he was keen to prove his eligibility. A year later, however, Mary had broken off the engagement.

Having nursed 'misgivings' about Harcourt for some time, Mary was further put off by his strident demands that she renew her promise of marriage. Harcourt had even presented her with a deadline by which she must do this – 2 October 1855. In the face of this ultimatum Mary chose to cut free.[21] Her insensitive suitor was not just disappointed, he was also publicly embarrassed; and in the following weeks he wrote to Lady Waldegrave describing his 'horrible' melancholia.[22]

Worse still, vicious rumours soon spread to his circle, compounding his misery. 'I hear,' he continued to his aunt, that 'Lady Elizabeth [Bulteel – Mary's mother] has been telling abominable lies about me, not the smallest of which is that from the first she was against the engagement'.[23] Harcourt's reaction to such idle spite was typical. He salved his pride by lashing out with true vindictiveness, circulating Mary's love letters to him among his relations. By the following spring, word had reached Mary's mother that one of Harcourt's sisters had been publicly quoting sentences from her daughter's private correspondence. Lady Elizabeth, outraged by Harcourt's lack of 'manly' feeling, recruited her brother, Henry, the 3rd Earl Grey to tackle him in person.[24] Outranked by the earl in seniority and social position, Harcourt backed down and returned Mary's papers. But his vindictive impulses remained.

Wary of the Bulteels' experience and of Harcourt's sulky indiscretions, Thérèse Lister's mother continued in 1859 to oppose the new match between them until Lady Waldegrave intervened. Only when Harcourt's aunt successfully persuaded her that his faults were actually 'on the surface and . . . far less apparent as you know him more' did she capitulate.[25] In the end she became rather fond of her new son-in-law and was rewarded soon after the marriage with the expectation of a new grandchild.

On 6 October 1860, Thérèse Harcourt gave birth to a baby boy. He was christened Julian, after Harcourt's 'choicest' of 'bosom cronies' from his university days, the 'startlingly handsome, incurable philanderer', Julian Fane, a diplomat and poet.[26] But like his namesake, the child Julian was delicate and in February 1862 the Harcourts returned from a business trip in Switzerland and Germany to find their son suffering from a fever and 'brain disorder' from which he failed to rally.[27] Julian Vernon Harcourt died on 2 March 1862, aged sixteen months.

Harcourt found the loss of his first son a 'heavy and bitter blow'.[28] In a letter to his friend Thomas Hughes, the author of *Tom Brown's Schooldays*, he described how he 'really [felt] as if all [his] heartstrings were snapped. My happiness was so wrapped up in the little boy that I feel it must be very long before either mind or body can rally from the shock'.[29] Julian Harcourt was buried at Nuneham Church, in the grounds of Nuneham House. A monument marking his passing still exists inside: a slumbering angel baby lying on a classical plinth. Hovering above, casting a faint shadow over his delicate face, another stone monument was soon to be added, marking the second tragedy that followed, swift as a hungry ghoul.

On 31 January 1863, an unblinkingly blue day, Thérèse gave birth prematurely to her second baby boy.[30] This time she did not survive the birth. She died the same day, only twenty-seven years old, and Harcourt was plunged into many more months of grief. 'I do very badly without her,' he wrote to his sister, 'the desolation of this house is quite unbearable to me'.[31] Harcourt sought relief in his daily legal work and, more slowly, in his love for his remaining new-born son – Lewis. He came to dote on 'Loulou', describing the child as both his 'trust and consoler' and agonizing daily over his wellbeing.[32] Lady St Helier, who often visited Loulou during his sickly boyhood, recalled the relationship between father and child.

> No more tender or devoted nurse ever watched over her child, and though his methods . . . were not perhaps in accord with the first principles of health, one cannot scrutinize too severely the regime which nurtured Mr. Lewis Harcourt.[33]

Throughout Loulou's childhood Harcourt indulged his son as his peer. He had 'at home' cards printed stating both his and his son's names and at Christmas the two would drink solemn toasts together, sitting at opposite ends of the dining table like husband and wife. Harcourt had found comfort in the fact that he could see traces of Thérèse in Loulou and almost a year after her death wrote to his friend Lady Minto:

> My dear little boy is all I could wish. Even apart from a father's fondness for an only child I think he is the . . . most beautiful boy you ever saw and withal his mother's smile, I quite feel as if he was her angel with me still.[34]

Harcourt spoiled Loulou in his childhood to assuage his own loss and loneliness, but also perhaps to relieve the boy of his leaden burden: that the price of his existence was the death of his mother. Likewise, as Loulou grew up, he will have understood that his father too had paid a heavy toll for his life, the loss of his young wife. As such, he indulged his father and the two came to rely upon each other rather too much. 'The death of a much-loved wife', writes their biographer Patrick Jackson, 'focused [Harcourt's] feelings on the child to an unnatural extent'.[35] In the absence of a spouse, the father turned for his emotional needs to his son, and Loulou had little choice but to willingly oblige.

*

In the bruising aftermath of Julian's and Thérèse's deaths, Harcourt remained a bachelor for thirteen years. Beyond Loulou he found solace in trusted friends, particularly Julian Fane and Richard Monckton Milnes. The three regularly met at Lady Waldegrave's salons, and Fane and Harcourt, who described his friend as a 'pard-like spirit beautiful and swift', were particularly close.[36] The three men also shared a bond beyond even Lady Waldegrave's reach, for they were all members of one of the most elite and clandestine male sects in England – the Cambridge Apostles.

This secret society was founded in 1820 and based in Trinity College, Cambridge University, which Harcourt, Fane and Milnes had all attended. The declared purpose of the Cambridge Apostles was to provide comradeship between intellectual, liberal-leaning undergraduates picked from the peerage and the professional (upper) middle class. The society held weekly debates on all manner of subjects, however taboo. Within this daring atmosphere, fraternal friendships created a 'freemasonry' of sympathy that lasted a lifetime.[37]

Their exclusiveness and secrecy re-enforced the Apostles' notion of themselves as distinct from, superior to, and independent of the world: extraordinary beings who occupied 'Reality' while all else was ordinary, commonplace, something they labelled the 'Phenomenal'.[38] The key requirement of Reality was absolute candour. Intellectually and sexually, the Apostles' search for truth, their search for the Real, had to be liberated from the trivial moral constraints that preoccupied the Phenomenal; and applying this dialectic, Apostles believed they could remain 'independent, yet public [and] be uncompromised, yet do one's duty'.[39] In other words, by separating public duty from private pleasures, a Cambridge Apostle felt he could do as he pleased.

One of the earliest Apostles was the poet Alfred Tennyson, who was famously believed to have conducted an intimate relationship with fellow Apostle Arthur Hallam, who also became engaged to Tennyson's younger sister Emily.[40] In later years, the more overt sexual libertinism of London's Bloomsbury group was informed by the Cambridge Apostles Lytton Strachey and Roger Fry.[41] Later still, during the cold war, the revelation of a Cambridge spy ring pivoted on two former Apostles, Guy Burgess and Anthony Blunt. In November 1963 *The Times* aggressively linked the 'homosexual culture' and 'arrogant cult of the intellect' formed in 'the Cambridge School' to Burgess and Blunt's treachery.[42]

One man who left an enduring legacy of his dedication to the experimental creed of the Cambridge Apostles was Richard Monckton Milnes. Known to all as 'Dicky Milnes', in the public sphere he was a social success and an influential and philanthropic literary patron. Like his friend Lady Waldegrave, Milnes 'knew everybody, talked of everything [and was] . . . a social power in London'. He was 'the cool of the evening', a 'maker of men', and a 'word from him went far'.[43] He counted Gladstone, Disraeli and Louis Napoleon as friends, as well as Tennyson, Thackeray and Carlyle. For many years he was also Florence Nightingale's most serious suitor and supporter. Nightingale, who decided she was unwilling to spend a 'life with [Milnes] in making society and arranging domestic things', eventually turned down his hand in marriage, though the two remained lifelong friends.[44] In an effusive letter after Milnes' death, Nightingale described to a friend how he once declared that 'if there is any good in me, it is that I would lay out my life in good service to others'.[45] She appears blissfully unaware that he also had a more voracious side, having rivalled Tennyson for Arthur Hallam's intimacy at Cambridge before embarking on a Byronic tour of sexual adventures in the Orient; or that in his private life, Milnes was a dark presence whose bullying wit goaded weaker men into pushing the moral boundaries he himself despised.[46]

In the library of his Palladian home, Fryston Hall, in the West Riding of Yorkshire, Milnes amassed what Harford Montgomery Hyde described in his *History of Pornography* as 'probably the largest collection of erotica ever assembled by a private collector or for that matter ever likely to be'.[47] Milne's world-class collection was matched only by that of another of his friends, Henry Spencer Ashbee (alias Walter, author of

My Secret Life). Much of Milne's obscene material was imported from the Continent via the Foreign Office in the 'diplomatic bag'. His collection ranged from eighteenth-century French classics like *Les Liaisons Dangereuses* by Choderlos Laclos and *La Pucelle d'Orléans* (a satire about the bawdy adventures of Joan of Arc) by Voltaire, to lesser-known gems such as *Les Yeux, Le Nez et Les Tétons* (Eyes, Nose and Nipples) or *Le Jou-jou des Demoiselles* (Lady's Toys).[48] He also amassed many homoerotic works and was perhaps best known for his obsession with sexual sadism in all its forms, which he also liked to experience in person. On one occasion, Milnes attended a brothel run by a 'Mrs Jenkins', where he beat a 'class' of naked thirteen-year-old girls until they bled.[49]

Milnes also counted in his coterie the ever-philandering Prince Edward and A. J. Munby, a Victorian diarist who sketched and fetishized working-class women, the dirtier the better. In his diary Munby records an afternoon spent with Milnes, who dominated his 'court' with his 'favourite subject' – pornography. Watching Milnes in his element, Munby found him 'sly, sensuous and potentially wicked'.[50] The Italian critic Professor Mario Praz went further, describing Milnes as a man of 'Mephistophelean malice' who crouched spider-like at Fryston, directing the interplay of his cohort's perversions for his own 'strange, weird comedy'.[51] Milne's many young acolytes included the poet Algernon Swinburne – a sado-masochist and alcoholic who became his literary protégé. Another was the future Home Secretary, Sir William Harcourt.

*

As Harcourt's faithful son Loulou hurried back from the Isle of Wight to London in response to his stricken father's telegram, uppermost in his mind was a concern for his young half-brother, Robert, born to his father's second wife, Elizabeth. Loulou was very fond of seven-year-old Robert and dreaded that another tragedy had returned to torment his father. By the evening, he finally reached his family's London home in Grafton Street, Mayfair. To 'his great relief' he found that here at least 'everyone was well'.[52] His father being still at the Houses of Parliament, Loulou continued his journey there through the late summer twilight. Over the Mall and into Parliament Square, up the House of Commons steps, down stone corridors, through wooden doors – until at last he would have his answer.

Sir William Harcourt had demanded his son's return from Cowes because he found himself in a most desperate and damaging fix. Thanks to the fervent, whispered determination of the ex-inspector Jeremiah Minahan, the Irish MP Philip Callan had ratcheted up his threats over Harcourt's conduct and the Jeffries case. Loulou's father had been informed that Callan next intended publicly to charge the former Home Secretary 'with having treated Minahan unfairly' to serve his own base and private means.[53] Harcourt had abused his position, he had punished an innocent man, stolen Minahan's pride and snatched his pension purely to secure his own. Because, alleged Callan, the ex-inspector had observed Harcourt in Chelsea, and regularly in Church Street. As Callan had it, Sir William Harcourt had ill-used Jeremiah Minahan solely to shield the fact that it was he who was 'in the habit of frequenting Mrs. Jeffries' brothel'.[54]

Chapter Thirteen

I And I Alone Am Responsible

> You ain't going to be able any longer to monopolise any fact of general interest, and it ain't going to be right you should, it ain't going to continue to be possible to keep out anywhere the light of the Press . . . We'll see who's private then, and whose hands are off, and who'll frustrate the People – the People *that wants to know*.
>
> George Flack, newspaper reporter in *The Reverberator*, by Henry James, 1888[1]

William Thomas Stead, editor of the *Pall Mall Gazette*, appeared overwhelmed by the effect of his summer toils. Standing on a platform in Hyde Park late in the afternoon of Saturday 22 August, he could see beneath him a rippling expanse of pale city faces. Their waving hats and handkerchiefs, hands and flowers and banners were raised amid a cacophony of cheers and shouts of admiration. Tens of thousands had come, wrote a correspondent from the *Manchester Guardian*, to witness 'the man who had literally set the world talking for the past two months'.[2] Thanks largely to Stead's *Maiden Tribute* revelations, the Criminal Law Amendment Act had entered the British statute books on Friday 14 August 1885. This 'Great Demonstration' in Hyde Park was both a celebration and an exhortation to the authorities to impose the new vice laws with vigilance. Stead was now the established leader of the summer's 'moral uprising', a crusader unshakeable in his desire to shield the children of the poor from the profligacy of the rich.[3] He was the man who promised to always 'speak the truth and shame the Devil', yet his demeanour on the speaker's platform was not one of triumph, but rather of a man marked by a silent, soul-searing dread.[4]

When it was time to speak, Stead held out his hand to silence the crowd. But it was a 'curious gesture', half-hearted and weak.[5] He tried to begin – twice – and stumbled – twice. Under the weight of the throng's great expectations, 'nothing more articulate came from Stead than a sort of gasp of pain', and in the unseemly seconds that followed, the *Manchester Guardian* newsman, standing close by, observed that Stead's forehead was corrugated 'all in perpendicular wrinkles . . . of anxiety' and that his face was 'deadly pale and his lips were almost white'. Such a sickly pallor must stem, the reporter presumed, from the overwhelming pride of such a moment; that as a 'small obscure country journalist [Stead] had moved down on London like a conqueror'.[6]

It was a generous thought. In fact, the real sources of Stead's strain were his professional rival, Thomas Catling, and *his* tenacious special correspondent Henry Hales. Though Stead always denied any allegations about the methods he employed during his *Maiden Tribute* investigations, his countenance at the Hyde Park event betrayed his misgivings. At the very least he was quick-witted enough to understand that there were gentlemen in London keen to push him from his righteous perch. And just hours before he was due to address the crowd in Hyde Park, Catling and Hales had informed him that they had the wherewithal to do just that.

*

Over the previous weeks, Henry Hales had unravelled a fatal flaw in Stead's *Maiden Tribute* report. As Hales had it, Eliza Armstrong was not 'sold' into iniquity by her heartless mother; rather Stead had tricked the girl away from her respectable parents on the promise of a 'place'; an act that the less generous might construe an abduction. He next subjected the girl to the intimate scrutiny of a French midwife, a measure that could certainly be considered an indecent assault, before having the child drugged in a Soho brothel – a crime so ignominious as to be unspeakable.[7] Worse still, despite several reports in *Lloyd's* over the previous weeks describing the efforts of Eliza's mother to retrieve her daughter, the thirteen-year-old girl still remained missing. Whatever Booth had claimed about keeping the child in 'safe keeping', he had yet to prove his words.[8] And as Catling and Hales understood it, it was actually William Stead and his shadowy accomplice Rebecca Jarrett who were last *seen* with Eliza in their hands.

The principal questions *Lloyd's* wanted answered now were where (and with whom) 'the girl passed the night' before being passed to Booth and what had really happened to her since?[9]

Catling and Hales were not alone in their curiosity. The several articles they had already published in *Lloyd's* and the subsequent discussions in Parliament had intensified the pressure on Stead to provide answers. On Friday 21 August, he had been a key speaker at a social purity event in Piccadilly, to promote the protection of girls. When he stood up to speak a lone heckle had shot across the vast conference hall:

'What about Lizzie [Eliza] Armstrong?'

To which Stead made a remarkable admission:

'I will tell you about Lizzie Armstrong . . . I and I alone, am solely responsible for taking Lizzie away from her mother's house . . . We took that child from a place that reeked with vice. We took that child from a mother who knew . . . her child was going to a brothel [and] we placed her in good and Christian guardianship.'[10]

The moral reformers in the crowd greeted the story of Eliza's salvation with enthusiastic cheers. Emboldened, Stead next disclosed that he had also taken Eliza 'to a brothel for about half an hour', but wholly failed to mention her examination, the chloroform, or his own presence in the bawdy house's bedroom.[11]

The following morning, ahead of Hyde Park, Stead ran into Catling and Hales at the Salvation Army offices of William Bramwell Booth. Having decided to visit his friend, he discovered him in a tight-lipped conflux with the two men from *Lloyd's*. Catling and Hales were delighted when Stead appeared and agreed to answer their questions. In response to their query as to 'where [Eliza] had passed the night', Stead disclosed that 'at around midnight' she was taken from Soho to respectable lodgings near Harley Street:

> After sleeping there with Rebecca Jarrett she was driven the next morning – Thursday June 4th – to Charing Cross Station, and handed over to one of the female members of the Salvation Army, by whom she was at once taken off to France, where she had since remained.[12]

With the help of Booth and his international network of Salvation Army staff, Eliza had been 'trafficked' at Stead's behest to the Continent in exactly the same way as Adelene Tanner and all the others who had gone before. In proving how easily this could be done, Stead had hoped to shock the nation into seeing the necessity of improving Britain's vice laws. Eliza had travelled to Paris by railway and steam packet across the Channel in the company of a Salvation Army woman named Madame Combe, and Rebecca Jarrett. Jarrett's presence was unplanned, but when Stead, Combe and she regrouped amidst the scurrying clerks and cuff-shooters at Charing Cross Station, Eliza balked at being parted from her new 'mistress'.[13] Rather than risk a scene or upset the girl,

Stead had decided to pay for Jarrett to accompany her to Paris. Jarrett then returned to England two days later.[14]

For the whole of June 1885, Eliza stayed in the Parisian Salvation Army headquarters in an old canal-side foundry in the working-class district of Quai de Valmy, to the north-east of the city.[15] In July, she was moved to Loriol, deep in the south of France, where she remained under the care of another family connected to the Salvation Army and their English governess. When the questions surrounding her disappearance intensified in Parliament and in the newspapers, Stead and Booth had returned her to Paris, to ease her probable return to London. Though confused by events, the sweet-tempered girl was unaware of her role at the centre of a growing police and Home Office investigation, and her presence in what was to prove one of the biggest newspaper sensations of the nineteenth century. Instead, Eliza had enjoyed the adventure of selling the *War Cry*, the Salvation Army newspaper, on the Parisian boulevards, and in the verdant environs of Loriol she had grown healthy working as a servant girl.[16]

For weeks Stead had reassured himself that Mrs Armstrong really was a callous mother who knowingly sold her daughter, only to claim innocence when she was caught. But inside the Salvation Army offices on Saturday 22 August, Thomas Catling was insisting that Mrs Armstrong was genuine and truly 'wished to have her child back'.[17] If Catling was proved right, Stead had flagrantly breached both the law and the sanctity of a family in order to score his political point. As a journalist he had also failed to check his facts, trusting instead to the word of Jarrett, a procuress he barely knew; and his failure to mention Madame Mourey or the doings in the brothel suggests a creeping doubt in his mind that his treatment of the girl was entirely justified. There is no evidence that Stead touched Eliza, but his anxiety about how his actions might be perceived can only have deepened when he heard Catling and Hales' less than altruistic interpretation of events. Yet Stead had little choice. If his career and his reputation were to survive the coming storm, he had to side with Jarrett against Mrs Armstrong. In the guise of the persecuted saint, he would brazen out his beliefs to the bitter end.

As soon as Catling and Hales departed to add Stead's admissions to their copy, the *Pall Mall Gazette* editor and the Salvation Army leader did their utmost to contain the dynamite *Lloyd's* would ignite the following day.

Booth sent word to France requesting that his Salvation Army colleagues return Eliza Armstrong from Paris to England immediately. She arrived in London next morning, Sunday, around the same time that *Lloyd's* hit the streets. While Booth did this, Stead wrote a letter to Eliza's parents:

> Pall Mall Gazette Office,
> Northumberland Street,
> Strand,
> August 22nd 1885.
>
> Mrs. Armstrong, Madam, I am informed today for the first time [by Thomas Catling] that you wish your daughter Eliza restored to you. She is well taken care of and very happy, but if you and Mr. Armstrong really wish to have her returned to you I am, and always have been, perfectly ready to comply with your request. As yet, however, you have not informed anyone with whom I have been in communication, either the police or the Salvation 'Army' people, that you desire her to be taken from a good situation in order to have her back at home.[18] If, however, you should now inform me that you want to have her back, I shall deliver her over on receipt of your letter to that effect . . .
>
> I am, yours truly, Chief Director[19]

The letter formed a brief defence of his actions and a means of staving off his panic, but it also added to the evidence being collated by the police and the Home Office, an investigation that had derived huge benefit from the assistance of Catling and Hales. Mr Jacques, Stead's accomplice and employee, delivered the letter, also on the Sunday, to 32 Charles Street, Lisson Grove.

'Would you like to see your daughter?' Jacques asked Mrs Armstrong.

'Oh yes sir, very much indeed,' she replied.

'Then you shall see her,' said Jacques.[20]

He promised to take Mrs Armstrong to Eliza 'on the morrow', Monday 24 August. They arranged to meet at eleven.

'Whatever you do,' said Jacques before taking his leave, 'do not say nothing about it to the police.'

'No,' said Mrs Armstrong.[21]

Then *Lloyd's* came out.

Next morning Mr Jacques returned to Lisson Grove at eleven to find Police Inspector Borner had arrived at the Armstrongs' lodgings at half-past nine. Inspector Borner had returned from his holiday in the Fens to resume his investigation of the Armstrong case, and Eliza's mother had shown him Stead's letter soon after Jacques left. Under Borner's supervision, Eliza was returned to her mother's care at Stead's house in Wimbledon that same day, with Stead's full guarantee that she was healthful, happy and most importantly – still a virgin. After providing a statement to the police at Scotland Yard, Eliza and Mrs Armstrong returned rather triumphantly to Charles Street with a police escort and there found hundreds of anxious well-wishers gathered to catch a glimpse of the new young celebrity. But it was not enough to save Stead.

*

It had taken an hour for the seventy thousand demonstrators, thirty-four brass bands, twenty-five wagonettes, private carriages, traps and dogcarts to process into Hyde Park at five o'clock on that Saturday afternoon.[22] Arriving from different routes and directions, some walking west along Pall Mall spotted the brothel-keepers' favourite MP, George Cavendish-Bentinck, watching them pass from a window of the Carlton Club, a sanctum of the Conservative Party.[23]

From his observation post, Cavendish-Bentinck saw trade unionists and artisan guilds, Repealers and Socialists, Christian Associations, Nonconformist chapel brethren, Sunday-school groups and hordes of women from Josephine Butler's Ladies' National Association passing by, their variant aims briefly united beneath the wan summer sky. Many of the women were dressed in black. They carried posies of white flowers; the men wore white rosettes or armbands. Some carriages were decorated with white lilies and roses, while one wagon was filled entirely with little girls all bedecked in white. Just as the red feather in Eliza's hat had symbolized immodesty and peril, here the colour white was for both purity and mourning.[24] Theirs was a lamentation for the lost virtue of London's children, sold to a destiny worse than death. 'Shall the innocent be slaughtered?' asked one banner, while another demanded: 'Men! Protect England's Girlhood'. More progressive still was the insistence that 'Representation [was] the Only Check for Irresponsible Power' and that there should be 'Equal Rights for Men and Women'.[25]

Across ten platforms set up in the eastern end of the park, fifty speakers advanced the banners' calls. Stentorian preachers such as James B. Wookey and the international evangelist Henry Varley demanded social purity; others attacked overcrowding, poverty and intemperance in the city. The speakers on the women's platform – largely organized by Jeremiah

Minahan's supporter, the authoress and campaigner Miss Bewicke – demanded female suffrage to end the pre-dominance of low masculine values.[26] At platform no. 3, a popular and crowded area, the Irish social campaigner (and former political lieutenant of Charles Parnell, MP) Michael Davitt roundly asserted that vice came from a society riven with social inequality:

> The working-classes [have been] defrauded and debauched by those who taught . . . that labour was debasing and that a descent from hereditary idlers [equated to] the right to rule the State. [We] should not rest with the rigorous application of the Criminal Law Amendment Act, [we] should go to the root of . . . poverty from the standpoint of the producers of all wealth, who were, nevertheless, the wage-slaves of the wealth thus created.[27]

Davitt's words were greeted with loud – and to some observers worrying – cheers. One society journal, the *World*, dismissed such voices with outright disdain:

> The fools and fanatics who have taken part in the . . . Demonstration have done what they can to degrade their country . . . These people can no more be kept from thronging round an unsavoury business than flies from lighting upon dungheaps. The *personnel* of the crowd [were] far inferior in quality to what one is accustomed to see upon these occasions.[28]

The demonstration, insisted the *Standard*, was made up of 'thousands of idlers', while the *Western Mail* found 'the spectacle of youths and girls laughing and joking with one another . . . not edifying'; and in a letter published by the *St. James Gazette*, 'An Accidental Demonstrator' opined that he 'believed himself to be the only respectable person present'.[29]

Such snobbish derision from the conservative press revealed its alarm over recent events in London. 'Some will say', predicted Stead, 'that there were about 500 people in the park today – and that speakers with one consent set class against class'.[30] Commentators and politicians had repeatedly accused Stead of stoking class antagonism in the wake of his *Maiden Tribute* campaign; his sweeping accusations against the dissolute ruling elite coupled with his assertion that the rights of any child should take precedence over the predilections of gentlemen had made him a swathe of enemies. But what his detractors were really railing against, and perhaps only dimly perceived, was a sea change in society far bigger than Stead and his hydra-headed mix of Socialists, Suffragists, Nonconformists and Radicals. For these seminal months of 1885 were the crested wave of a decade that rose and broke over England, pulling influence from the hands of the aristocracy and depositing it instead on the shores of the rising middle classes.[31] This was the summer that marked the turning point in a very tacit, slow-creeping, Victorian revolution.

*

The passing of the Criminal Law Amendment Act on Friday 14 August 1885 was just one of several fronts on which the middle classes had trumped aristocratic mores. The new law signified the ascent of bourgeois respectability over the louche and outmoded libertinism long enjoyed by wealthy, high-born men like Richard Monckton Milnes. As if to acknowledge the end of his era, the seventy-six-year-old Milnes died on 11 August 1885, three days before the Bill passed into law. It was his successors who would feel its sting. The Act increased the age of consent to sixteen; provided the police with the power to raid brothels and restrict soliciting; and introduced new penalties against *placeurs* and abusers, and against parents who allowed their children to be sexually exploited.[32]

Joining the judiciary and the police in enforcing the new moral dawn was an embryonic tabloid press. While England's conscience continued to reel in the wake of Stead's *Maiden Tribute* revelations, canny editors who had witnessed the *Pall Mall Gazette*'s peak in sales also turned their efforts to sensationalism. Stead's public-spirited but sex-centred campaign spawned numerous imitators after 1885, which culminated in the cheap, scandal-mongering press of the twentieth century.[33] The journalist Kennedy Jones, who worked on the *Sun* before launching the *Daily Mail* in 1896, attributed his industry success to the inspiration of Stead:

> The simplest way to collect a crowd in London is to shout loud enough from a top-floor window 'Murder! Fire! Thieves!' So to an upper casement Stead went and raised the old scream at the top of his voice:
>
> 'Babylon! Babylon! The Mother of Harlots! The Great City of Babylon!'
>
> He got his crowd.[34]

Lower-class readers of the penny and ha'penny 'rags' were treated to tales about the private lives of public figures, the upper class and the celebrated: privileged people who came to despise the menace of living under such scrutiny.

In his 1888 novella *The Reverberator*, Henry James explored the peril of this new form of journalism. He had spent much of the summer of 1885 in England and in the company of his friend and fellow writer Robert Louis Stevenson.[35] Both authors witnessed the social upheaval created by Stead's *Maiden Tribute* campaign and appear inspired by its cultural significance: Stevenson's *Jekyll and Hyde* – published in January 1886 – implied that the double lives upheld by gentlemen like the late Richard Monckton Milnes (or indeed the late Professor Risley) had now become untenable; while James took the rise of the scandal sheets as his inspiration for *The Reverberator*.[36] According to James, such newspapers wrought 'the invasion, the impudence and shamelessness . . . the extinction of all sense between public and private' upon society.[37] It was an encroachment propelled by the cultural influence and the 'familiarity' of the lower classes, or as James put it, the 'democratization of the world'.[38] During such a levelling process, James also understood that it was the wealthy and powerful who felt they had the most to lose. 'Oh *they* can be fixed you'll see!' his upstart reporter in *The Reverberator*, George Flack, declares of the 'prominent members' of the 'society-news'.[39]

One of the first to be 'fixed' by the nation's new moral mood was Sir William Harcourt's friend and colleague, the Liberal MP for Chelsea, Sir Charles Dilke. Before the *Maiden Tribute* series was published, Sir Charles was the rising star of the Liberal Party, touted to be party leader and eventually Prime Minister. But on 18 July 1885, Dilke was cited as co-respondent in the high-profile divorce case of Virginia and Donald Crawford – also a Liberal MP. Crawford's young wife alleged an affair between herself and Dilke and despite his later protestations of innocence, the politician immediately understood that during such charged times (and with Stead sharpening his pen over this latest 'Great Social Scandal') his career was effectively over.[40] On 23 July 1885 Dilke wrote in his diary:

> Left for the last time the House of Commons . . . It is curious that only a week ago Chn. [Joseph Chamberlain MP] & I agreed at his wish that I shd. be the future leader, & only three days ago Mr. G. [Gladstone] had expressed the same wish. A sudden fall indeed![41]

Dilke's demise was followed in 1890 by that of the Irish

Nationalist MP Charles Parnell who, similarly embroiled in a divorce scandal, lost his political leadership. Five years on, the 1895 trials revealing the homosexuality of the great playwright and society wit Oscar Wilde also brought about his public ruin.

The newspapers that profited most from such downfalls were owned and operated by men who presented yet another threat to upper-class authority. The gentry had long justified their powers by claiming that their land ownership was tantamount to an investment in the country they governed out of loyalty and duty.[42] By contrast, or so the aristocracy felt, the new and emerging generation of plutocrats were businessmen on the make, who operated with little consideration for the nation that funded their fortunes. Brash financiers, capitalists and speculators were buying their way into the Commons and the Lords and once there, using their political influence with a view to profit rather than principle. Their presence was increasingly pervasive and for the first time, during the 1880s, peerages were regularly bestowed on men of a non-landed background.[43]

Amongst the plutocrats, it was the press barons who were feared the most, since not only did they dine out on disgrace, they also held huge political sway over England's lower-class voters. One of the most successful newspaper proprietors during this period was Alfred Harmsworth (later Lord Northcliffe), who launched his first populist magazine in 1888, aged just twenty-three. Harmsworth then went on to own the *Daily Mail*, the *Express*, the *Observer* and the ultimate organ of Empire and Establishment, *The Times*.[44] By exercising their monopoly over the populace, Harmsworth and his successors came to exert an unprecedented control over politicians, making and breaking party policies, Prime Ministers and even governments.[45]

While the plutocrats wrested power from the top, it was

ordinary men, from the respectable working-class up, who seized the political initiative from the bottom. The passing of the Third Reform Act of 1884–5 had finally tilted the balance of the constitution from notables to numbers and as a result of this too, patrician dominance in the House of Commons began to fade.[46] The 'class' of the marchers at Hyde Park may have been deemed 'inferior' by certain commentators, but the demonstrators' voting power, their motivation and their moral standards now represented a serious cultural and political challenge to their patrician 'betters'.

So when William Stead insisted, as he had in his *Maiden Tribute* articles that July, that 'the future' belonged to 'Democracy and Socialism' or that, as he continued to suggest in the *Pall Mall Gazette* on Saturday 22 August, the nation was venturing into 'great experiments in social reconstruction', he touched a nerve already deeply aggravated. Entitled observers like Cavendish-Bentinck may have felt a certain foreboding over Stead's popularity. In a matter of weeks this nobody from the North Country had indeed 'conquered' London, and could now garner crowds of seventy thousand. Some witnesses suggested the real total at Hyde Park that day was closer to a quarter of a million.[47] Could this forthright idealist, this God-fearing messenger with messianic eyes actually be a revolutionary leader in the making? The answer was no. For thanks to the findings published next day in *Lloyd's*, Stead was thoroughly felled before his 'moral uprising' could swell any further.

*

On Sunday 23 August, Catling turned his latest revelations on 'The Armstrong Mystery' into an entire '*Lloyd's* Special Edition' and clearly implicated Stead as ringleader in the strange disappearance of Eliza Armstrong.[48] Catling also identified William Bramwell Booth and Josephine Butler as sharing

Stead's connection with the disreputable Rebecca Jarrett. In the same report, *Lloyd's* revealed that Jarrett had attempted to steal other girls too, including a thirteen-year-old from Winchester. When asked by the girl's frantic mother what business she had with the child, the 'startled' Jarrett replied:

'Well I was going to take her up to a situation in London.'

'I think you might have consulted me about it first,' complained the mother, 'it is a great liberty to take her up to London without my authority, and we have been hunting all day long for her.'

'I did not know she had a mother,' said Jarrett.[49]

Jarrett later explained to the same family why she was 'stealing' girls, saying that:

> She had been engaged by some people in London who wanted to prove that girls could be stolen and that mothers would sell their children and no further enquiries would be made about them. They also wanted to show that they could be sent from one country to another.[50]

*

Jarrett's lonely conversion from drunken prostitute to abstemious rescue-worker had only begun a few months before she met Stead. By the time she reached her mid-thirties, she had been a hard drinker for over two decades and was warned by doctors that she would die if she did not stop. In November 1884, she had tried to improve her situation by moving away from London to the market town of Northampton. It was there that she saw a street sign advertising a Salvation Army meeting. Curious, she went inside and sat quietly at the back, but her bright dress and blue bonnet with its long matching feather loudly announced her status to the Salvationists inside. When, overcome by hunger and failing health, Jarrett collapsed unconscious in the middle of the meeting, her dramatic rescue under the auspices of the Salvation Army began. Over the following months the Salvationists nursed Jarrett away from alcoholism and into Christian temperance. At the Army's Rescue Home for Women at 212 Hanbury Street, in the East End of London, she became close to Booth's wife, Florence. The Booths introduced her to Josephine Butler, who helped her establish Hope Cottage in Winchester.[51] In late May 1885, when the campaign to pass the Criminal Law Amendment Bill had seemed lost and hopeless, Butler had arranged Jarrett's journey from Winchester to Stead's newspaper offices in London. On the May Whitsun weekend, both Butler and Stead, who shared an 'intense desire to reform [the] system, urged [Jarrett] to make reparation for her past life and do what was required'.[52] Guilt-ridden and needy, Jarrett placed herself at their disposal. 'They let Mr. Stead have me,' she later recalled, 'to be the poor tool to show it up'.[53] Stead instructed Jarrett to purchase a young virtuous girl like Eliza Armstrong then hand her back to him to be 'trafficked' to the Continent.

Focused on their own issues, neither Stead nor Butler anticipated the risks Jarrett was taking on their behalf. The purchase of Eliza forced the former alcoholic to return to the stews and drinking dens she had sworn off just months before, and in Whitechapel, Jarrett broke her sobriety to appear credible to the stooges inside the bad house at Lady Lake Grove.[54] When she returned to Lisson Grove in Marylebone she risked encountering her mother and her brothers, who now ran a brothel in the district. The family feared Jarrett's new-found Christianity, worrying she might open their business to scrutiny, while her former 'husband', a man named Sullivan, missed living off her harlotry.[55] Jarrett may have successfully dodged their sights during her flits in and out of Charles Street, but word soon reached her kin that she had been back.

After Jarrett purchased Eliza Armstrong and handed the girl over to Stead and his Salvation Army friends, she sent the letter to Nancy Broughton reassuring that Eliza 'was alright and doing well', and suggesting she would visit Nancy again 'if you will let me'.[56] But she also included her address, and soon after received an unwanted visit from 'her brothers' and Sullivan at Hope Cottage, Winchester.[57] Barging into the small country house, the men had tried to coax her back to London and her old life, then harassed and insulted her, and when she rejected them, smashed several windows.[58] Butler was so concerned that on 11 July 1885, she and Booth helped Jarrett flee to Jersey in the Channel Islands and then to Colchester in Essex.[59] Booth wrote to Stead, describing his involvement: 'I sent a man to remove Rebecca to a place of safety – he has done so & I have a telegram today saying that four persons arrived there last night seeking her!'[60]

Jarrett's flight from her former 'friends' was the reason why Hope Cottage was found to be 'closed' up when Inspector Borner visited on 15 July, though her absence was later interpreted as a means of evading the police investigation.[61]

*

According to the men from *Lloyd's*, Jarrett was a genuine product of 'Outcast London', barely educated, fatalistic and drink-damaged. It was upon the warrant of a woman like this, their article insinuated, that Eliza Armstrong's mother had suffered 'terrible accusations' and had 'been for six weeks striving to regain possession of her child'.[62] It was also wholly on the word of Jarrett that Stead had hinged his shocking account of Eliza (alias 'Lily'), the 'Child of Thirteen Sold for £5'. Stead's report had shamed the nation and changed the course of English law. Now *Lloyd's* was suggesting that it appeared an improbable and embarrassing fabrication.

When Stead finally managed to utter some words at the Hyde Park demonstration, he chose *not* to mention the case of Eliza Armstrong. Instead he praised his listeners for their 'glowing hearts' and their new-found voice of 'truth and earnestness'.[63] Theirs was a warmth that contrasted with the 'men' whose 'papers circulate by their hundreds of thousands [and] . . . who have nothing but words of contumely and reproach for the great cause'.[64] Men who would soon join the politicians chastened by Stead into hurrying through new legislation, the upper-class libertines whose wings he had clipped, the police force he had accused of corruption and the family he had shamed, into using Catling and Hales' revelations to reap their revenge.

Chapter Fourteen

Men of Derby! The Time Has Come!

> If ever there was a man who ruthlessly . . . strangled the friendships he professed to desire . . . that man is 'William Harcourt' . . . If ever there was a Man who had the persuasion of an Angel with the deceit of the Devil that man is 'William Harcourt.'
>
> William Harcourt, c. 1855[1]

In Derbyshire the rain beat down mercilessly: slicking the red gold leaves, staining the mills and manufactories, drenching the rich green earth. It poured all day on Friday 23 October, continued overnight and through to the following day. The River Derwent and its numerous relatives burst their banks. Fields, cellars and homes were immersed in near four feet of soft peaty water.[2] To risk the streets of Derby in such weather was to invite a sodden, relentless drubbing. It was enough to deter the strongest of spirits from his plans, but not Sir William Harcourt, who sought the votes of his Derby constituents; and not Jeremiah Minahan, who had doggedly followed him there.

Despite Jeremiah's August plotting with the Irish MP Philip Callan, by the autumn of 1885, Harcourt's reputation remained frustratingly intact. Very early on Friday 7 August, Callan had indeed risen as threatened in the House of Commons with the apparent intent of revealing to one and all that the former Home Secretary was a regular habitué of Mary

Jeffries' Chelsea brothel. But it soon became clear that the Irish Party member had undergone a strange change of heart.

When Callan eventually stood up to speak it was two o'clock in the morning. The House was edging towards the end of another marathon debate on the Criminal Law Amendment Bill and most ministers were more interested in retreat than in hearing this Irish MP's rambling tirade. Still, undeterred by muted groans, Callan did launch into a vent against Harcourt, who sat listening on the Liberal bench, braced for his bombshell.[3]

Callan opened his statement by accusing the Chelsea police of having 'connived at – and having connived with the late Home Secretary – [in] hushing up the case of Mrs. Jeffries'.[4]

Harcourt had readied himself for this charge and appears to have made eleven pages of notes in anticipation. These notes, still kept in Harcourt's papers, are written in his rushed, forward-slanting hand and go roughly through Jeremiah Minahan's case from 1883 to 1885. Even by Harcourt's standard, the hurried scrawl is mostly illegible; illustrative perhaps of the same panic that had summoned Loulou to race back from the Isle of Wight the day before.[5]

To Callan's allegations of connivance, Harcourt's prepared response – in note form – was to include:

> [Jeffries] Pleaded guilty
> She had no defence
> Not I only but judge attacked
> He is accused of improper conduct
> That I asked it
> Not true.[6]

When Callan argued that because 'many of Mrs Jeffries' clients were of the highest order' it 'was not considered prudent . . . to allow the case to go so far', and that this was why the issue was covered up; Harcourt's scribbles foresaw this too:

> It is alleged that the Prosecution decided to hush up the case?
> Read speech for Counsel for Prosecution.
> . . . I have now gone through this case.
> I have laid upon you the whole truth as I know it.[7]

In the midst of these assertions Callan also announced that he now had the names of Jeffries' clients 'in his possession'.[8] This was what Harcourt had really been dreading, that his name might appear on that list. According to his notes, he had planned several different denials with which to appeal to his fellows in the House:

> The House will appreciate the position in which I stand. They will recognise the peril in which any man may be placed who discharges without flinching a public duty.

And:

> If I had not thought it right to support the authority of the police in a matter when I believed them right this false charge would never have been brought.

And:

> What can a man rely upon except upon the conduct of his word or character? And I am confident that I can rely on the House of Commons [to] accept my word and to protect my character against this false aspersion.[9]

But Harcourt need not have worried. Despite his threat the day before, Callan chose not to accuse him directly. Instead he admitted to the Commons that while 'yesterday he *had intended* to call the attention of the House to the misconduct of – thank God! – the late Home Secretary', something had changed his mind.[10] The question is: what?

From his statements, Callan seems confident he had the 'evidence' to back his claims and parliamentary privilege shielded him from slander, yet still he gifted Harcourt a reprieve. It is possible that Harcourt or Loulou had used their knowledge of the adulterous affair of Callan's party leader, Charles Parnell, to douse Callan's fire. Callan had known of Parnell's intrigue with Mrs O'Shea for at least two years, but it remained in Callan's interest, just three months before the 1885 general election, to protect his leader's position.[11]

Whatever had deterred Callan, he watered down his former menace to a series of intimations about Harcourt so vague that they provoked the ire of the Speaker of the House, Arthur Wellesley Peel. Amidst dull 'cheers' and fatigued 'hear hears' from the other ministers, Peel demanded that Callan cease 're-trying a case already settled in court' and eventually ordered the Irish MP to 'resume his seat' on grounds of 'tedious repetition' and 'irrelevance'.[12] Callan did as he was told. Unfortunately for Jeremiah, he was well known for being intoxicated while in the House and this shuffling, late-night meander lacked the necessary punch to fell the ex-inspector's foe.[13] But despite his ineloquent delivery, Callan did manage two intriguing statements, the first of which must have made Harcourt wince. Callan informed the house that Jeremiah's initial belief that Jeffries kept a 'brothel for the aristocracy . . . was to some extent a mistake, because, from the evidence adduced, [he was now] able to say that it was largely supported by what he might call the wealthy Members of the Radical Party' – that is to say, the Liberal wing of the Commons.[14] He also alleged that 'during the progress of the [Jeffries] trial officials connected with the Home Office visited Mrs. Jeffries' establishment'. Was there any record, Callan asked, of the Home Office visitors' report, a visit of which *he* 'had evidence'?[15]

But this last, sticky question came too late. Peel stopped Callan in his tracks and soon after, at three in the morning, the House was adjourned. Jeremiah's chances in Parliament were gone for good.

Nonetheless, Harcourt kept his eleven pages of notes and placed them inside a long envelope for portability and protection. Across the front, he wrote 'Minahan'. Instinctively, he understood that his relations with the ex-inspector were not over yet.

*

Following Philip Callan's failure, Jeremiah might have been tempted to return to another of his powerful allies, William Stead, except that before August was out, he too had been successfully undone. Stead's confession of responsibility over Eliza Armstrong, combined with the girl's own statement, led to the arrest of Rebecca Jarrett and the summons of Stead, William Bramwell Booth, Mr Jacques, Madame Combe and the French midwife Louise Mourey to the Bow Street police court – Jeremiah's former workplace – on Monday 7 September. The six defendants faced charges of the abduction and indecent assault of Eliza, and evidence against them was to be assessed during five pre-trial hearings throughout September by the Bow Street magistrate, Mr Vaughan.[16]

Hundreds of protestors from all over England petitioned the Home Office in support of Stead. They complained that his prosecution was, as Alfred Dyer put it, an effort to 'crush the editor because he has exposed the vices of those in the rank of Cabinet Ministers'.[17] But just as many people turned against him and in Bow Street the crowds were hostile. Stead, Booth and Jarrett were booed, pushed and physically attacked as they battled their way in and out of the police court. Their effigies were paraded through the streets and rotten eggs thrown by the crowd were supplied by Mary Jeffries from her brougham carriage.[18] At home in Wimbledon, Stead woke one morning to find another crude manikin, a mock-up of his auburn-haired self, hanged from his garden tree.[19] On 26 September all six defendants were bound over to appear for criminal trial at the Old Bailey on Friday 23 October, during the same week that Harcourt and Jeremiah descended on Derby.

*

In the wake of the resignation in July 1885 of Gladstone and his Liberal Cabinet, a general election was called for 24 November to 18 December 1885 to establish a new government.[20] Since it was the first to incorporate around two million more working-class men newly enfranchised by the Third Reform Act, the outcome of the vote was too unpredictable for politicians to be complacent. Particularly as Liberal fortunes were still being damaged by the Irish Party leader, Parnell, who had instructed all Irish Catholics to vote Conservative in the belief the Tories would support Irish Home Rule.[21] Parnell's edict caused Liberal ministers to work extra hard at the hustings and Harcourt was busy throughout the autumn of 1885 on the Liberal campaign trail.

DERBY BOROUGH ELECTION, 1885

DRILL HALL, DERBY

ON FRIDAY, OCTOBER 23RD,
THE ELECTORS of the BOROUGH of DERBY
will be ADDRESSED by the Parliamentary
Representative of the Borough,
THE RIGHT HON.
SIR W.V. HARCOURT, MP

The chair will be taken at 7.30[22]

Alongside three or four thousand Derby voters, Harcourt would be forced to accommodate two far less welcome visitors to the Drill Hall on that wretched, rain-soaked October night: Jeremiah and his latest partner in protest, the international preacher Henry Varley – alias the 'Butcher's Evangelist'.

Like Jeremiah, Varley was a tough man of working-class origin, the youngest son of a brewer and maltser. His mother was a devout Anglican evangelical who died when he was ten. A year later he left home to find work in London and there, aged sixteen, experienced an evangelical conversion that would change his life. He went on to establish a successful butcher's trade in Notting Hill, but his daily business was soon eclipsed by his success as a plain-speaking itinerant preacher, independent of any church.[23] Between 1874 and 1885, Varley's talent took him preaching around the world, until he learned of Stead's *Maiden Tribute* campaign and returned from America to lend his support.[24] In an article on 21 August 1885 in the *Pall Mall Gazette*, Varley boasted of being another in possession of the dreaded 'list of names' of Jeffries' clientele. These were men, he wrote, who purchased 'mere children' to sate their 'rapacity' and he would 'not consent to be silent' when such men, some of whom were of the 'highest rank and position', were 'still at large'.[25] With his indignation stoked to a 'red heat' and Jeremiah by his side, Varley arrived in Derby with a vengeful purpose: to 'prevent, if it were possible, the re-election of Sir William Harcourt'.[26]

In the days leading up to Harcourt's appearance at the Drill Hall on 23 October, Henry Varley distributed pamphlets all over the East Midlands town and espoused 'allegations of an extraordinary nature against the personal character of [Derby's] senior member'.[27] He caused a sensation. One of his pamphlets, under the heading 'Reasons why the Liberal

Electors of Derby should not return Sir William Harcourt as their Representative', laid out a blistering list of Harcourt's deficiencies as both a politician and a gentleman.[28] Varley charged Harcourt with failing to prevent the 'buying, selling and exportation of little girls and women for vile . . . purposes' by taking 'no interest in advancing or passing' the Criminal Law Amendment Bill.[29] The former Home Secretary's refusal to prosecute the 'notorious Mrs. Jeffries' served only to shield 'a number of high-class criminals whose hands are red with the blood of dishonoured girls and women'.[30] Furthermore, rather than 'institute an inquiry into Inspector Minahan's case' Harcourt instead used the 'cowardly tactics of traducing his character in the House of Commons [and] stated things of him that were utterly untrue'.[31] Finally, Varley argued that Harcourt's failings over the cases of Jeffries and of Jeremiah Minahan had forced Stead and his Secret Commission to take the drastic action that resulted in their criminal trial. 'Harcourt' wrote Varley was thus 'morally responsible' for the prosecution of Stead, and 'whatever the verdict, Mr. Stead stands acquitted before the nation, and Sir. W. Harcourt condemned'.[32]

Harcourt's name was then further compromised before the Derby electorate in Varley's series of 'public lectures', the first of which took place on Monday 19 October at Derby's Temperance Hall. Thanks to the controversy whipped up by his pamphlets, Varley's event attracted a 'very large audience'.[33] The Temperance Hall's floor and narrow, wrap-around galleries were 'completely packed' and 'consisted almost entirely of working men and their wives'.[34]

Having declared to the crowd that nothing would deter him from subjecting public figures to needful criticism, Varley, who was a fat-fingered man with a square face and stubborn countenance, introduced the two beside him on the platform as the ex-inspector Jeremiah Minahan and George

Bellchambers, the former coachman to Mary Jeffries. Both were greeted with loud cheers. 'The ex-inspector', noted the *Derby Daily Telegraph*, 'is a smart looking, well favoured man of about 45, while Bellchambers is probably ten years younger, of the true coachman type and a cockney to the manor born'.[35] The meat of Varley's public lecture was a detailed analysis of Jeffries' brothel business: her purchase of young girls from their mothers, her dealings with Belgian royalty, her overseas trade and the stifling of facts at her trial. Varley then interrogated Bellchambers about his experiences. Jeffries' coachman described her three connected houses on Church Street as 'like a rabbit warren – you could go in at one end and out the other – just as you liked'.[36] He also reiterated that Jeffries' clientele were fetched from 'West End clubs' and her 'ladies' from 'St. John's Wood and elsewhere'.[37] The necessity of venting such details in public was justified by Varley as his 'duty' in bearing 'witness against such evil'.[38]

The preacher then moved on to the imminent trial of his fellow moral crusader, William Stead. Varley suggested that instead 'of putting [Stead] in a criminal court he should be sent to Parliament'.[39] 'Send him here!' responded the crowd, aptly bringing Varley to his real point, which was that Harcourt's moral laxity should mean he forfeit his position as representative of the people of Derby.[40] By displacing Harcourt in the forthcoming general election, argued Varley, the Derby townsfolk would demonstrate their 'reproof of evil', and in a show of hands, 'nearly the whole of the people in the hall favoured his suggestion'.[41]

Though he had stood beside Varley and Bellchambers throughout, Jeremiah remained silent. His contribution was saved for Varley's second 'lecture', held the following night at the smaller Gospel Hall, an old converted theatre in the city. This time Jeremiah regaled the crowd with the tale of his own experiences, his career in the force and his suspension by the Assistant Commissioner. To the delight of his audience, Jeremiah reiterated Colonel Labalmondiere's blatant hypocrisy word for word:

'Brothels for the nobility,' Labalmondiere had told him, 'that is most improper.'

'Oh! Oh!' cried his Derby crowd.[42]

Jeremiah then went on to describe how he was 'treated unjustly and unfairly' by Derby's Liberal MP. Again, Varley took this as his cue to suggest to Derby's voters that they 'turn Sir William out'. 'We will not have him in Derby!' cried the audience. 'We will turn him out!'[43]

Varley and Jeremiah's incendiary activities resulted in a flurry of correspondence in the Derby newspapers. 'His coming here and vilifying an ex-Minister of whom Derby is proud . . . is simply shameful', wrote 'An Alderman' on Thursday 22 October.[44] 'I went to the Temperance Hall on Monday,' wrote J. Lambert, who objected to 'Mr. Varley's base *insinuations* upon the character of an eminent statesman'.[45] 'An Unbiased Liberal' was more circumspect, asking why 'we should shrink from the charges leveled against Harcourt [who] as a lawyer of the first rank [was] well able to defend himself if the charges were unfounded'.[46]

Harcourt was indeed bombastic enough to defend himself against all comers, but his real response to Varley's attacks was rather cowed, though still characteristic. He sent spies. A Mr Moody infiltrated Varley's first meeting and reported back to Harcourt immediately afterwards:

> Mr. Tetley, myself and Partners have just returned from the meeting at the Temperance Hall, certainly a very crowded one not a few women. The only reference to yourself was purely in your official position and not in anyway affecting your private character.[47]

As well as disclosures about his 'private character', Harcourt was clearly concerned about further revelations concerning Jeffries' brothel. Of these, Mr Moody reassured him that 'the Coachman' George Bellchambers' testimony 'went to show that he had taken letters to Clubs etc. but nothing about you'.[48]

Jeremiah and Varley's smear campaign certainly succeeded in undermining Harcourt's election chances in Derby, as well as his peace of mind. On 9 November 1885, Loulou Harcourt wrote about the voters in his journal: 'we are likely to lose a large number. All the Irish and Catholics will vote against us and we shall lose a good many Church people'.[49]

For a Bible-thumper like Henry Varley, the antics in Derby were all part of his 'holy war' against 'deep-dyed sinners', but what was Jeremiah's real motivation now, almost two years after losing his original appeal for justice?[50] Why was he still so desperate to undermine the position of such a formidable and vindictive man? In his written word and his rare speeches, Jeremiah comes across as an articulate, balanced and intelligent man. His sentences are spare and rational: at no point does he invoke the righteous tone of men like Varley or the wordy ebullience of Stead. Jeremiah was not a religious zealot. His pride and sense of justice had first propelled him into Sir William's path; and yet with each of their subsequent encounters he had become more resolute and wayward, relentless even, in his desire to ruin Harcourt. What did Jeremiah know about Harcourt that drove him to such obsession?

Both in life and after his death, Harcourt's reputation was cultivated and protected by the vigilance of his son, Loulou. Harcourt's first biographer, A. G. Gardiner, explained how 'the principal occupation of [Loulou's] life in the years following his retirement from office was the accumulation and arrangement of the mass of material bearing upon his father's career'.[51] Loulou gave himself ample opportunity to destroy any evidence that might harm his father in posterity, but he had no such figure in his own life, no guardian to protect his reputation. His less careful legacy is a window into his father's private world: so too, as they were so intertwined, is that of the man Harcourt mentored from youth – Reginald Baliol Brett, the 2nd Viscount Esher. Reginald (Regy) and Loulou lived well into the early twentieth century. Letters, memoirs and the recollections of their contemporaries reflect the openness of this more brightly lit world – a world beyond the unspeakable shadows of their father's.

*

High-society whisperings frequently bracketed Regy and Loulou together.[52] Regy was a slim, wary looking man with a large, straight nose, a fine moustache and a receding hairline. He was also nine years Loulou's senior, but the two shared certain private peccadilloes.

Harcourt, Regy and Loulou first met in 1872, when Loulou was a boy of nine and Regy a young man studying at Trinity College, Cambridge. Lady Ripon, who became a friend and adviser to Harcourt after Thérèse's death in 1863, introduced the three.[53] Regy was the son of Sir William Brett (later Viscount Esher), a successful barrister, judge and a Conservative MP. Both Regy and Loulou attended Eton, where Regy became particularly close to the charismatic tutor William Johnson, known to his pupils as 'Tute'. In the same year Loulou met Regy, William Johnson was forced to resign from the school when the homoerotic nature of his relations with some of the boys was uncovered. Before going up to Cambridge, Regy was one of Johnson's favoured Eton boys; he later supported Johnson through his 'disgrace' and the two remained close for the rest of their lives.[54] Johnson was also, like Sir William Harcourt and Richard Monckton Milnes, a

Cambridge Apostle. In 1872, Regy Brett was selected to join them.[55]

With Loulou still a boy, Regy's first relations were with his father, who became his acknowledged patron. By 1872, Harcourt was a highly successful barrister as well as the MP for Derby, and three years earlier had been made the Professor of International Law at Cambridge. In return for a few lectures a year, Harcourt was allotted rooms at Trinity College that he barely used. These he offered to Regy Brett on condition he might also occupy them when he had to visit.[56] After Regy's graduation, Harcourt continued to patronize him, assisting him in securing his first position at Westminster, as the Liberal Cabinet minister Lord Hartington's private secretary. Harcourt relayed the news of Regy's appointment in a letter to his parents at Christmas 1877, expressing his hope that the position would be a 'substantial advantage to the future of your boy, in whose welfare I have long taken much interest'.[57]

As well as sharing the favour of Lady Ripon, the young man was also a regular guest at the political salons of Harcourt's aunt, Lady Waldegrave. Regy himself was rather sniffy about the Waldegrave set. Still, there was something in this aloofness and in Regy's 'genius' for 'influencing people' that attracted others.[58] Four years after Regy began his political career, the precocious young Loulou joined him in Parliament, acting as private secretary to his father.[59]

Though occasionally critical of each other, circumstance threw Loulou and Regy close together. Both were highly cultured, socially smooth men; both married relatively late and each sired four children. The two also shared a love of history and the arts and in 1912 established the Museum of London together. Privately, however, they shared a more furtive bond: a desire for young male flesh.

Society gossips were well aware of Loulou's and Regy's

inclinations, and the mothers of Eton boys even warned their sons against taking solitary walks with either man.[60] Of the two, Regy was far less outwardly predatory. But beyond 'Tute' and a few boyfriends in his youth, one of the greatest loves of Regy's life was his own youngest son, Maurice or 'Molly'.

Largely ignoring his other three children (he had an older son named Oliver and two daughters, Dorothy and Sylvia), Regy focused his attention on the 'affectionate, weak and easily malleable' Molly to an abnormal extent.[61] Letters from Regy to Molly when he was just thirteen years old contain clinging interrogations into the child's development, with Regy often asking his son, whose pet name was 'Fatty', whether anyone had attracted him at school, whether he had lost his heart or fallen in love yet?[62] When Molly wrote telling Regy that 'Ainger', his tutor at Eton, had entered his school bedroom and lain closely on his bed beside him, caressing him and 'cuddling' up to him, his father is only amused, describing Molly's night time experience as 'fun', and joshing about how 'elephantine' Ainger must have felt, fumbling about in bed with Molly.[63] Later he reminds his son covetously that it was actually he who instigated Molly's earliest sensual experiences, insisting that he was the first person to kiss Molly properly and was certainly the one to initiate Molly into kissing 'passionately'; before adding how he still loved 'to linger' over the memory of these illicit intimacies.[64] But Regy was not nearly so amused or dreamy when someone more threatening than 'Ainger' made a pass at Molly – Loulou Harcourt.

Loulou was so corrupt in adulthood that he even gave Regy 'the creeps'.[65] Gaunt, beaky and famously ugly, Loulou was well known as a pederast, but he did not limit his preying to boys. Shortly after his attempt on Molly, he tried for Regy's daughter Dorothy, who he caught at fourteen, alone in a farmhouse on Regy's land. She remembered Loulou as being 'a very tall man, well over six feet' and someone she had known since she was 'two':

> It was a dampish day so he had on a Burberry – the kind with false pockets. He took hold of my hand and pulled it through the pocket. I suddenly felt something burning hot and soft . . . I tore my hand away and turned to run. I was not quick enough. He was on me, he caught hold of me from behind and held me in a grip of iron, and began kissing the back of my neck . . . I kicked and kicked and kicked myself free . . . For years I would never let a man come near me.[66]

When Regy eventually learned of Loulou's attempt to molest his daughter, he responded with shocking casualness, remarking only to Molly in a letter of 20 September 1902 that such antics were typical of Loulou, who 'for years' had preyed upon both girls and boys. Regy did sound one note of concern however, about the risks Loulou took to fulfil his needs, particularly as he was by now a Cabinet Minister.[67]

The 1885 Criminal Law Amendment Act had increased society's awareness that coital relations between adults and children were a form of abuse, both illegal and immoral. One year later, the German sexologist Dr Krafft-Ebing explored the sexual 'inversion' of men like Loulou in his book *Psychopathia Sexualis: A Medico Forensic Study*. In his chapter on the 'Violation of Individuals Under the Age of Fourteen', he attributed some cases of child abuse to people who had 'suffered shipwreck in [their] sphere of morality and potency': 'monsters' who inspired 'revolt' in 'normal members of human society'. To more extreme cases he applied a new term: *paedophilia erotica*.[68] A decade on, the psychoanalytic studies of Sigmund Freud initiated further discussions about child abuse, both real and imagined.[69] As the public consciousness of sexual misconduct increased so too did the likelihood that Loulou would eventually be found out.

Edward James, the son of a socialite named Evelyn Forbes, was 'twelve or thirteen-years-old' when he and his mother passed a weekend with Loulou (then Lord Harcourt) at Nuneham House in 1921.[70] Having spent the time deflecting the gropes of this 'hideous and horrible old man' Edward was sent alone by his oblivious mother to bid Loulou farewell:

> I came in at one end of a long room and [Loulou] was lying in bed . . . He said, 'Come nearer, child!' . . . So I came a little nearer and made my [goodbye] speech . . . Suddenly he threw back the bedclothes revealing a large and hideous erection . . . I ran out of the room.[71]

When Edward confessed the incident to his mother, the affronted Evelyn told 'all her women friends' and the tale became the talk of London, making its slow social descent until it reached the police.[72] On the morning of 24 February 1922, Loulou, who was said to have been 'looking preoccupied for days', was found dead in his dressing room at 69 Brook Street, Mayfair.[73] He had swallowed a whole bottle of Bromidia, a sleeping draught. Although the coroner returned a verdict of misadventure, it was widely received in society that Loulou, fearful of an impending scandal over Edward James, had committed suicide.[74]

After Loulou's death, Regy Brett attempted to protect his reputation by going through Loulou's archives and extracting his store of child pornography.[75] In a letter, Molly wondered whether he might next inherit Loulou's 'improper' hoard, for certain 'objects' were rather rare and valuable.[76] Loulou's collection was said to be one of 'the best in the world', the adage applied to the reams of erotica once held by his father's mentor and friend, Richard Monckton Milnes. It is possible that some items of the collections were one and the same, passed down through the years between a close cabal who shared similar sexual appetites.[77] Milnes was a sado-masochist known to enjoy beating girls and to collect pornography about boys; Loulou was a child-molester; and Regy, who next took over the collection, abused his own son. In the midst of these three debauchers stood Sir William Harcourt.

During his own examination of the individuals he found afflicted with *paedophilia erotica*, Dr Krafft-Ebing found that in all his cases, the men were 'tainted by heredity'; that the 'perversion' appeared somehow to be passed down the family line, as in for example, from father to son.[78] The cyclical nature of sexual abuse was fully established long after Krafft-Ebing's demise, but both he and his English contemporary, Havelock Ellis, noticed that 'the hereditary character of [sexual] inversion is a fact of great significance'.[79]

In 1916 Sir William Harcourt's first biographer, A. G. Gardiner, referred to his relations with Loulou as 'unusual'. In 2004 his second biographer, Patrick Jackson, described them as 'unnatural'.[80] It is possible that the true nature of Harcourt's emotional dependence on his son revealed itself in Loulou's sexuality, just as, with the damaged logic of the victim, Loulou dedicated his life to shielding and protecting his abuser.

Harcourt was a man who referred to himself as having the 'the persuasion of an Angel with the deceit of the Devil', a man confused about his true sexual nature: on the same fragment of paper he described himself as 'incomprehensible' as either a man or 'a woman'.[81] A later letter addressed to his old friend Robert Lytton gives a fuller picture. The letter was written on 7 January 1881, four years into Harcourt's marriage to Elizabeth Cabot Ives and three years before Jeremiah Minahan began to investigate Mary Jeffries and her regular clientele. It escaped Loulou's grasp.

Dear Robert Lytton

You don't know how happy your letter makes me. By no means come to a pompous dinner. I am obliged to dine *en ceremonie* Wednesdays and Saturdays and I do not know which is the more detestable.

But on the other days of the week I almost always dine at home . . . If you come you will always find broken meats, ramshackle company, an odd Radical, an old Whig, a strong Tory, and occasionally a Traverser (some masculine, feminine Traviata) picked up on the spot in the H of C and served hot and hot. If this menu with a bottle of claret smiles upon you, you will find it on all profane days at 7 Grafton Street . . .

Yours affectionately

WVH[82]

By 'Traviata' Harcourt is referring to a 'fallen woman' or prostitute, after Verdi's 1852 opera, *La Traviata*. He did not mind whether his whore was 'masculine' or 'feminine', so long as they were 'served hot and hot', like his 'broken meats'.

*

When Jeremiah stood in the green shadows of Church Street watching Mary Jeffries' brothel, and when he befriended and questioned the procuress's servants old and new, he may well have heard their whisperings about Harcourt and his son Loulou. Unseen but watchful, the servants observed human sexuality in all its forms, both in overcrowded childhood homes and later in the luxury of their masters'. They cleared and scrubbed undergarments and sheets and in the case of Mary Jeffries' maids washed the dirt from a purchased child, wiped the tears from their eyes and remedied their resultant diseases. Jeremiah was an experienced policeman, more immune than most to the realities of Victorian vice, but one of the first concerns he reported about Jeffries' prostitutes was that they were 'youthful'.[83] As such her infamous charges would have matched Harcourt and Loulou's tastes precisely, for she traded pretty boys replete with patent shoes as well as young girls.[84]

By the autumn of 1885, though Jeremiah had fought for many months to expose Harcourt's low hypocrisy, all his attempts through Dyer, then Stead, then Callan had been in vain. Yet the election campaign in Derby offered something he could not resist, a chance to face Harcourt man to man. Here he might look straight into Harcourt's eyes and challenge his secret disgrace. And so Jeremiah went to the Drill Hall on Friday 23 October, and no torrents or floods could stop him.

Chapter Fifteen

Tell Him Not to Grieve

> Nowadays with our modern mania for morality, everyone has to pose as a paragon of purity, incorruptibility and all the other seven deadly virtues – and what is the result? You all go over like ninepins – one after the other.
>
> Oscar Wilde, *An Ideal Husband*, 1895[1]

Built in 1869, Derby's Drill Hall was one hundred and fifty feet long and seventy-five wide.[2] It had a span roof with a glazed centre, supported by prominent, curved iron girders.[3] On Friday 23 October 1885, the noise of torrential rain against the glass intensified with the shouts from the steaming throng below. At the far end of the hall, Derby's mayor, its aldermen, councillors and other local dignitaries were seated on the raised stage alongside Sir William Harcourt and his wife, Elizabeth. Immediately below them at floor level was a large table surrounded by newspaper reporters. Behind this group were several rows of chairs occupied by the more genteel members of local society; and beyond this fragrant front line, three or four thousand Derby folk were packed so tightly into the rear space they appeared like 'herrings in a barrel'.[4] Several agile youths climbed the girders under the ceiling to escape the crush below. One man stayed there, nonchalantly smoking his pipe. Hundreds more remained outside, straining for a few precious inches.

Over the last twenty-four hours, word had gone out across the city that the ex-inspector Jeremiah Minahan and the evangelist Henry Varley intended to present themselves at the Drill Hall to confront Sir William Harcourt face to face. The web of controversy spun by these two men in the previous four days had guaranteed the meeting's large attendance. All were alive to the possibility of a scrap, and 'it was evident from an early hour that there would be considerable excitement'.[5]

Audaciously, Varley seated his working-class self upon the stage, on an equal footing with Sir William and his wife.[6] The ex-inspector Minahan, 'with the discretion which popular opinion often ascribes to his order', stood instead by the 'reporters table' at the front of the hall, where he might look directly at Harcourt.[7]

The chairman of the meeting, Alderman Renals, announced that *only* members of the Derby electorate would be allowed to ask questions, thus excluding Varley and Jeremiah.[8] But when Harcourt stood up to speak shortly after 7.30 p.m., the groans of Varley's supporters countered the cheers for the MP. This surging and shoving between the two camps continued throughout his electoral address, as if Harcourt were a captain on a ship's bridge, facing down a rough sea. It was to prove a stormy voyage.

Harcourt began with a series of flat denials against Varley's public charges, his pamphlets and lectures. Listening, Varley smiled blandly and drolly shook his head. Amidst the rising turmoil and chaffing in the hall, Harcourt then moved on to Jeremiah Minahan.

'He is over there!' shouted a voice. 'The bobby! The bobby!' cried others, at which point Jeremiah presented his six-foot-two-inch self in a space allowed by the crowd at the front of the hall.[9] His imposing physique and smart demeanour could now clearly be observed by the adjacent reporters, the frontline ladies and, most importantly of all, by his arch traducer, Harcourt.

'I could not,' explained Harcourt, as if directly to Jeremiah, 'and do not undertake the discipline of the police. It would be very improper that I should do so . . .'[10]

But Harcourt's rehashed excuses were now drowned in a chaotic scene of 'prolonged disorder'.[11] Frantic struggles and fights broke out around the hall. The stifled spectators at the rear pushed hard against their fellows in front to gain space and air. Harcourt droned on. At his feet, half those seated on the chairs were thrown from their comfort by those standing and, indignant at being forced upright, they too now turned and joined the fracas. Their empty chairs were hurled about the vast room, over people's heads and to the floor. People began smashing them into splintered pieces, then throwing them into a hotchpotch barricade in the corner of the hall by the stage.

In the chaos, one young fellow decided that Henry Varley must be the root cause of the panic and grabbed the evangelist by his collar. With the help of several others, Varley was forced out of the Drill Hall and into a dripping back alley. Jeremiah did not go to his aid. No one touched him. He remained rooted, listening to Harcourt, until around the rock of the ex-inspector a final monstrous heave unseated all those still left in the chairs. In an undignified rush, these reputable locals and ladies climbed right over the reporters, across their table and up to the relative safety of the stage. For their own protection they gathered behind Harcourt, while Jeremiah remained immutable, a ragged rebellion at his back.

*

Before ten o'clock the meeting was ended and the gasping herrings were released onto the soaking streets. Two hundred and fifty-eight broken chairs and fifteen dismembered benches commemorated the evening.[12] It is hard to judge who precisely was the hero of the night: Harcourt, who had continued to speak, completely unheard by his electorate, for almost two hours; or Jeremiah Minahan, whose mere presence had caused several thousand Derbyites to erupt into riot.

Jeremiah could do no more. His attempts to derail Harcourt's return to power were now taken over by his former employer Alfred Dyer, a measly 'creature', Loulou described without irony, with a 'sneaking' countenance.[13] In November 1885 Dyer offered himself as an alternative parliamentary representative to the voters of Derby, standing in the general election as an independent Liberal, a direct challenger to Harcourt.[14] But before the polling places even opened on the 24th of the month, Jeremiah and Harcourt faced another potential round in the public ring. William Stead had called both as witnesses at his Criminal Court trial over the abduction of Eliza Armstrong.

*

On the day of the Drill Hall debacle, a courtroom at London's Old Bailey was filled with dozens of barristers, solicitors, reporters and friends of the Armstrong defendants. Anyone with a place in the public gallery had secured their ticket from one of the under-sheriffs, City of London officials resplendent in crested frills and carrying silver swords. The majority of the trial took place in the Old Court, located through the street entrance, across a large open yard and up a flight of stairs.[15]

The proceedings of the first morning were slowed slightly by the late arrival of Rebecca Jarrett, who joined Stead, Booth, Mr Jacques and Madame Combe in the dock. All five were charged with abduction. Madame Mourey, the French midwife, was to be charged later with indecent assault alongside Stead, Jarrett and Jacques.

The new attorney-general, Sir Richard Webster, led the prosecution. Balding, clean-shaven and thoughtful in countenance, Webster was a former athlete and an incisive, talented barrister. In his opening speech he identified the crux of the case for the prosecution and the essential weakness of the defence. 'Whatever,' Webster announced, 'might be said about the motive, nothing could justify the taking away of a girl without outward consent and without the will of the father'.[16] The judge, Mr Justice Lopes, reinforced Webster's line, insisting that 'the consent of the mother was nothing [and] the consent of the father was everything'.[17]

On hearing Webster's strategy, William Stead almost immediately changed his plea to guilty.[18] It had never occurred to him to gain Eliza's father's consent. As far as he knew, Charles Armstrong had received the news of Eliza's departure with 'indifference, without even inquiring where she was going to' and in his own words, it was Mrs Armstrong 'who [had] full power to act for me in these things'.[19] The supervision of Victorian children was women's work, unless it suited the attorney-general to insist otherwise.

Webster's first witness was Eliza Armstrong. At the police court, the reporters had noted that Eliza's figure was still 'undeveloped' and she barely looked thirteen. Her 'brown hair [was] plaited in a short pigtail and [she] was dressed in a large and somewhat battered black velvet hat with a big gilt buckle'.[20] The gaudy purple dress bought for her by Rebecca Jarrett on Derby Day had 'faded' and was now worn beneath 'a brown jacket'.[21] At the Old Bailey she was self-possessed and consistent in her account, which revealed that with the exception of her molestation by Madame Mourey, Eliza appeared untroubled by her 'abduction'. In the hands of Jarrett and the Salvation Army she had felt happy and secure. She had in fact written to her mother on 22 July 1885:

> I am a long way in France. This is a very good place. I will come and see you soon. I is a very good girl . . . I have good food and everything I want. I hope you and my sisters and brothers are well.[22]

Eliza's letter was initially addressed care of William Bramwell Booth, who passed the letter on to Stead, who in turn delayed in passing it to Mrs Armstrong. By the time Eliza's mother received her daughter's message, she was ensconced with Henry Hales and *Lloyd's Weekly* – regularly accepting their shilling in return for her compliance and public outcry.[23]

When Mrs Armstrong appeared for her cross-examination in the witness box on the second day of the trial, Saturday 24 October, she looked a 'respectable working woman': 'short and stout, with black hair and a reddish complexion'.[24] In the more familiar surrounds of the Bow Street police court Mrs Armstrong had been full of bravura, playing to the guffaws of the gallery during the pre-trial hearings. When she caught sight of Jarrett across the courtroom she had shaken her fist and exclaimed: 'Oh you beauty! I should like to get hold of you! You would want to join the Salvation Army if I got hold of you!'[25] At the Old Bailey however, her maudlin tears returned.

During her cross-examination by Stead (who had chosen to represent himself), Eliza's mother denied that Jarrett had placed a sovereign in her palm in exchange for her daughter, insisting instead that she had only ever received a shilling with which she 'bought a comb for Eliza and a pair of socks for the baby. I paid six pence for the comb, five pence three farthings for the socks.'[26]

'So there was a farthing left?' asked Stead.

'Yes,' Mrs Armstrong replied, 'and I got drunk on it.'[27]

A farthing was a quarter of a penny. A quart of beer in 1885 was priced at around four pence, a quart of gin at around six pence.[28] Mrs Armstrong was so inebriated on Derby night that she was arrested for being drunk and disorderly, the third time she was charged with such an offence.[29] On this occasion she was also bailed out, rather kindly, by the landlord of the Marquis of Anglesea, her local pub.[30]

'You got drunk on a farthing?' asked Stead.

'Well according to you,' Mrs Armstrong replied, 'I was supposed to be always intoxicated.' She then broke down in tears for the second time, prompting the intervention of Mr Justice Lopes.

'Do you mean to say that you spent the farthing on drink?' he asked.

'No my lord,' she said.

'Did you spend any portion of the money?'

'No.'

'Did you buy drink that day?' asked Stead.

'Not that day.'

'That night?'

'Yes.'

'Where did you get the money?'

'My husband gave me money.'

'To get drunk on?'

'No.'

'Was it your housekeeping money?'

'I'm not going to tell you.'[31]

As well as peppering her evidence with shady contradictions, Mrs Armstrong also opened to several outright lies. In the pre-trial hearing she had denied telling Henry Hales that Eliza had been destined for the iniquitous Albany Street, something Hales' notes might contradict. When Stead reminded her of this she changed her mind, 'If I said that,' she admitted, 'it was a lie.'[32]

'It is true,' continued Stead, 'that Jarrett asked if Eliza was a pure girl?'

'Yes,' replied Mrs Armstrong.

'Then if you denied that when I asked you the question at the police court, that is a lie?'

'Of course it's a lie if I said so, for she did ask me.'[33]

Mrs Armstrong also admitted that she had immediately identified Eliza as 'Lily' in Stead's *Maiden Tribute* article, 'A Child of Thirteen Sold for £5', from its reference to the school trips taken by the child to Richmond and Epping Forest. Eliza had been on exactly the same outings.

'The story,' said Stead, was 'published in the paper and you never got your husband or the inspector to inquire [after Eliza] at the *Pall Mall Gazette* office?'

'If I had thought you knew anything about the child I should have called upon you,' replied Mrs Armstrong.[34]

The connection between Eliza, her alias 'Lily' and the *Pall Mall Gazette* may have been obvious to Stead, the perpetrator of the link, but not to Mrs Armstrong or even the investigating officer, Inspector Borner. 'Nothing was said,' Borner explained, 'about the *Pall Mall Gazette* being able to give that child back.'[35] Both appear to have assumed that a newspaper solely reported crimes and did not actually commit them. Which is why Mrs Armstrong and Inspector Borner focused their attention instead on Rebecca Jarrett and later William Bramwell Booth. It took seasoned newsmongers like Henry Hales and Thomas Catling to understand that a fellow hack might stray into transgression in pursuit of sensation.

On the third day Nancy Broughton took the stand. Caught between a ferocious neighbour and a former friend, she spoke in such timid whispers that she was repeatedly asked to speak up. Some of her answers contradicted those of Mrs Armstrong: others suggested she knew deep down that Jarrett intended Eliza for dark purposes: 'I told,' she said, 'the mother to go and make the bargain herself – I was not responsible for it – I did not want to be blamed . . . if wrong was to come of the girl.'[36] Nancy remained adamant that she had received no money for Eliza. Like Mrs Armstrong and her stretched 'shilling', Nancy claimed she believed Jarrett's two sovereigns were gifted in kindness for the support she had shown her friend in the past. The whereabouts of the other two sovereigns Jarrett said she had spent on Eliza, plus the one she was alleged to have given Mrs Armstrong for the girl, bringing the total to £5, was still disputed and never wholly clarified.

Despite their wrangles and lies, Mrs Armstrong and Nancy had at least bolstered each other's sworn belief that Eliza was wanted for a maid rather than brothel stock. This intensified the pressure on Rebecca Jarrett to prove otherwise. Only she could save herself and in doing so, save Stead.

Poorly dressed in a plain trimmed hat and an old green overcoat, when Jarrett took the stand on Friday 30 October she was wracked from months of anxiety. A fallen woman thrust under the public eye like a dirty rag, her name now generated disgust, suspicion and hate; hisses followed her every step, in the courts, on the streets, even at Christian meetings, which cut her to the quick.[37] In the Old Bailey's public gallery, her Salvation Army friends prayed, while those from her former life 'jeered' and whispered that she might yet escape and come away with them.[38]

This was one of Webster's first questions: 'Have you ever been married?'[39]

He had gone straight to Jarrett's weak point, her respectability and trustworthiness.

'Never,' she replied.[40]

Jarrett carried the ignominy of her past like a disfigurement. Letters written to Florence Booth during the summer of 1885 refer constantly to her dread that as a result of her involvement with Stead everything about her would be exposed. 'You know,' she wrote, 'when I first entered into this work I was promised my history should never be entered into, but I find that is not so.'[41] Now dozens of reporters vied to embarrass her and she was caught in the irony of being 'condemned by the people' for having turned her back on vice.[42] 'Had I not been *converted*,' she wrote in retrospect, 'nothing would have been said I could have taken [Eliza] away and done just what I liked with her.'[43] Sometimes she suspected she was safer in the netherworld.

'Your first acquaintance with Mrs Broughton,' continued Webster, 'was at Claridge's Hotel? . . . Had you been in service before that?'[44]

'Yes,' Jarrett replied, 'to try and get myself up.'

'You say,' replied Webster, 'that previous to your going to Claridge's you kept a gay house?'

'In High-Street, Marylebone.'

'What number?'[45]

Jarrett hesitated. To answer Webster's question truthfully might reveal the villainous crib of her own family, as well as other sinister men like the mysterious Mr Sullivan. If Sullivan was willing to travel the sixty miles to Winchester to warn her off, it was highly likely he was present at the Old Bailey, his eyes riveted upon her.

'Now sir,' she tried, 'I told you I led a bad life. I beg of you that my past life may not come up here.'[46]

'The number please?'

'No. 23, Sullivan rented it.'[47]

This was untrue. Within seconds of her cross-examination Jarrett had broken her oath and though he had yet to discover his triumph, Webster made easy work of her now. He produced letters revealing her vulgarity. In one, supplied by Nancy Broughton, Jarrett had joked that she was not getting any 'toast'.[48] Painfully, Webster forced her to explain that she and her co-workers at Claridge's used the term to describe their 'romping' with male staff; an activity that made them 'warm as toast'.[49]

Later, Webster returned to the address Jarrett had given for the Marylebone brothel. Having privately found her out, Webster now publicly pressed Jarrett as to its accuracy, until she 'blurted forth' that he had 'forced that lie' out of her, before refusing to answer more.[50] Mr Justice Lopes advised the jury to draw their own conclusions about her falsehood.[51]

Referring to Stead's version of Eliza's purchase in the *Pall Mall Gazette*, the unravelling Jarrett next admitted that 'there were some slight mistakes'.[52]

'Did Stead,' asked Webster, 'write down what you told him?'

'No sir,' she said.[53]

When Stead's turn came, he confirmed that Jarrett – now a proven liar – was his sole source of information.

'Except for what Jarrett told you,' Webster asked Stead, 'had you any authority for the statements made in the article in the *Pall Mall Gazette*?'[54]

'None whatever,' he replied.

'So far as the purchase of the child was concerned, you had Jarrett's word for it, and Jarrett's word only?'

'Yes.'[55]

'From such worthless lips as hers,' sneered Thomas Catling in *Lloyd's Weekly*, 'Mr. Stead derived the hideous details set forth in his revelations.'[56]

A week before the jury even retired to consider its verdict, the journalist Arnold White wrote to his friend Sir William Harcourt from his club in St James's.

> Saturday 31 October [1885]
> Private
>
> Dear Sir W Harcourt
>
> . . . With regard to your letter of yesterday. I may inform you confidentially that Stead's case has broken down. He informed me yesterday afternoon that he should probably call no more evidence . . . Under no circumstances will you be called . . .
>
> I am
>
> Your faithful servant
>
> Arnold White[57]

Harcourt had been subpoenaed to attend the Armstrong trial on 8 October.[58] After Stead confirmed this in court during his opening speech for the defence, Harcourt knew he had no choice but to appear, as 'it would never have done for me to seem to hold back or to wish to beg off'.[59] But luck was on his side.

If Stead had not stood Harcourt down, Mr Justice Lopes would probably have disallowed him as he did with the majority of Stead's defence witnesses, on grounds of irrelevance. Only those who might shed light on the actual 'abduction' of Eliza Armstrong were admitted. Josephine Butler, William Bramwell Booth and Benjamin Scott all testified to their involvement in the Secret Commission, but Jeremiah Minahan did not appear. Stead claimed to have wanted Jeremiah to reveal 'the names of lords and members [of Parliament] who were the patrons of Mrs. Jeffries'', but was either unable or unwilling to actually follow through with his threat.[60] Lopes had warned that Stead was not at liberty to 'show the jury the whole operations of which the alleged abduction formed one part'; the only question the jury needed to consider was 'whether in carrying out his good motives [Stead] had overstepped the law'.[61]

When the jury retired at twenty minutes to four on Saturday 7 November, the silence of the court was abandoned. Some 'two dozen be-wigged barristers were scattered around' while ladies chatted in the best seats and the court aldermen lounged in their furred robes.[62] In the dock, the defendants talked among themselves or leaned over the bar to speak to their barristers and friends. Josephine Butler engaged in a quiet conversation with Jarrett. Stead, who now believed the verdict a foregone conclusion, set about writing a series of farewells to his supporters, apologizing for making 'such a mess of things'.[63] Others, like Thomas Catling, were less certain of the jury's sentiment. Catling worried they might have been swayed by Stead and the other defence barristers' 'eloquent, ardent and impassioned appeals'.[64]

'Shortly after half past five the judge returned' and after whispered words with a clerk, 'smiled'.[65] At half-past six, the defendants shared a bowl of grapes to still their appetites. At half-past seven there was a sudden stir 'which thrilled like an electric flash through the throng' and all were ordered to take their seats as the jury returned.[66]

The clerk stood and turned to the foreman. 'Did Stead or Jarrett take Eliza Armstrong out of the possession of her father against his will?' he asked.

'Yes, Stead did,' he replied.

'Then about Jarrett? [sic]' asked Mr Justice Lopes.

'Yes, my Lord,' replied the foreman, 'and Stead was misled by Jarrett.'[67]

William Bramwell Booth, Mr Jacques and Madame Combe were found not guilty of Eliza's abduction. In a brief, second trial, Madame Mourey, Jacques, Jarrett and Stead were all found guilty on the charge of indecent assault. Jacques was sentenced to one month in prison, Mourey to six months with hard labour – she died in prison. Stead received a sentence of three months and Jarrett was to spend six months in Millbank prison without hard labour.[68]

At the close of the trial, the foreman approached William Stead's wife in apologetic tears and tried to explain the guilty verdict. 'Tell him not to grieve,' Stead wrote to his wife, 'if I had been in his place I should have done as he did.'[69] Stead had read his scripture. He knew the Messiah's tale always ended in martyrdom.

The day after the trial, most Sunday newspapers described Stead's guilty verdict with undisguised glee. On its front page, *Lloyd's Weekly* revelled in the fact that its own Henry Hales' series of summer reports were vindicated in court. 'The jurymen', ran its editorial, 'have done their duty in a way that establishes . . . the inviolability of English homes, be they ever so humble'.[70] Better still, the 'dreadful crimes' reported by the *Pall Mall Gazette* and with which 'England was held up to the execration of the world' were now proven to be ' . . . no more truthful than the alleged sale of Eliza by her mother'.[71] With one competitive swoop of his pen Catling had undone the entire findings of the Secret Commission. On the same Sunday the *Observer* opined that it was 'not the duty of the journalist to act as a literary knight errant [and] editors are neither missionaries nor evangelists'.[72]

*

The condemnation of Stead soon spread to undermine the entire social-purity movement. 'The offspring of the poorest', argued the *Daily Chronicle*, 'are as much entitled as the rich to be exempt from the experiments of busybodies'.[73] 'The truth is,' stated the *Spectator*, 'that the fanatical religious movement with which this crusade has been bound up has seriously tainted it'.[74] It is true that the movement's response to the backlash was, unfortunately, to become more repressive and conservative. With Stead in prison, religious extremists took over the campaign through the newly established National Vigilance Association (NVA), which did pressure the police to implement the new vice laws, but focused most of its attention on the prostitutes and brothel-keepers. Between 1885 and 1914 approximately 1,200 brothels were prosecuted in England and Wales each year, fourteen times as many, on average, as before.[75] But brothel closures were not supplemented by improvements in the working conditions of women, and some women's groups accused the NVA of persecuting 'the poorest, most helpless and forlorn of womankind'.[76] Many more were now forced to supplement their wages on the streets, which exposed them to the menace of figures like Jack the Ripper, who killed his first victim in 1888.

The NVA also engaged in the suppression of theatres, music halls and 'obscene' literature, including pamphlets on birth control. Josephine Butler resigned from the NVA in protest, but there was little she could do to prevent its fanaticism discrediting a once-progressive movement; and her warning against 'the fatuous belief that you can oblige human beings to be moral by force' went unheeded.[77]

Other middle-class intellectuals shared Butler's horror. The loucheness of the aesthetic movement formed one provocative response, countered in 1895 by the prosecution of its lodestar, Oscar Wilde.[78] The Irish playwright and socialist George Bernard Shaw, a former employee and supporter of William Stead, channelled his own disgust into his two most famous plays. The first, *Mrs Warren's Profession* (1893), featured a wealthy brothel-keeper and 'white slaver' akin to Mrs Jeffries, a successful businesswoman who had chosen prostitution over noxious, ill-paid factory work.[79] The play was banned from public performance for thirty years, a victim of the puritanical censorship Shaw came to despise.

The second was a satire, *Pygmalion*, and it is to this play that the case of William Stead and Eliza Armstrong bears more than a passing resemblance.[80] Although Shaw did not complete *Pygmalion* until June 1912 – two months after Stead died – he had begun planning it many years earlier.[81]

The spirit of Stead appears in *Pygmalion* in the guise of an impassioned but myopic phoneticist named Henry Higgins, who attempts to pluck a young girl from her working-class life and reform her by altering her accent, her manners and her clothes. The girl's name was Eliza Doolittle. Like Eliza Armstrong, she came from Lisson Grove and was purchased by Higgins from her parents for £5. Further references to the Armstrong case abound: 'I've heard', Eliza tells Higgins, 'of girls being drugged by the like of you.'[82] When Higgins' housekeeper warns, 'You can't take a girl up like that as if you were picking up a pebble on the beach,' Higgins replies, 'Why not?' 'Why not!' the housekeeper replies. 'Why you don't know anything about her. What about her parents?'[83]

Throughout the play, Shaw makes comedy of the parallels between moral reformers and sexual predators. Like Stead, Higgins did not seek to defile Eliza but to improve her. His interference, predicated on his assumption of class and moral superiority, is nonetheless fraught with peril. He is accused of 'playing' with his 'live doll' with no thought to consequence, and Eliza soon realizes that in becoming 'middle-class', she has forfeited a great deal, namely her identity and her independence.[84] 'I sold flowers,' she said, 'I didn't sell myself. Now you've made a lady of me I'm not fit to sell anything else.'[85]

Shaw's disdain for middle-class hypocrisy was shared by other – upper- and lower-class – victims of their moral, 'kill joy', interventions, reaffirming class animosities that would resonate for decades.[86] Or as he put it in his preface to *Pygmalion:* 'it is impossible for an Englishman to open his mouth without making some other Englishman despise him'.[87]

*

One of the main beneficiaries of Stead's downfall was Sir William Harcourt. Through the autumn of 1885, he continued, like Stevenson's Dr Jekyll, to 'plod in the public eye with a load of genial respectability'.[88] The black fog of suspicion that had surrounded him dissipated after Stead's prosecution, just in time for the forthcoming general election. Stead's claim that his *Maiden Tribute* series had secured the passing of the Criminal Law Amendment Act was revised as bunkum in the mainstream press, while Harcourt's assertion that he had always been determined to pass the Bill and 'was proud to have initiated the measure' was now accepted as genuine.[89] And while Stead languished in his freezing prison cell, Harcourt trumped Alfred Dyer at the Derby polls by 7,548 votes to 1,239.[90] In February 1886, he returned to the pinnacle of the English Establishment as Chancellor of the Exchequer in the newly elected Liberal government. Over the following years, he and Loulou refocused their ambition on what Harcourt desired most, to become Prime Minister. Harcourt had passed through the fiery furnace and emerged without a scorch.

As the charged middle months of 1885 faded into a harsh and prolonged winter, Jeremiah Minahan finally yielded to his fate. His best efforts spent, he turned his thoughts to home, and waiting patiently there, his wife Barbara. The couple's solution to their months of turmoil was to flit quietly away from the metropolis to the south coast, and the picturesque town of Bexhill-on-Sea.[91] Long renowned as an area of 'pastoral solitude', offering 'serener air' and a 'perpetual feast' of 'green', the locale seemed the perfect retreat from the madding city – but London's reach remained.[92]

Like the swelling sea clouds that regularly dampened the town's warm promise, Jeremiah's memories still crowded in. Now he might swallow the sour draught of his recent defeats, the knowing that he had failed to crush his enemy and that his youth and future hopes had already ebbed beyond the horizon. His lifetime's losses shaded his mind and darkened his thoughts, until, surrounded by the south coast's solid cliffs and sparkling waves, the rock that once stood firm inside Derby's Drill Hall slowly dissolved to sand.

Epilogue

Shocking Affair at Haywards Heath

SUSSEX EVENING TIMES, FRIDAY APRIL 5 1895

A WOMAN FOUND MURDERED
THE HUSBAND ARRESTED

> The body of a woman named Minahan was found in Ashenground Wood this morning. There was a large wound in the throat. This afternoon her husband, recently an inmate of the Haywards Heath Asylum, was arrested after a prolonged and fierce struggle.[1]

Julia Field remembered the first scream as 'a sort of hallooing' and the girls in the woods as an 'hoi'; but none felt it a 'cry of a person in distress or danger'.[2] It must, they all presumed, be schoolboys. Sometimes boys would gather at the bridge and scream at the trains beneath, thundering between London and the south coast.

Shortly after 12 p.m. on Friday 5 April 1895, Barbara and Jeremiah Minahan had set off together for Haywards Heath railway station, walking the scenic route through Ashenground Woods. A sumptuously green and wooded town, Haywards Heath was built up and down the small hills that hugged the new railway line. Its main gravelled thoroughfares, South Road, Perrymount and Boltro, were lined with trees and dotted with new Victorian villas. From any of the town's peaks were grand views across the South Downs, rolling away in the haze towards the sea.[3] It was a glorious spring day, the kind that breaks winter's steely hold and beckons in summer. Jeremiah had just regained his job as a canvasser for an assurance agent in nearby Brighton and he and Barbara had settled, over the past four months, to a fresh start in this small Sussex town, making new friends through St Wilfrid's Anglican church.[4]

At around 12.30 p.m. they reached the approach to Ashenground Bridge, a pedestrian crossing over the railway line, marking the entrance to the woods. This was when Barbara screamed. Her cry was heard by the Hudson girls, gathering primroses beneath the beech trees with their nursemaid, and by Julia Field, who lived close by the bridge in Ashenground Cottage. Julia was twenty-nine years old and lived with her elderly widowed father, John, the gamekeeper at Ashenground.[5] A few minutes earlier she had seen Barbara and Jeremiah walk past the cottage from an upstairs bedroom window. Barbara was tall and 'a fine woman for her age'.[6] She wore a mantle with a dark dress and black kid gloves. Just a yard or so behind her was a big man Julia had noticed passing her cottage many times before, on his way to stroll in the quiet woods.

The scream left Julia with a 'sort of strange impression' so she went outside to look.[7] Her cottage gave onto Ashenground Road, a narrow dirt track, more like a bridleway than a proper road. Down the hill to her left she could see the railway bridge and woods beyond, but there was nobody there.

Two or three minutes later, back inside the cottage, Julia heard a second scream. The nursemaid, Emily Mills, and the Hudson girls, Amy, Gladys and Dorothy, heard it too. This time they were closer and from the shade of their woodland track, they saw two figures on the railway bridge. One of them, a woman, was leaning against the blackened bridge wall. Close by her, watching, was a 'big tall man'.[8] Emily knew he was called Minahan, 'or something like that', and

Amy was aware he was 'not supposed to be quite right in the head'.[9]

Briefly Jeremiah looked towards them. 'Let's go up to them,' said Amy, but Emily refused.[10] She was frightened of the man and pulled Amy back. Fearing Jeremiah might follow, they stole away together, back into the darkness of the trees.

*

Four months earlier, Jeremiah Minahan had been released from the East Sussex County Lunatic Asylum. The year before he had suffered an attack of 'mania' lasting a whole week, and had been committed to the asylum as a pauper lunatic. The asylum's 1894 Register of Admissions lists his former abode as the 'Brighton Workhouse', and that he was sent to the asylum under the authority of the Brighton magistrate, Mr C. E. Heathcote.[11] A former medical superintendent of the Sussex Asylum, Dr Samuel Williams, described in the *Journal of Mental Science* how an educated, middle-class man might come to enter his asylum in such a way:

> [He] becomes insane [and] becomes aggressive in the public thoroughfares. His relations, from various reasons, refrain to take the necessary steps to place him in safety. He falls into the hands of the police; is brought before two justices, who call to their assistance a medical man. He is undoubtedly insane and a danger to the public. They sign a [Section] order for his removal to the County Lunatic Asylum.[12]

While these arrangements were being made between the police and the magistrate, the 'insane' were usually held at the local workhouse.

Before succumbing to his 'mania', Jeremiah had been living first in Bexhill-on-Sea and then in Brighton, where he had family connections.[13] Living at 1 Hampton Place, a five-minute walk from the seafront, was Jeremiah's young copper-haired Limerick cousin, Margaret Austin (née Hayes), and her husband, Lionel. Margaret was in her early twenties, Lionel a few years older, and the couple had a reputation for benevolence: one relative remembers that there were 'always tramps' sitting on the steps of their pretty townhouse, awaiting Margaret's frequent charity.[14] In 1891, the Brighton census lists Jeremiah Minahan, by then forty-eight, at Hampton Place with Margaret and Lionel, but Barbara is strangely absent. She appears instead to have been lodging, 'on her own means', in a modest house in Devonport (near Plymouth), over two hundred miles away.[15] Barbara and Jeremiah's seaside hopes, which had begun in 1886 with their lease of Rose Cottage in Station Road, Bexhill-on-Sea, had not been entirely fulfilled.[16]

*

The Sussex Asylum at Haywards Heath was opened on 25 July 1859, after an Act which compelled every county and borough in England and Wales to provide adequate accommodation for all pauper lunatics.[17] Built for four hundred and fifty patients, in cheerful red and ochre brick, it was designed to maximize its aspect over the South Downs.[18] Dozens of south-facing windows allowed patients spectacular views of the rolling, ever-changing countryside. 'I never saw a building', wrote its first medical superintendent, Dr C. Lockhart Robertson, 'look less like an asylum'.[19]

Beyond sedation by cannabis or morphia, patients like Jeremiah Minahan were offered 'moral treatments' rather than medical. Improving distractions and entertainments were provided in the form of a library and school as well as dances and visits by local bands. The patients were kept to a daily routine and provided with a decent diet – fresh meat, rice, barley and vegetables served in broths and pies – and an opportunity to learn or work a trade. In the asylum grounds there was a tailor's shop, a shoemaker's shop, a baker's, a blacksmith's and a carpenter's as well as a twelve-acre vegetable garden.[20]

Yet a reporter from the *Brighton Gazette* wrote that 'notwithstanding all the kindness we saw', he had still left the asylum after an official visit ' . . . under feelings of a painful depression, an indescribable feeling of pity for the unhappy inmates'.[21] As well as the more pleasant amenities, he had seen the padded room, 'a sure preventative of self-mischief from even the most violent', and patient records dating to the mid-1890s suggest how strange, noisy and disturbing it must have been there, particularly at night.[22] The following phrases frequently appear in relation to Jeremiah's fellow inmates: 'impulsive and violent', 'very restless and unsettled', 'destructive and uses very foul language' and 'very dirty in habits'.[23] Other notes hint at underlying brutality: 'has a left black eye' and 'says an attendant struck [another patient] five or six times'.[24]

Still, five months after entering the asylum Jeremiah was deemed to have made 'a good recovery' and once discharged on 28 November 1894, he found Barbara back and waiting for him.[25]

Together again, the two cautiously chose to remain in Haywards Heath and for several months things went well. Jeremiah's neighbours found him a 'genial man of excellent education and good conversation' and the couple seemed 'comfortable,' 'quiet' and 'happy together'.[26] It also appears that since the death of her father, Bishop Joshua Hughes, in January 1889, Barbara had made some reparation with her family. Her younger sister, Alicia Hughes, was on her way to visit them by rail from Malvern, which was why Barbara and Jeremiah were crossing Ashenground railway bridge together on Friday 5 April 1895. They were on their way to collect Alicia from the station, but the happy meeting was not to be.

*

With her second scream Barbara collapsed to the ground. Jeremiah knelt down beside his wife and reached out to touch her. The pale Sussex dust clung to her black gloves; her face was dirty and her eyes were wide and empty. Alone at the entrance to the ancient woods, Jeremiah 'did not know what to do'.[27] He needed to think, but the shock was too much. His 'mania' was coming back.

Crouched beside his dying wife, it seemed to a delusional Jeremiah that the only possible cause of Barbara's sudden, unexpected death could be poisoning.

His next, less illogical thought was that if Barbara had been poisoned, he must have been poisoned too. He needed to act quickly. He needed to find water.

Back inside Ashenground Cottage, Julia Field was alone in the washhouse when she heard a knock on the front door. A huge man stood outside, and she recognized him instantly as the one who had walked past earlier with a woman.[28] Oddly, though, he was now alone.

'Will you give me a glass of water, please?' he asked.

'Yes sir,' said Julia, who went to fetch a drink from the kitchen. Jeremiah waited on the mat.

'They have been trying to poison me,' he said, as Julia returned. He put out his tongue. 'Look, it's all white.'[29]

Julia looked. She assured him his tongue looked quite 'natural', though it was now becoming clear there was something 'the matter' with this big powerful man.[30] Jeremiah then came inside the cottage and pushed the door closed behind him.

'You know the angels are coming from heaven?' said Jeremiah. 'Would you like me to kill you?'

'No sir,' said Julia.

'If you like I will kill you,' said Jeremiah, who now seemed to Julia 'very excited', ' . . . if you give me a knife or a gun or a rifle or a musket or anything.'[31]

Somehow Julia manoeuvred round him and out through her own front door. Outside, she stopped by the garden gate and turned, ready to run.

Jeremiah drank the water from her glass, then started walking across the garden towards her. She was trapped between the cottage and the gate. He raised his arm. He handed her the empty glass.

'You would not like me to kill you now,' he said. 'Then, goodbye my angel,' and taking her hand, he gently shook it. 'Will you telegraph my wife to send out the guards?'

'Yes,' said Julia.[32]

With that he turned and walked up the Ashenground Road in the direction of the town, away from the dark woods and into the light.

Julia locked herself inside the cottage. She thought for a moment then put on her outdoor clothes and left in the opposite direction from Jeremiah, heading down the slope towards the woods. On the ground ahead of her she could see something dark 'lying partly on the road and partly in the bushes'.[33] As she neared, it came into focus. She saw the feet and legs of a woman. She could not see a head and she did not want to look. For several minutes she stood beside the legs. Nothing stirred. She then hurried on, across the bridge, through the woods and north towards the police station on the Paddockhall Road.[34]

Jeremiah, meantime, went home to his lodgings at St Wilfrid's Villas. He paced in the sitting room then rang the bell. Expecting that Mr and Mrs Minahan were wanting 'dinner', the landlady, Mrs Jane Shelton, appeared with food – but Jeremiah had other things on his mind. 'If you receive a telegraph from London,' he said, advancing towards her, 'send word back to say I am the King of England, and my wife is the Baroness Burdett-Coutts.'[35] Up until this moment Jane Shelton had found Jeremiah to be 'most quiet and gentlemanly'.[36] Rather shocked by his new manner, she put the dinner plates down. 'Don't speak nonsensically,' she told him, and left.[37]

Jeremiah couldn't eat, and he didn't settle. Instead he went out again and while he walked, word spread of the body in the woods. Julia Field had reported her experiences to the Haywards Heath police and soon two officers began pursuing him. They followed him to another lodging house run by a Mrs Meads, where Jeremiah and Barbara had resided in the past. Shaking hands with his former landlady, Jeremiah sat down in her armchair and told her he 'had come into millions of money'.[38] He then also asked her to telegraph his wife and 'complained of pains in the back of his head' and that 'his hands were hot'.[39] Mrs Meads, apparently unperturbed, was in the process of making Jeremiah a comforting cup of tea when the two policemen entered her house. As soon as Jeremiah realized he was being handcuffed he began to struggle violently and continued to resist the officers for the entire half-mile back to the police station.

At around three o'clock that afternoon, Dr Alfred Newth attended to the body in the woods and officially pronounced Barbara Pennant Minahan dead.

The following morning, Saturday 6 April, Jeremiah was formally charged on suspicion of murdering his wife. Too distraught and incoherent to be placed in the dock of the police court, he was charged instead inside his cell. After a post-mortem carried out by Dr Newth, Barbara's body was removed to the nearby Sussex Hotel, to await an inquest that same day. It would be up to a jury of local citizens now to decide exactly how she came by her demise.

*

Many of the Sussex Asylum's records from this period have been lost, including the case notes on Jeremiah Minahan. Without them, it is impossible know whether his madness might have rendered him capable of killing, but the hints and scraps of remaining evidence do suggest two possible theories about his mental illness: one physiological, the second psychological.

Jeremiah's claims to kingship and his delusions of grandeur are symptomatic of the behaviour accompanying the 'tertiary' or final stage of syphilis, the dreaded and incurable disease that fuelled Mary Jeffries' trade in virgins. Syphilis was notoriously difficult to diagnose because of its ability to mimic many other conditions, which might range from rheumatism, arthritis, gout and epilepsy to mania and depression, and in 1879 it was dubbed the 'Great Imitator'.[40] It also lurked hidden in the body for years after initial infection. The tertiary stage, writes the historian Deborah Hayden, often 'begins with a dramatic episode characterised by delusions; grandiosity; identification with religious, mythic or royal figures; and sometimes rage and violent acts'.[41] In Jeremiah's lifetime, patients in the tertiary stage were diagnosed as suffering from 'general paralysis of the insane'.

Since Jeremiah did not marry until the age of thirty-nine, it is possible that in the course of earlier encounters he became infected. Was his righteous campaign in the 1880s the repentant action of a guilty, ailing man? Did he obsessively pursue Sir William Harcourt because he was slowly succumbing to the madness of 'general paralysis'? Prior to its onset, warning signs of the disease's progression might only be obvious to a patient's family and friends, who observe sporadic episodes of 'bizarre, uninhibited, even criminal' behaviour in their loved ones. Yet none of Jeremiah's *known* activities appear to have been bizarre or uninhibited. He was passionate in his pursuit of justice between 1883 and 1885, but not unhinged. During his week in Derby he deliberately distanced himself from the excesses of Henry Varley and remained calm in the midst of a riot at the Drill Hall. It is of course possible that he was then still in a sentient phase of his illness, but it is equally possible that Jeremiah's insanity stemmed from psychological strain rather than a physiological trigger.

On the 1894 asylum Register of Admissions, one word remains in explanation of the 'supposed cause' of Jeremiah's 'insanity'. This word is: 'Worry'.[42]

The leading psychiatrist of the late-Victorian era, Dr Henry Maudsley, described the effect of 'mental trials' upon individuals in an 1878 article for *Popular Science Monthly* magazine. He linked mental trauma to the kind of delusions suffered by Jeremiah Minahan, citing the 'disorder of the sensory centres' prompted by anxiety or shock – something we might refer to today as nervous breakdown or stress disorder. In his article Maudsley cites the case of 'Nicolai, a bookseller of Berlin' who suffered hallucinations after having been 'exposed to a succession of severe trials which had greatly affected him'.[43]

The medical superintendent who oversaw Jeremiah Minahan's care when he was first admitted to the asylum was Dr Charles Saunders. Dr Saunders remembered Jeremiah as a man of 'splendid physique and pleasant personality' whose essential delusion was that 'he was followed by detectives'.[44] Saunders presumed these hallucinations stemmed from Jeremiah's former life in the police force, and in examining the impact of his past, Saunders was on the right track. But there was a more sinister possibility. For there were two men who did still have reason to watch Jeremiah: Sir William Harcourt and his unscrupulous son, Loulou.

Sir William Harcourt was certainly not averse to having his enemies followed. During the 1880s, he had gained great advantage by having Irish Party members, including Parnell, under surveillance, as far away as Paris. Detectives also watched William Stead and other reporters from the *Pall Mall Gazette* for many months after the *Maiden Tribute* campaign (though under whose orders is unclear); and if Harcourt was willing to send spies to Varley and Jeremiah's Derby meetings, he may well have had them followed during 1885 and after.[45] Such an arrangement, as Harcourt and Loulou well knew, served two purposes: information-gathering and intimidation.

Certainly, Jeremiah seems to have believed that the knowledge he gathered while investigating Mary Jeffries' brothels rendered him a permanent threat to Harcourt's political objectives. He had never personally revealed what he knew about Harcourt's and Loulou's sexual proclivities; instead he had tried to be wise. He had passed his information to more robust men protected by public opinion. But William Stead's prosecution had presented a fearful lesson, that even fame and public support were not always enough. Stead's imprisonment in 1885 can only have enhanced Jeremiah's 'worry'. The months he had served as Alfred Dyer's private detective meant that he knew too much, and it was a burden he would carry for the rest of his life.

Dr Maudsley referred to the kind of 'prolonged anxiety' suffered by Jeremiah as 'moral shock'; and found that it affected different people in different ways. While one man might 'go to sleep and recover his equanimity' another might go 'mad in consequence'.[46] 'Life,' he explained, 'is always surrounded by forces that are tending to destroy it, so it is with the mind'; those who can no longer accommodate the 'continued warfare' of living may be overcome. Maudsley called it the 'moral cause of insanity'.[47]

Thirty years before, Jeremiah Minahan had journeyed from Limerick to London with little more than a few belongings and the plain ethics of his rural Catholic childhood. Intelligent and competent but poor, he had joined the police force on the promise of progression and security, and perhaps even to assist in the implementation of the justice he so believed in. Instead he found himself ensconced within an institution already decayed by corruption, a condition seemingly propped up by its master, the Home Secretary, Sir William Harcourt. Jeremiah may have believed that his moral strength was enough to fell such a man, but he was no match for Harcourt's pragmatism and realpolitik. It was Jeremiah's idealism and his ordinary faith in the narratives of justice that were his greatest strength and his most profound weakness. He might have been magnificent and courageous and clever, but next to the ruthless and powerful Harcourt, he was simply naive. His protest had brought only stress, loss and fear.

*

The inquest into Barbara Minahan's death was held at the Sussex Hotel on Saturday 6 April. This was a landmark inn in Haywards Heath, standing at the narrow corner between two roads that led up to the Sussex Asylum. Inquests in pubs and inns represented the last vestige of a long judicial tradition, in which they had often hosted petty sessions under the magistrate, providing a large space with the facility to accommodate groups for long periods. By 1895, only inquests continued to be held amidst the unseemly 'odour of gin and smell of tobacco smoke' once complained of by Charles Dickens.[48]

It seems clear from the newspaper reports that despite

knowing he had been in the asylum, Jeremiah's neighbours found it difficult to conceive of him as a murderer. He always behaved, said a juryman named Mr Jinks, 'in the most respectful manner'.[49] Of the several witnesses, the nursemaid, Emily Mills, and her young charge, Amy Hudson, proved key to Jeremiah's fate. They had seen Jeremiah and Barbara at Ashenground Bridge and though they had felt afraid of Jeremiah and were disturbed by what they saw, had seen no struggle between husband and wife. Jeremiah was standing close by Barbara when she fell to the ground, but was not touching her, and Emily Mills was certain she had 'not seen the man use any violence towards the woman'.[50] Dr Newth, who had observed the death scene and carried out a post-mortem, confirmed what Emily and Amy said. There were no external marks on the body 'beyond a slight bruise on the right temple', which may have been caused by the fall. The 'blood' on her neck amounted to a small scratch. According to Dr Newth, 'there was not the slightest sign or trace of any violence used', either at the death scene or on Barbara's body.[51] Her lungs were extensively diseased, her heart was dilated, her liver, kidney and spleen congested and she was suffering from gallstones. His theory was that Barbara was overcome with syncope (a fainting fit) caused by the 'failure of the heart's or brain's action'.[52] She had then fallen forward into some loose earth on the woodland path and become asphyxiated by inhaling the sandy soil. Mr Hillman, the Sussex coroner, reinforced Newth's findings by comparing a case where 'a man had fallen forward into three inches of water, and being helpless to move died drowning'.[53] Jeremiah had not been sentient enough to understand that Barbara could not breathe. Instead he had moved her off the pathway, laid her in the shelter of some bushes and turned her face to the sun.

The inquest jury concluded that Barbara died of natural causes. She was fifty-six years old. Jeremiah's status immediately shifted from murderer to widower, but this did not ease his torment. On Monday morning, 8 April, a 'few morbid spectators' gathered outside the Haywards Heath police court to watch him being taken back inside.[54] A reporter for the *East Sussex News* watched with them as 'this tall, fine man' still struggled 'in the hands of his captors'.[55] Little did the reporter suspect how terrified Jeremiah was, back in the hands of the uniformed men he had learned to distrust so many years before. The magistrate charged him not with murder but with being a 'lunatic at large'.[56] Jeremiah's response was largely incoherent beyond one warning: 'They are going to blow up the Houses of Parliament with dynamite.'[57] He was then manoeuvred back outside and into a waiting cab. He kept shouting for his wife, while the cab bore him on to his final destination.

Three months later, Sir William Harcourt and his Liberal Party suffered a sensational defeat in the general election of July 1895. Harcourt's one chance to become Prime Minister had been fought and lost to the dashing young Lord Rosebery, despite Loulou's backroom intrigues over Rosebery's sexuality. Indeed, Loulou Harcourt's skulduggery during the political contest, writes Rosebery's biographer, Robert Rhodes James, was so ruthless that it 'was to poison the Liberal Party for the next decade'.[58] His father spent the rest of his life in opposition and died on 1 October 1904, his ultimate ambition unfulfilled.

*

Jeremiah Minahan remained at the Sussex Asylum until his death on 23 August 1897. His death certificate cites: 'brain softening – 3 months'.[59] This was a lose term that could imply that Jeremiah died from either syphilis or stroke, with the qualification of '3 months' suggesting the latter – that he had suffered a stroke and had failed to rally. The Sussex Asylum doctors were also in the habit of using the term 'general paralysis of the insane' on the death certificates of those actually diagnosed with syphilis.

Three days later, Jeremiah was buried in the grounds of the asylum. At his funeral, his attendant 'friends' appear to have included his kindly cousin Margaret Austin. She and her husband were practising Catholics and a priest was specially brought in to conduct the service.[60] Jeremiah might not have returned to Ireland, but he was returned to the faith that reared him.

The Sussex Asylum's old cemetery still commands a 'beautiful prospect', albeit overgrown now with shrubbery and trees.[61] Standing and gazing across the South Downs on Thursday 26 August 1897, Margaret saw summer trees, hedgerows and flower meadows reminiscent of the Minahan family's former Limerick townland; and in the distant Sussex hills, an echo of the brooding Knockfierna, Ireland's Hill of Truth.

Afterword

Nine months after the passing of the Criminal Law Amendment Act, on 14 May 1886, a letter to Stead's *Pall Mall Gazette* from Thomas W. Snagge, the barrister who had investigated the traffic in English girls to Brussels for the Home Office in 1880–81, reported triumphantly that 'no woman of English nationality [was now] inscribed under the control of prostitution in Brussels'.[1] This is not to say that the trade had stopped, rather that it had moved to less vigilant pastures. A decade on, the first of many multinational conferences against international trafficking, or white slave trading, was held in London.[2] In 1912, the Bishop of London still claimed that 'for one great city alone 5,000 girls were procured every year' and that the 'traffic had spread all over the world'.[3]

Within England and Wales, the number of sexual-assault cases tried in the courts doubled in the immediate aftermath of the Criminal Law Amendment Act, the majority involving child victims.[4] By making his stand, Inspector Jeremiah Minahan lost everything, but the change of consent law he helped engender continues to this day to protect Britain's children.

*

William T. Stead was released from prison on 18 January 1885. Thereafter he marked the anniversary of his Old Bailey conviction by commuting to his newspaper offices 'clad in his prison garb, a remarkable figure in the streets'.[5] Unwavering in his belief that his good motives outweighed the 'mess' of the Armstrong case, Stead always insisted that his *Maiden Tribute* campaign was a triumph for altruism and the power of popular journalism. He died on the *Titanic* in April 1912. Survivors reported that he made no attempt to board the lifeboats and was last seen praying on deck. With his dramatic death, his *Maiden Tribute* errors were forgotten and he became lionized by social reformers and feminists, who continued to campaign against the sex trade and for women's rights.[6]

After the 1885 abduction trial, a testimonial fund was set up to assist Eliza Armstrong and her family. Eliza attended the Princess Louise's Home for the Protection and Training of Young Girls. She was granted two and a half years' more schooling and then placed in service. Charles Armstrong was supplied with 'two sets of sweeping machines, capable of reaching to the tops of the highest chimneys built'.[7] His family were meant to be re-housed and were offered assistance in paying their rent, but in February 1886 were still living in Charles Street, Lisson Grove, when Charles was accused in court of assaulting a female neighbour.[8] After this, the family dissolved back into anonymity. Eliza married, but was said by Stead some years later to have been widowed with five children and left 'very insufficiently provided for'.[9]

Adelene Tanner died in New Cross, South London, on 18 November 1890. She was thirty and died of 'apoplexy', the same death that took her father and protector Edwin Tanner thirteen years earlier. She never married.[10]

In September 1887, Chelsea's most famous madam, Mrs Mary Jeffries, was arrested and charged under the Criminal Law Amendment Act with keeping a brothel in Knightsbridge.[11] Dressed in black silk and a bonnet with feather trimmings, the sixty-eight-year-old was sentenced on 25 November by Judge Edlin – the same judge who let her off with a fine in 1885 – to six months in prison.[12] She died on 20 March 1891. The total proceedings of her estate went to her unmarried niece, Charlotte Barrowcliffe, and were valued at £4,450 (more than £250,000 in today's money).[13]

Despite her punishment and one or two relapses into alcoholism, Rebecca Jarrett did not return to her nefarious ways. She eventually settled in Hackney, east London, where she remained under the care of William and Florence Booth and of the Salvation Army. She died on 20 February 1928, leaving behind at least two autobiographies and two biographies, all of them different.[14]

Appendix One

A note about the weather

Unless otherwise indicated, weather conditions have been taken from *The Times* or the *Graphic*.

A note about money then and now

The figures below are based on the currency converter produced by the National Archives and available at www.nationalarchives.gov.uk/currency.

Value Then (1880)	*Value Now (2005)*
A farthing, a quarter of a penny	5p
Ha'penny	10p
One penny	20p
One shilling (12 pence)	£2.42
Ten shillings	£24.16
One pound (20 shillings)	£48.31
Five pounds	£241.55
Ten pounds	£483.10
Fifty pounds	£2,415.50
One hundred pounds	£4,831.00
Five hundred pounds	£24,155.00
One thousand pounds	£48,310.00
Ten thousand pounds	£483,100.00

Appendix Two

An outline of Jeremiah Minahan's career in the Metropolitan Police Force (1863–1883)

Jeremiah Minahan, officer no. 43862, joined the Metropolitan police force on 27 April 1863. He was first stationed in G: Division, Finsbury.

On 8 September 1870 he was promoted to sergeant and transferred to B: Division, Westminster.

On 17 November 1873 he transferred to P: Division, Camberwell and remained there for seven years, being promoted from sergeant to inspector (third class).

On 23 June 1880, having passed the necessary examinations, he was promoted again, to second-class inspector, and transferred to L: Division, Lambeth. Five months later, in the police orders of 10 November 1880, the officers of Minahan's Lambeth division were commended three times for catching and convicting local criminals. Minahan may have been seen as part of his division's success, because the following day he was swapped for another inspector from E: Division, Holborn, and transferred to Bow Street, one of the biggest and most important police stations in the Metropolitan force.

After sixteen months in E: Division, however, he was transferred out to T: Division, Chelsea, on 11 April 1882.

On 1 December 1883, he was demoted from second-class inspector to sergeant.

On 2 December 1883, he submitted his resignation, forfeiting his pension.

On 3 December 1883, he left the force.

Bibliography

Books

Ackroyd, Peter, *London: The Biography* (London: Vintage, 2000)

Acton, William, *Prostitution, Considered in its Moral, Social and Sanitary Aspects* (London: John Churchill, 1857)

Adams, Henry, *The Education of Henry Adams: an autobiography* (Boston: Houghton Mifflin, 1918)

Amos, Sheldon, *A Comparative Survey of Laws in Force for the Prohibition, Regulation and Licensing of Vice in England and Other Countries* (London: Stephens and Sons, 1877)

Anonymous, 'A Magistrate', *Metropolitan Police Court Jottings* (London: Horace Cox, 1882)

Arnold, Matthew, *Complete Prose Works* (Ann Arbor: University of Michigan Press, 1977)

Balch, William, *Ireland as I saw It* (New York: Putnam, 1850)

Begbie, Edward Harold, *Painted Windows; a Study in Religious Personality, by a Gentleman with a Duster* (New York: G. P. Putnam's Sons, 1922)

Belien, Paul, *A Throne in Brussels: Britain, the Saxe-Coburgs and the Belgianisation of Europe* (Exeter: Imprint Academic, 2005)

Bell, Ian, *Robert Louis Stevenson: dreams of exile* (London: Headline, 1992)

Bignell, John, *Chelsea seen from 1860 to 1980* (London: Studio B, 1978)

Booth, Charles, *Life and Labour of the People in London*, vol. I (London: Macmillan, 1892)

Booth, William, *Twenty One Years Salvation Army* (London: Salvation Army, 1887)

Born, Daniel, *The Birth of Liberal Guilt in the English Novel: Charles Dickens to H.G. Wells* (North Carolina: University of North Carolina Press, 1995)

Brassey, Mrs Annie, *Voyage in the Sunbeam* (Chicago: Belford Clarke, 1881)

Briggs, Asa, *History of Birmingham*, vol. II (Oxford: Oxford University Press, 1952)

———, *Victorian People: A Reassessment of Persons and Themes (1851–1867)* (University of Chicago Press, 1975)

British War Office, *A List of the Officers of the Army and the Corps of the Royal Marines* (London: Pinkney, 1839)

Buchanan, Robert, *The Poetical Works of Robert Buchanan* (London: Chatto and Windus, 1884)

Burleigh, Michael, *Blood and Rage: A Cultural History of Terrorism* (London: Harper Perennial, 2009)

Burnand, Sir Francis Cowley, *The Catholic Who's Who and Year Book* (London: Burnes and Oates, 1939)

Butler, Josephine, *Personal Reminiscences of a Great Crusade* (Tennessee: General Books, 2010)

Calder, Jenni, *RLS: a life study* (Glasgow: Richard Drew, 1990)

Cannadine, David, *The Decline and Fall of the British Aristocracy* (London: Picador, 1991)

Carpenter, Edward, *Loves Coming of Age* (South Carolina: Forgotten Books, 2010)

Catling, Thomas, *My Life's Pilgrimage* (London: John Murray, 1911)

Cavanagh, Timothy, *Scotland Yard Past and Present* (London: Chatto and Windus, 1893)

Chapman, Jane L., *Journalism Today: A Themed History* (Chichester: John Wiley & Sons, 2011)

Chase, Karen, *The Victorians and Old Age* (Oxford: Oxford University Press, 2009)

Clarke, W. S. *The Suburban Homes of London: A residential guide to favourite London localities, their society, celebrities and associations with notes on their rental, rates and house accommodation* (London: Chatto and Windus, 1881)

Clarkson, Charles and Hall Richardson, J., *Police!* (New York: Garland, 1984)
Collier, Richard, *The General Next to God: the story of William Booth and the Salvation Army* (London: Collins, 1968)
Corbin, Alain, *Women for Hire: prostitution and sexuality in France after 1850*, trans. Alan Sheridan (Cambridge, Mass.: Harvard University Press, 1996)
Croot, Patricia E. C., ed., *A History of the County of Middlesex: Volume 12: Chelsea* (Woodbridge: Boydell & Brewer, 2004)
Curtis, L. P., *Anglo-Saxons and Celts: A Study of Anti-Irish Prejudice in Victorian England* (Berkeley: University of California Press, 1968)
Davies, Owen, *Murder, magic and madness: the Victorian trials of Dove and Wizard* (Essex: Pearson Education, 2005)
Dellamora, Richard, *Masculine Desire: the sexual politics of Victorian aestheticism* (University of North Carolina Press, 1990)
Dickens, Charles, *Bleak House* (London: Penguin Classics, 1996)
———, *Speeches Literary and Social* (Adelaide: ebooks@adelaide, 2005)
———, ed., *Household Words*, vol. 2 (London: Bradbury & Evans, 1882)
Ditmore, Melissa Hope, *Encyclopedia of Prostitution and Sex Work*, vol. I (Connecticut: Greenwood Publishing, 2006)
Dodd, George, *Chambers Handy Guide to the Kent and Sussex Coast* (Edinburgh: Chambers, 1863)
Doré, Gustave and Jerrold, Blanchard, *London: A Pilgrimage* (London: Anthem Press, 2005)
Dyer, Alfred, *The European Slave Trade in English Girls: a narrative of facts* (London: Dyer Bros., 1885)
Dyos, H. J., *The Victorian City* (Oxon: Routledge, 1999)
Eder, Franz, *Sexual Cultures in Europe: themes in sexuality* (Manchester: Manchester University Press, 1999)
Ellis, Havelock, *Studies in the Psychology of Sex: sexual inversion* (Google Books: The Minerva Group Inc., 2001)
Fielding, Stephen, *Class and Ethnicity: Irish Catholics in England,*

1880–1939 (Buckingham and Philadelphia: Open University Press, 1993)

Ford, Wyn K., and Gabe, A. C., *The Metropolis of Mid Sussex: A History of Haywards Heath* (Haywards Heath: Clarke, 1981)

Ford, Wyn K., and Rogers, Lillian, *The Story of Haywards Heath* (East Sussex: S. B. Publications, 1998)

Fraser, Peter, *Lord Esher: A Political Biography* (London: Hart-Davis, MacGibbon, 1973)

Fraxi, Pisanus, *Encyclopedia of Erotic Literature: Index Liborum Prohibitum* (New York: Documentary Books, 1862)

Gardiner, A. G., *The Life of Sir William Harcourt*, vol. I, *1827–1886* (London: Constable, 1923)

Gardner, James, *Sweet Bells Jangled Out of Tune: A History of the Sussex Lunatic Asylum, Haywards Heath* (Brighton: James Gardner, 1999)

Gaskell, Elizabeth, *Mary Barton: a tale of Manchester Life* (Leipzig: Tauchnitz, 1849)

Geduld, Harry M., ed., *The Definitive Dr. Jekyll and Mr. Hyde Companion* (New York: Garland, 1983)

Gibson, Ian, *The Erotomaniac: The Secret Life of Henry Spencer Ashbee* (London: Faber, 2001)

Gleadle, Kathryn, *The Early Feminists: Radical Unitarians and the Emergence of the Women's Rights Movement, 1831–51* (New York: St. Martin's Press, 1995)

Goncourts, *Journal*, vol. II, 1862, www.gutenberg.org

Graham, Clare, *Ordering Law: the architectural and social history of the English law court* (Hants: Ashgate, 2003)

Greenwood, James, *The Seven Curses of London* (London: Fields Osgood, 1869)

Gull, Cyril Arthur, *The Great Acceptance: The life story of F.N. Charrington* (London: Hodder and Stoughton, 1913)

Gwynn, Stephen, *The Life of the Rt. Hon. Charles W. Dilke, Bart*, vol. I (London: John Murray, 1917)

Hall, Catherine, ed., *Defining the Victorian Nation: race, class, gender and the British Reform Act of 1867* (Cambridge: Cambridge University Press, 2000)

Harman, Claire, *Robert Louis Stevenson: A biography* (London: Harper Perennial, 2005)

Harrison, Brian, *Drink and the Victorians: the Temperance Question in England* (London: Faber & Faber, 1971)

Hattersley, Roy, *Blood and Fire: William and Catherine Booth and their Salvation Army* (London: Little, Brown, 1999)

Hayden, Deborah, *Pox: Genius, Madness and the Mysteries of Syphilis* (New York: Basic Books, 2003)

Hekma, Gert et al., *Gay Men and the sexual history of the political left*, Part 1 (London: Routledge, 1995)

Hewett, Osbert Wyndham, *Strawberry Fair: A Biography of Frances, Countess Waldegrave 1821–1879* (London: John Murray, 1956)

Hibbert, Christopher, *Edward VII: The Last Victorian King* (Basingstoke: Palgrave Macmillan, 2007)

Hignett, Sean, *Brett: from Bloomsbury to New Mexico, a biography* (London: Hodder and Stoughton, 1984)

Hill, Jacqueline, *From Patriots to Unionists: Dublin Civic Politics and Irish Protestant Patriotism* (Oxford: Oxford University Press, 1997)

Hill, Octavia, *Homes of the London Poor* (London: Frank Cass, 1970)

Hochschild, Adam, *King Leopold's Ghost: a story of greed, terror and heroism in Colonial Africa* (London: Macmillan, 2006)

Hollingshead, John, *Ragged London in 1861* (London: Smith, Elder, 1861)

Hubbard, Louisa M., *Work and Leisure*, vol. II (South Carolina: Bibliobazaar, 2008)

Hutchinson, Horace Gordon, *Portraits of the Eighties* (London: T. Fisher Unwin, 1920)

Hyde, Harford Montgomery, *A History of Pornography* (London: Four Square, 1964)

Jackson, Louise A., *Child Sexual Abuse in Victorian England* (London: Routledge, 2000)

Jackson, Patrick, *Harcourt and Son: A political biography of Sir William Harcourt, 1827–1904* (Madison: Fairleigh Dickinson University Press, 2004)

———, *Loulou: Selected extracts from the Journals of Lewis Harcourt (1880–1895)* (Madison: Fairleigh Dickinson University Press, 2006)

Jackson, Stanley, *The Life and Cases of Mr. Justice Humphreys* (London: Macmillan, 1952)

Jalland, Patricia, *Death in the Victorian Family* (Oxford: Oxford University Press, 2000)

James, Edward, *Swans Reflecting Elephants: my early years* (Weidenfeld and Nicolson, 1982)

James, Henry, *The Notebooks of Henry James*, ed. F. O. Matthiessen and Kenneth B. Murdock (Chicago: University of Chicago Press, 1981)

———, *Portrait of a Lady* (London: Penguin Classics, 2003)

———, *The Reverberator* (Los Angeles: Aegypan Press, 2010)

James, Lawrence, *The Middle-class: A History* (London: Little Brown, 2006)

Johnson, George W., ed., *Josephine Butler: an autobiographical memoir* (Bristol: J. W. Arrowsmith, 1911)

Jones, Gareth Stedman, *Outcast London: A Study in the Relationships between Classes in Victorian Society* (London: Penguin, 1971)

Jones, Kennedy, *Fleet Street and Downing Street* (London: Hutchinson, 1920)

Jordan, Jane, ed., *Josephine Butler and the Prostitution Campaigns: Diseases of the Body Politic*, vol. IV, *Child Prostitution and the Age of Consent* (Oxon: Routledge, 2003)

Jump, Harriet Devine, ed., *Women's writing of the Victorian period, 1837–1901* (Edinburgh: Edinburgh University Press, 1999)

Kaplan, Joel H., *Theatre and Fashion: Oscar Wilde to the Suffragettes* (Cambridge: Cambridge University Press, 1995)

Kern, Stephen, *A Cultural History of Causality: science, murder novels and systems of thought* (Princeton: Princeton University Press, 2006)

Kinealy, Christine, *A Death-Dealing Famine: the Great Hunger in Ireland* (London: Pluto, 1997)

Kleiner, Fred S., *Gardner's Art through the Ages* (Boston: Cengage Learning, 2008)

Knight, Charles, *Knight's Cyclopaedia of London* (London: Charles Knight, 1851)

Krafft-Ebing, Dr R. V., *Psychopathia Sexualis: A medico forensic study* (Pioneer Publications: New York, 1947)

Lees, Lynn Hollen, *Exiles of Erin: Irish Migrants in Victorian London* (Manchester: Manchester University Press, 1979)

Lees-Milne, James *The Enigmatic Edwardian* (London: Sidgwick & Jackson, 1986)

Leighton, Denys P., *The Greenian Moment: T.H. Green, Religion and Political Argument in Victorian Britain* (Exeter: Imprint Academic, 2004)

Liggins, Emma, *George Gissing, the working woman and urban culture* (Farnham: Ashgate, 2006)

Linton, Elizabeth Lynn, *Modern Women and What is Said of Them: Reprint of articles from the Saturday Review (London)* (New York: Redfield, 1868)

Lubenow, William C., *The Cambridge Apostles, 1820–1914: Liberalism, imagination and friendship* (Cambridge: Cambridge University Press, 1998)

Lucy, Henry William, *Later Peeps at Parliament from Behind the Speaker's Chair* (Newnes: London, 1905)

Lytton, Robert, *Julian Fane: A Memoir* (London: John Murray, 1871)

McCarthy, Justin, *British Political Portraits* (New York: Outlook Company, 1903)

McKenna, Neil, *The Secret Life of Oscar Wilde* (London: Arrow Books, 2004)

McLaren, Angus, *Sexual Blackmail: A Modern History* (Cambridge, Mass.: Harvard University Press, 2002)

Marshik, Celia, *British Modernism and Censorship* (Cambridge: Cambridge University Press, 2006)

Maudsley, Dr Henry, *Body and Mind: an inquiry into their connection and mutual influence specially in reference to mental disorders* (New York: D. Appleton, 1890)

Mayhew, Henry, *London Labour and the London Poor*, vol. IV (London: Griffin, Bohn, 1862)

Middlemas, Keith, *The Life and Times of Edward VII* (London: Weidenfeld and Nicolson, 1972)

Middleton, Judy, *Around Haywards Heath in Old Photographs* (Gloucester: Sutton, 1989)

Mill, John Stuart, *The Subjection of Women* (London: Longmans, Green, Reader and Dyer, 1870)

Mitchell, Sally, *Daily Life in Victorian England* (Oxford: Greenwood Publishing, 1996)

Moore, Wendy, *The Knife-Man* (London: Bantam, 2005)

Morris, Robert John, *Class, sect and party: the making of the British middle-class: Leeds 1820–1850* (Manchester: Manchester University Press, 1990)

Mort, Frank, *Dangerous Sexualities: medico-moral politics in England since 1830* (Oxon; Routledge, 2000)

Mullen, Richard, *The Smell of the Continent: the British discover Europe 1814–1914* (London: Macmillan, 2011)

Murdoch, Lydia, *Imagined Orphans: poor families, child welfare and contested citizenship in London* (New Jersey: Rutgers University Press, 2006)

Myers, John E. B., *Evidence in Child Abuse and Neglect Cases*, vol. I (Aspen Publishers Online, 1997)

Neely, W. G., *Kilcooley: Land and People in Tipperary* (Belfast: Universities Press, 1983)

Nelson, Claudia, *Family Ties in Victorian England* (Santa Barbara: Greenwood Publishing, 2007)

Nicholls, David, *A Lost Prime Minister: a life of Sir Charles Dilke* (London: Hambledon Press, 1995)

Nightingale, Florence, *Ever Yours: selected letters* (Cambridge, Mass: Harvard University Press, 1990)

———, *Florence Nightingale on Society and Politics, Philosophy, Science, Education and Literature*, vol. 5 (Ontario: Wilfrid Laurier University Press, 2003)

O'Donnell, F. Hugh, *A History of the Irish Parliamentary Party*, vol. 1 (London: Longmans, Green, 1910)

Orr, Clarissa Campbell, *Wollstonecraft's Daughters: womanhood in England and France, 1780–1920* (Manchester: Manchester University Press, 1996)

Pardon, George Frederick, *The Popular Guide to London and its Suburbs* (London: Routledge, 1862)

Parris, Matthew, *Great Parliamentary Scandals* (London: Robson Books, 1997)

Pearson, Michael, *The Age of Consent: Victorian Prostitution and its Enemies* (Newton Abbot: David and Charles, 1972)

Pease, Edward P., *The History of the Fabian Society* (New York: E. P. Dutton, 1916)

Pellow, Jill, *The Home Office 1848–1914: from Clerks to Bureaucrats* (London: Heinemann Educational Books, 1982)

Perkin, Harold, *The Rise of Professional Society: England since 1880* (London: Routledge, 1989)

Petrie, Glen, *A Singular Iniquity: the campaigns of Josephine Butler* (London: Macmillan, 1971)

Plowdon, Alison, *The Case of Eliza Armstrong* (London: BBC Books, 1974)

Poirteir, Cathal, *Famine Echoes* (Dublin: Gill and Macmillan, 1995)

Pope-Hennessy, James, *Monckton Milnes: The flight of youth, 1851–1885* (London: Constable, 1951)

Praz, Mario, *The Romantic Agony* (London: Oxford University Press, 1951)

Railton, George, ed., *The Truth About the Armstrong Case and the Salvation Army: Mr Stead's Defence* (London: Salvation Army, 1885)

Reid, T. Wemyss, *Life, Letters and Friendships of Richard Monckton Milnes*, vol. 2 (New York: Cassell, 1890)

Rice-Jones, Rev. D., *In the Slums: Pages from the Notebook of a London Diocesan Home Missionary* (London: Nisbet, 1884)

Richards, Grant, *Memories of a Misspent Youth 1872–1896* (London: Heinemann, 1932)

Rimbault, Edward Francis, *Soho and its Associations: Historical, Literary and Artistic* (London: Dulau, 1895)

Rintoul, M. C., *Dictionary of Real People and Places in Fiction* (London: Routledge, 1993)

Ritchie, J. Ewing, *Days and Nights out in London* (London: Tinsley, 1880)

Roberts, Nickie, *Whores in History* (London: Harper Collins, 1992)

Rodrick, Anne B., *Self-Help and Civic Culture: Citizenship in Victorian Birmingham* (Hants: Ashgate, 2004)

Roscoe, Henry, *A Digest of the Law of Evidence in Criminal Cases* (Philadelphia: T. & W. Johnson, 1840)

Ross, Ishbel, *Child of Destiny: the life story of the first woman doctor* (London: Victor Gollancz, 1950)

Roth, Michael P., *Historical Dictionary of Law Enforcement* (Connecticut: Greenwood Publishing, 2001)

Rowe, Richard, *Life in the London Streets* (London: J. C. Nimmo and Bain, 1881)

Sala, George, *Gaslight and Daylight* (London: Chapman and Hall, 1859)

———, *Breakfast in Bed, Or Philosophy Between the Sheets* (New York: John Bradburn, 1863)

Sala, George Augustus, *Twice Around the Clock, or The Hours of Day and Night in London* (London: Richard Marsh, 1862)

Schlesinger, Max, *Saunterings in and about London* (London: Nathaniel Cook, 1853)

Schults, Raymond L., *Crusader in Babylon: W.T. Stead and the Pall Mall Gazette* (Lincoln: University of Nebraska Press, 1972)

Scott, Benjamin, *Six Years' Labour and Sorrow* (London: Dyer Bros., 1885)

Scott, J. R., *The Family Guide to Brussels* (London: Edward Stanford, 1883)

Scott, J. W. R., *Life and Death of a Newspaper* (London: Camelot Press, 1952)

Shanley, Mary Lyndon, *Feminism, Marriage and the Law in Victorian England 1850–1895* (New Jersey: Princeton University Press, 1989)

Sharp, Ingrid, ed., *Josephine Butler and the Prostitution*

Campaigns: Diseases of the Body Politic, The Moral Reclaimability of Prostitutes, vol. I (London: Routledge, 2003)

Sharp, Joanne P., ed., *Entanglements of Power: geographies of domination/resistance* (Oxon: Routledge, 2000)

Shaw, George Bernard, *Unpublished Shaw* (Pennsylvania: Penn State Press, 1996)

———, *Pygmalion* (London: Penguin Books, 2003)

Shirley, W. Shirley, *Leading Cases in the Criminal Law* (New Jersey: Read Books, 2007)

———, *A Sketch of the Criminal Law* (South Carolina: Bibliobazaar, 2009)

Shpayer-Makov, Haia, *The Making of a Policeman: a social history of a labour force in metropolitan London, 1829–1914* (Aldershot: Ashgate, 2002)

Smith, J. A., *Henry James and Robert Louis Stevenson: a record of friendship and criticism* (London: Rupert Hart-Davis, 1948)

Snell, Lord, *Men, Movements and Myself* (London: J. M. Dent, 1936)

Spellissy, Sean, and John O'Brien, *Limerick: The Rich Land* (Clare: Spellissy/O'Brien, 1989)

Stafford, Ann, *The Age of Consent* (London: Hodder and Stoughton, 1964)

Stead, Estelle W., *My Father: Personal and Spiritual Reminiscences* (London: Heinemann, 1913)

Stevenson, Robert Louis, *Strange Case of Dr Jekyll and Mr Hyde* (Oxford: World's Classics, 2008)

Swift, Roger, *The Irish in the Victorian City* (Oxford: Taylor & Francis, 1985)

Tames, Richard, *The Victorian Public House* (Osprey Publishing: London, 2008)

Taylor, David, *The New Police in Nineteenth-Century England: crime, conflict and control* (Manchester: Manchester University Press, 1997)

Terrot, Charles, *The Maiden Tribute* (London: Frederick Muller, 1959)

Thackeray, William Makepeace, *Irish Sketch Book of 1842* (New York: J. Winchester, 1848)

Thayer, Stuart, *American Circus Anthology: Essays of the Early Years*, © Stuart Thayer and William L. Slout, 2005, www.circushistory.org)

Thomas, Donald, *Swinburne: the poet and his world* (London: Allison & Busby, 1999)

Thomson, Basil, *The Story of Scotland Yard* (New York: Country Life Press, 1935)

Thornbury, Walter, 'Paternoster Row', *Old and New London*, vol. 1 (1878, www.british-history.ac.uk)

———, and Walford, Edward, *Old and New London*, vol. 3 (1878, www.british-history.ac.uk)

Tosh, John, *Masculinity and the Middle-Class Home in Victorian England* (London and New Haven: Yale University Press, 1999)

Ugolini, Laura, *Men and Menswear: sartorial consumption in Britain 1880–1939* (Hants: Ashgate, 2007)

Varley, Henry, Jnr., *Henry Varley's Life Story: by his son* (London: Alfred Holness, 1916)

Walford, Edward, 'Chelsea: Cremorne Gardens', *Old and New London*, vol. 5 (London: Cassell, Petter, & Galpin, 1878)

———, *Londoniana*, vol. 2. (South Carolina: Bibliobazarre, 2008)

Walker, Pamela J., *Pulling the Devil's Kingdom Down: the Salvation Army in Victorian Britain* (Berkeley: University of California Press, 2001)

Walkowitz, Judith R., *Prostitution and Victorian Society: Women, Class and the State* (Cambridge University Press, 1980)

———,*City of Dreadful Delight: Narratives of Sexual Danger in Late-Victorian London* (Chicago: University of Chicago Press, 1992)

Welsh, Alexander, *George Eliot and Blackmail* (Cambridge, Mass.: Harvard University Press, 1985)

White, Chris, *Nineteenth Century Writings on Homosexuality: a source book* (London: Routledge, 1999)

Whyte, Frederic, *The Life of W.T. Stead*, vols. I and II (London: Jonathan Cape, 1925)

Wilde, Oscar, *An Ideal Husband,* (Boston: John W. Luce & Co., 1906)

Wilde, Oscar, *The Soul of Man Under Socialism* (New York: Max N. Maisel, 1915)

Williams, Chris, *A Companion to Nineteenth Century Britain* (Oxford: Wiley-Blackwell, 2004)

Williams, Montagu, QC, *Leaves of a Life* (London: Macmillan, 1891)

———, *Round London: Down East and Up West* (London: Macmillan, 1893)

Wohl, Anthony, *The Eternal Slum* (New Jersey: Transaction Publishers, 2002)

Wright, Julia M., *Ireland, India and nationalism in nineteenth-century literature* (Cambridge: Cambridge University Press, 2004)

Wroth, Warwick, *Cremorne and the Later London Gardens* (London: Elliot Stock, 1907)

Yates, Edmund Hodgson, *The Business of Pleasure* (South Carolina: Bibliobazarre, 2008)

Zola, Émile, *Nana* (London: Penguin Classics, 1972)

Archives Used

Birmingham City Archives

Bodleian Library Special Collections, University of Oxford

Churchill Archives Centre, Churchill College, Cambridge (CC)

East Sussex Records Office, Lewes (ESRO)

Hansard, www.hansard.millbanksystems.com

Manuscripts Department, Cambridge University Library

Metropolitan Police Historical Collection, London

Parliamentary Archives, House of Commons, London

Registry of Deeds, Dublin

Religious Society of Friends Archive, London

Salvation Army International Heritage Centre, London (SAC)

Somerset Heritage Centre, Taunton

The National Archives, Kew (TNA)

Trinity College Archives, Dublin

University of Durham Library, Special Collections
Women's Library, London Metropolitan University

Manuscript Collections

Barker Ponsonby Papers, Trinity College Dublin
Churchill College Archive (CC)
Earl Grey Papers, Durham University Library
Harcourt Papers, Bodleian Libraries, University of Oxford
Home Office Archives, Kew (TNA) (HO)
House of Commons Parliamentary Papers (HCPP)
McKenny Hughes Archive, Cambridge University
Metropolitan Police Archives, Kew (TNA) (MEPO)
Papers of Rebecca Jarrett (SAC)
Papers of the Strachie Family of Sutton Court, Pensford, Somerset
Sussex County Lunatic Asylum Records (St. Francis Hospital)
Women's Library, Metropolitan University London

Online Sources

www.archive.org
www.gutenberg.org
www.victorianlondon.org
www.british-history.ac.uk
www.attackingthedevil.com

Libraries

British Library
Newspaper Library, Colindale
Haywards Heath Library
Limerick Local Studies Library
Religious Society of Friends Library, London
Kensington Central Library, Local Studies Department
Derby Local Studies Library

Notes

Prologue

1. 'Mother Seeking a Lost Child', *Lloyd's Weekly*, London, Sunday 12 July 1885.
2. George Augustus Sala, *Twice Around the Clock, or The Hours of Day and Night in London* (Leicester: Leicester University Press, 1971), p. 327.
3. 'The Maiden Tribute of Modern Babylon', *Pall Mall Gazette*, 6–9 July 1885. The word 'trafficker' was not widely used in this context until late 1885. One of the first instances I have found was in the pamphlet *Six Years' Labour and Sorrow* by Benjamin Scott, which was published after the summer of 1885. I have therefore used the earlier term *placeur* (usher).
4. Report from the Select Committee of the House of Lords on the Law Relating to the Protection of Young Girls, House of Commons Parliamentary Papers (HCPP), HC 448 (1881), ix. 355 and HC 344 (1882) xiii. 823.
5. The Earl of Dalhousie, 'Motion for a Select Committee', Hansard, HL Deb, 30 May 1881, vol 261 cc1603–13, hansard.millbanksystems.com.
6. 'Mother Seeking a Lost Child', *Lloyd's Weekly*, Sunday 12 July 1885.
7. Lydia Murdoch, *Imagined Orphans: poor families, child welfare and contested citizenship in London* (New Jersey: Rutgers University Press, 2006), pp. 104–5.
8. Clare Graham, *Ordering the Law: The Architectural and Social History of the English Law Court to 1914* (Hants: Ashgate, 2003), p. 192.
9. Anonymous, 'A Magistrate', *Metropolitan Police Court Jottings* (London: Horace Cox, 1882), p. 9.
10. Alison Plowdon, *The Case of Eliza Armstrong* (London: BBC Books, 1974), p. 25.
11. 'Mother Seeking a Lost Child', *Lloyd's Weekly*, Sunday 12 July 1885.

12 Ibid.
13 Ibid.
14 Anonymous, op. cit., p. 37.
15 'Mother Seeking a Lost Child', *Lloyd's Weekly*, Sunday 12 July 1885.
16 'Letters to the Editor', *The Times*, London, Monday 20 and Saturday 25 July 1885.
17 'Mother Seeking a Lost Child', *Lloyd's Weekly*, Sunday 12 July 1885.
18 HH, 'Letter to the Editor, "Street Ruffians" ', *Daily News*, Friday 20 August 1869, London.
19 Birmingham, Parish of St George, *Census Report*, 1841; Justin McCarthy, *British Political Portraits* (New York: Outlook Company, 1903), p. 77.
20 'Charles Street – Lisson-Grove', *British Architect*, Friday 4 November 1881, p. 544.
21 Octavia Hill, *Homes of the London Poor* (London: Frank Cass, 1970), p. 40.
22 Ibid., p. 89.
23 Marylebone, St Barnabas Parish, *Census Report*, London, 1881. Mrs Armstrong also had another daughter, four years older than Eliza, who was in service but who occasionally returned to live with the family.
24 Trial of Rebecca Jarrett et al., t18851019-1031, www.oldbaileyonline.org.
25 Letter, Mary A. Spibey to William Stead, 22 October 1885, Churchill Archives Centre, Cambridge (CC), Papers of William Stead, STED 1/9 Correspondence B, Part 7.
26 'Mother Seeking a Lost Child', *Lloyd's Weekly*, Sunday 12 July 1885.
27 Ibid.
28 Ibid. When quoting Mr Broughton's words, Hales stated that Jarrett's name was 'Rachel' not Rebecca. Whether Hales simply misheard Mr Broughton or was misled by him is unclear.
29 Ibid.
30 Ibid.
31 Trial of Rebecca Jarrett et al., op. cit.
32 Ibid.
33 Ibid.
34 'Mother Seeking a Lost Child', *Lloyd's Weekly*, Sunday 12 July 1885.

Notes

Chapter One: Serious Charge against the Police

1 James Greenwood, *The Seven Curses of London* (London: Fields Osgood, 1869), pp. 142–3.
2 Pamphlet, Jeremiah Minahan, *How an Inspector of the Metropolitan Police was punished for faithfully performing his duty to the public*, 1884 (Women's Library, London Metropolitan University) (WL), Printed: 350 420941 JOS.
3 Ibid.
4 Ibid.
5 *Glasgow Herald*, Monday 27 March 1882.
6 *Daily News*, London, Monday 10 April 1882.
7 G: Division Register, 1863, Metropolitan Police Historical Collection, London.
8 By 1882 the London force was policing almost five million people using 11,234 men, of which 605 were inspectors like Jeremiah Minahan. See E. Y. W. Henderson, *Report of the Commissioner of Police of the Metropolis for the year 1881*, London, 1882, Printed 3AMS/B/05/21 (Women's Library, London Metropolitan University).
9 Walter Thornbury and Edward Walford, *Old and New London*: vol. 3 (1878), pp. 197–218, www.british-history.ac.uk.
10 Rev. D. Rice-Jones, *In the Slums: Pages from the Notebook of a London Diocesan Home Missionary* (London: Nisbet, 1884), p. 26.
11 Ibid.
12 Ibid., p. 27.
13 Henderson, op. cit.
14 *Daily News*, London, Monday 3 April 1882; *Standard*, London, Monday 10 April 1882.
15 Ibid.
16 Henderson, op. cit.
17 Ibid.
18 *Daily News*, London, Monday 3 April 1882.
19 Ibid.
20 Rice-Jones, op. cit., p. 196. I have taken Rice-Jones' description of a 'Metropolitan Police Station' to be Bow Street station as it was situated in the centre of the slums he described. The glass partition is also shown in the architect's plan of the new Bow Street Police Court and Station, 1876–81, see Clare Graham, *Ordering the Law: The Architectural and Social History of the English Law Court to 1914* (Hants: Ashgate, 2003), p. 184.
21 Rice-Jones, op. cit.; Richard Rowe, *Life in the London Streets* (London: J. C. Nimmo and Bain, 1881), p. 31.

22 *Standard*, London, Monday 10 April 1882.
23 'The Police of London', *Quarterly Review* (London: John Murray), vol. 129, no. 257, July 1870.
24 Peter Ackroyd, *London: The Biography* (London: Vintage, 2000), p. 583.
25 Ibid., p. 655.
26 *Morning Chronicle*, London, Monday 15 July 1850.
27 Haia Shpayer-Makov, *The Making of a Policeman: a social history of a labour force in metropolitan London, 1829–1914* (Aldershot: Ashgate, 2002), p. 44.
28 Ibid.
29 Ibid., p. 47.
30 Ibid., p. 49.
31 'Police 'Prentices', *Cassells Family Magazine* (London: Cassell, 1875), pp. 308–10.
32 Shpayer-Makov, op. cit., p. 49.
33 *Metropolitan Police Instruction Book for the Use of Candidates and Constables of the Metropolitan Police Force 1871* (London), Metropolitan Police Historical Collection, London.
34 Shpayer-Makov, op. cit., p. 33.
35 Ibid., pp. 220–21.
36 G: Division Register, op. cit.
37 George Frederick Pardon, *The Popular Guide to London and its Suburbs* (London: Routledge, 1862), p. 27.
38 Shpayer-Makov, op. cit., p. 166.
39 Timothy Cavanagh, *Scotland Yard Past and Present* (London: Chatto and Windus, 1893), p. 45.
40 Shpayer-Makov, op. cit., pp. 246–9.
41 Henry Mayhew, *London Labour and the London Poor* (Herts: Wordsworth Editions, 2008), pp. 19–20.
42 *Reynolds's Newspaper*, London, Sunday 6 March 1864.
43 Shpayer-Makov, op. cit., p. 147; *Lloyd's Weekly*, London, Sunday 12 September 1880 (author's italics).
44 *Reynolds's Newspaper*, London, Sunday 5 November 1876.
45 Shpayer-Makov, op. cit., p. 193.
46 Ibid., pp. 248–9.
47 Martin Fido and Keith Skinner, *The Official Encyclopedia of Scotland Yard* (London: Virgin, 1999), p.218.
48 Minahan, op. cit; Police Orders, 8 September 1870 (TNA: PRO copy), MEPO7/32.
49 *Lloyd's Weekly*, London, Sunday 18 September 1881.
50 *Morning Post*, London, Friday 11 November 1881.
51 *Bradford Observer*, Thursday 8 October 1874.

52 *Morning Post*, London, Friday 11 November 1881; *Daily News*, London, Monday 17 October and Monday 24 October 1881.
53 *The Times*, Friday 11 November 1881.
54 *Morning Post*, London, Friday 11 November 1881.
55 Ibid.; *The Times*, Friday 11 November 1881.
56 Ibid.

Chapter Two: The Same Old Game of Revenge and Tyranny

1 *Anthropological Review*, London, January 1866.
2 Jeremiah Minahan, Church Baptism Records, Patrickswell Parish, Co. Limerick, 16 October 1842; Gerard Beggan, *In the Barony of Pubblebrien, Patrickswell and Crecora* (Galway: Clodoiri Lurgan, 1991), p. 92.
3 Dr Mainchin Seoighe, *Famine in Limerick*, Transcript of lecture given at the County Library Limerick, October 1995, Dooradoyle Library, Limerick City.
4 *Griffith's Valuation of Ireland*, 1848-1864, Jeremiah Minahan (snr), Co. Limerick, Barony of Pubblebrien, Parish of Croom, Lissaleen, www.askaboutireland.ie.
5 John O'Connor, 'Patrickswell Village', *Pubblebrien Journal*, vol. 1, issue 1, Limerick.
6 *Griffith's Valuation of Ireland*, op. cit.
7 Sean Spellissy and John O'Brien, *Limerick: The Rich Land* (Clare: Spellissy/O'Brien, 1989), p. 116.
8 Research trip by the author, March 2010.
9 William Makepeace Thackeray, *Irish Sketch Book of 1842* (New York: J. Winchester, 1848), pp. 64–6.
10 Ibid.
11 Ibid.
12 L. P. Curtis, *Anglo-Saxons and Celts: A Study of Anti-Irish Prejudice in Victorian England* (Berkeley: University of California, 1968), p. 27.
13 Stephen Fielding, *Class and Ethnicity: Irish Catholics in England, 1880–1939* (Buckingham and Philadelphia: Open University Press, 1993), p. 9.
14 *The Times*, London, 20 January 1846.
15 Fielding, op. cit., p. 8.
16 Curtis, op. cit., p. 52.
17 William Balch, *Ireland as I saw It* (New York: Putnam, 1850), p. 242.
18 Ibid., p. 247.
19 Christine Kinealy, *A Death-Dealing Famine: the Great Hunger in Ireland* (London: Pluto, 1997), pp. 16-20, 32-36.

20 *Griffith's Valuation of Ireland*, op. cit.
21 W. G. Neely, *Kilcooley: Land and People in Tipperary* (Belfast: Universities Press, 1983), p. 97.
22 Letter, Richard Wicklow to William Barker, 4 October 1835, Trinity College Dublin (TCD), MS Barker Ponsonby Deposit, P3/7/12.
23 Letter, Richard Wicklow to William Barker, ibid., 14 December 1835.
24 Letter, Richard Wicklow to William Barker, 4 October 1835, op. cit.
25 Ibid.
26 Balch, op. cit., p. 47.
27 Kinealy, op. cit. pp. 56–7, 72–6.
28 Ibid.
29 Ibid., pp. 77–81.
30 Seoighe, op. cit.
31 Ibid.
32 Cathal Poirteir, *Famine Echoes* (Dublin: Gill and Macmillan, 1995), p. 90.
33 Spencer T. Hall, 'Life and Death in Limerick', *Old Limerick Journal – Famine Edition*, Winter 1995, no. 32, Limerick, p. 160.
34 William Barker to the Commission for Public Works: Order for a Public Loan, 23 November 1847, Registry of Deeds, Dublin.
35 Kinealy, op. cit., p. 151.
36 Seoighe, op. cit.
37 Interview between Joe Daley and his mother, Anna Minahan Daley, aged ninety-five, 25 March 1979, passed to the author by Maresa McNamara.
38 Haia Shpayer-Makov, *The Making of a Policeman: a social history of a labour force in metropolitan London, 1829–1914* (Aldershot: Ashgate, 2002), p. 56.
39 Ibid, p. 38.
40 Ibid, p. 204.
41 Basil Thomson, *The Story of Scotland Yard* (New York: Country Life Press, 1935), p. 333.
42 Police Orders 9–11 November, 1880 (TNA: PRO copy), MEPO 7/42.
43 Lynn Hollen Lees, *Exiles of Erin: Irish Migrants in Victorian London* (Manchester: Manchester University Press, 1979), p. 64.
44 Roger Swift, *The Irish in the Victorian City* (Oxford: Taylor & Francis, 1985), p. 4.
45 Lees, op. cit., p. 44.
46 Pamphlet, Jeremiah Minahan, *How an Inspector of the Metropolitan Police was punished for faithfully performing his duty to the public*, 1884, Printed: 350 420941 JOS.

47 *Mid-Sussex Times*, Haywards Heath, Tuesday 9 April 1895.
48 Jacqueline Hill, *From Patriots to Unionists: Dublin Civic Politics and Irish Protestant Patriotism* (Oxford: Oxford University Press, 1997), p. 306.
49 Letter, Daniel O'Connell to Thomas McKenny, 19 February 1821, McKenny Hughes Archives, Cambridge University, Cambridge, Add. 9557/11/2.
50 Letter, E. H. Harty to Barbara Hughes, n.d. c. 1878, McKenny Hughes Archives, Cambridge University, Cambridge, Add. 9557/11/8(i).
51 Minahan, op. cit.
52 Ibid.
53 *Standard*, London, 10 April 1882.
54 Ibid.
55 Ibid.
56 Anon., *The Revolution in the Police and the Coming Revolution of the Army and Navy*, Penny Pamphlet, c. 1872 (TNA: PRO copy), MEPO 3/131.
57 Ibid.

Chapter Three: The Curse of Chelsea

1 Pamphlet, Jeremiah Minahan, *How an Inspector of the Metropolitan Police was punished for faithfully performing his duty to the public*, 1884, Printed: 350 420941 JOS.
2 Ibid.
3 Gustave Doré, and Blanchard Jerrold, *London: A Pilgrimage* (London: Anthem Press, 2005), p. 45.
4 Minahan, op. cit.
5 London Census, 1881.
6 John Bignell, *Chelsea seen from 1860 to 1980* (London: Studio B, 1978), pp. 63–88.
7 Metropolitan Police Orders (TNA: PRO copy), MEPO 7/35 and MEPO 7/42, 1873 and 1880.
8 A. R. Buckland, 'Hughes, Joshua (1807–1889)', *Oxford Dictionary of National Biography* (Oxford: Oxford University Press, 2004), pp. 2004–12; letter, Alfred Hughes to his father Joshua, 18 May 1871, McKenny Hughes Papers, Cambridge University Library, MS Add. 9557/10/26.
9 Document entitled *Executor of Joshua Hughes Will* signed by Thomas McKenny Hughes, 24 February 1890, McKenny Hughes T., Papers, Cambridge University Library, MS Add. 9557/11/11.
10 Alfred Hughes, op. cit.

11 Letter, H. Sandwith to T. McKenny Hughes, 31 July 1870, Cambridge, Sedgwick Museum Archive, McKenny Hughes Correspondence, DDF Box 736.
12 Julia M. Wright, *Ireland, India and nationalism in nineteenth-century literature* (Cambridge: Cambridge University Press, 2004), pp. 81–4.
13 Ibid.
14 *News of the World*, London, Sunday 7 April 1895.
15 Census Report, Great Malvern parish, Worcestershire, 1891.
16 Diary of Carrie Hughes, 23–24 February 1891, McKenny Hughes, T., Papers, Cambridge University Library, MS Add. 9557/8B/1-15.
17 Chelsea Register of Voters, 1887, Uverdale Road, Kensington Central Library, Local Studies Department.
18 Drainage Plans, 2 Uverdale Road, Chelsea, Kensington Central Library Local Studies Department P. H/A 2141 (2), December 1931. These plans are to put 'inside' toilets into the houses – they show what I believe to be the original layout of the house and I have assumed that no building renovations had been done prior to this date – it does not appear to have been extended.
19 Census Reports, Uverdale Road, Chelsea, 1881 and 1891. The even house numbers on Uverdale Road do not appear in the 1881 Census because the street was still under construction. The 1891 Census reveals the more middle-class occupations of the street's new residents.
20 Now Old Church Street, Chelsea.
21 Census Records, Melcombe Regis, 1851 and 1861.
22 Melissa Hope Ditmore, *Encyclopedia of Prostitution and Sex Work*, vol. 1 (Connecticut: Greenwood Publishing, 2006), p. 248.
23 Death certificate, Sarah Barrowcliffe, 5 June 1866 (General Register Office), DYC 829860.
24 'The Maiden Tribute of Modern Babylon', *Pall Mall Gazette*, London, Wednesday 8 July 1885.
25 Chelsea Rate Books, Ward One Church Street, Kensington Central Library Local Studies Department, 1876 and 1881.
26 *Reynolds's Newspaper*, London, 2 October 1887.
27 *Pall Mall Gazette*, Wednesday 8 July 1885, op. cit.
28 Ibid.; Hodson Stanley vs. Edward Ledger, London Central Criminal Court, Monday 12 January 1880, t18800112-142, www.oldbaileyonline.org.
29 Pamphlet, William Stead, *The Armstrong Case: Mr Stead's Defence in Full*, 1885 (CC) Papers of William Stead, GBR/0014/STED 4/2.
30 Ibid.
31 Mr R. M. Morrell to Select Committee on Sale of Liquor on

Sundays Bill, House of Commons Papers, V14 (London: HMSO), 8 June 1868, p. 283.

32 Edmund Hodgson Yates, *The Business of Pleasure* (South Carolina: Bibliobazarre, 2008), p. 13.

33 Edward Walford, *Londoniana*, vol. 2 (South Carolina: Bibliobazarre, 2008), p. 189.

34 Joanne P. Sharp, ed., *Entanglements of Power: geographies of domination/resistance* (Oxon: Routledge, 2000), p. 61.

35 William Acton, *Prostitution, Considered in its Moral, Social and Sanitary Aspects* (London: John Churchill, 1857), p. 103.

36 Asa Briggs, *Victorian People: A Reassessment of Persons and Themes (1851–1867)* (Chicago: University of Chicago Press, 1975), p. 298; John Hollingshead, *Ragged London in 1861* (London: Smith, Elder, 1861), p. 7.

37 Edward P. Pease, *The History of the Fabian Society* (New York: E. P. Dutton, 1916), p. 10.

38 Harold Perkin, *The Rise of Professional Society: England since 1880* (London: Routledge, 1989), pp. 36–7.

39 Ibid., pp. 28–31.

40 Gareth Stedman Jones, *Outcast London: A Study in the Relationships between Classes in Victorian Society* (London: Harmondsworth, Penguin, 1976), p. 4.

41 Ibid., pp. 281–2.

42 J. Ewing Ritchie, *Days and Nights Out in London* (London: Tinsley, 1880), p. 117.

43 Ibid.

44 Rev. Andrew Mearns, *The Bitter Cry of Outcast London: An Inquiry into the Condition of the Abject Poor* (London: James Clarke, 1883), pp. 9–10.

45 Mearns, op. cit., pp. 11–12.

46 Anthony Wohl, *The Eternal Slum* (New Jersey: Transaction Publishers, 2002), p. 211.

47 William Stead, 'Is it not time?', *Pall Mall Gazette*, London, Tuesday 16 October 1883.

48 Wohl, op. cit., p. 214.

49 William Stead, 'Outcast London – Where to Begin', *Pall Mall Gazette*, London, Tuesday 23 October 1883.

50 Perkin, op. cit., p. 125.

51 Ibid., pp. 116–19.

52 Pease, op. cit., p. 28.

53 Ibid., p. 18.

54 Sharp, op. cit., pp. 46–7.

55 'To the Editor of the Times', *The Times*, London, 18–24 October 1871.

56 Ibid.
57 Sharp, op. cit., pp. 47–61.
58 Ibid.
59 W. S. Clarke, *The Suburban Homes of London: A residential guide to favourite London localities, their society, celebrities and associations with notes on their rental, rates and house accommodation* (London: Chatto and Windus, 1881), p. 89.
60 Sharp, op. cit., p. 59.
61 Ibid., p. 60.
62 *The Armstrong Case: Mr Stead's Defence in Full*, op. cit.
63 Ibid.
64 Chelsea Rate Books, op. cit.
65 The Armstrong Case, op. cit.
66 Trial of Jeffries (TNA: PRO copy), HO 144/468/X124.
67 Ibid.
68 *The Armstrong Case*, op. cit.
69 Ibid.
70 Deborah Hayden, *Pox: Genius, Madness and the Mysteries of Syphilis* (New York: Basic Books, 2003), p. 45.
71 Quoted in Pisanus Fraxi, *Encyclopedia of Erotic Literature: Index Liborum Prohibitum* (New York: Documentary Books, 1862), p. 117 and p. 125.
72 Ian Gibson, *The Erotomaniac: The Secret Life of Henry Spencer Ashbee* (London: Faber, 2001)
73 Walter, *My Secret Life* (New York: Grove Press, 1966), vol. 9, p. 1873.
74 Nickie Roberts, *Whores in History* (London: Harper Collins, 1993), p. 198.
75 Ibid., p. 199.
76 'Maiden Tribute of Modern Babylon', *Pall Mall Gazette*, London, Monday 6 July 1885.
77 *The Armstrong Case*, op. cit.
78 Louisa M. Hubbard, *Work and Leisure*, vol. II (South Carolina: Bibliobazaar, 2008), p. 168; W. Shirley Shirley, *A Sketch of the Criminal Law* (South Carolina: Bibliobazaar, 2009), pp. 19–20.
79 Ibid.
80 Supt. Joseph Dunlap, 19 July 1881, Report from the Select Committee of the House of Lords on the Law Relating to the Protection of Young Girls (HCPP), HC 448 (1881), ix. 355, pp. 76–83.
81 W. Shirley Shirley, *Leading Cases in the Criminal Law* (New Jersey: Read Books, 2007), p. 36; Henry Roscoe, *A Digest of the Law of Evidence in Criminal Cases* (Philadelphia: T. & W. Johnson, 1840), p. 744.

82 Dunlap, op. cit., ix. 355, pp. 76–83.
83 The Armstrong Case, op. cit.
84 Ibid.
85 Photographs of Chelsea Police Station, 1910 (TNA: PRO copy), MEPO 14/28.
86 Warwick Wroth, *Cremorne and the Later London Gardens* (London: Elliot Stock, 1907).
87 Edward Walford, 'Chelsea: Cremorne Gardens', *Old and New London*, vol. 5 (London: Cassell, Petter, & Galpin, 1878), pp. 84–100.
88 Patricia E. C. Croot, ed., *A History of the County of Middlesex: Volume 12: Chelsea* (Woodbridge: Boydell & Brewer, 2004), pp. 2–13.
89 Ibid., pp. 156–65.
90 Minahan, op. cit.
91 Croot, op. cit., pp. 217–33.
92 Ibid.; drainage plans, 385–389 King's Road (Kensington: Kensington and Chelsea central library), 1949. The original police station near the corner of Milman's Street was extended east into the adjacent corner building in 1897; these 'drainage plans' actually show a 'Proposed Conversion of [the] Old Police Station, King's Road' and it is possible to see the layout of the two original buildings in the drawing. I have also referred to exterior photographs of the buildings as an additional guide, see Photographs of Chelsea Police Station, 1910, op. cit.
93 The Boltons, Chelsea Census, 1881.
94 Minahan, op. cit.
95 Josephine Butler, *The Shield*, London, Saturday 16 May 1885.
96 Minahan, op. cit.
97 Ibid.
98 Police Orders, Tuesday 4 August 1868 (TNA: PRO copy), MEPO 7/30.
99 *Report by the Committee on Intemperance for the Lower House of Convocation of the Province of Canterbury* (London: Longman, Green Reader and Dyer, 1869), p. 55 and pp. 75–90.
100 Minahan, op. cit.
101 Ibid.
102 Ibid.
103 Ibid.
104 Police Orders, Tuesday 5 August 1890 (TNA: PRO copy), MEPO 7/52.
105 David Taylor, *The New Police in Nineteenth-Century England: crime, conflict and control* (Manchester: Manchester University Press, 1997), pp. 58–61; Haia Shpayer-Makov, *The Making of a*

Policeman: a social history of a labour force in metropolitan London, 1829–1914 (Aldershot: Ashgate, 2002), pp. 79–83.

106 Anon., *The Revolution in the Police and the Coming Revolution of the Army and Navy*, Penny Pamphlet, c.1872 (TNA: PRO copy), MEPO 3/131.

Chapter Four: It is Not In London Only that I Carry on the Business

1 Alfred Dyer, *The European Slave Trade in English Girls: a narrative of facts* (London: Dyer Bros., 1885), p. 18.

2 Trial of Jeffries (TNA: PRO copy), HO 144/468/X124.

3 Hodson Stanley vs. Edward Ledger, London Central Criminal Court, Monday 12 January 1880, t18800112-142, www.oldbailey online.org; *Reynolds's Newspaper*, London, Sunday 31 May 1885.

4 Hodson Stanley vs. Edward Ledger, op. cit. Mrs. Jeffries' surname is spelt in varying ways in the press reports and other documents: Jeffries, Jeffreys and Jefferies. Jeffries is the most common.

5 Ibid.

6 Pamphlet, Jeremiah Minahan, *How an Inspector of the Metropolitan Police was punished for faithfully performing his duty to the public*, 1884, Printed: 350 420941 JOS.

7 Trial of Jeffries, op. cit.

8 *Pall Mall Gazette*, London, Thursday 29 September 1887.

9 *Derby Daily Telegraph*, Tuesday 20 October 1885.

10 Pisanus Fraxi, *Encyclopedia of Erotic Literature: Index Liborum Prohibitum* (New York: Documentary Books, 1862), p. xliii.

11 Minahan, op. cit.; trial of Jeffries, op. cit.

12 Chelsea Rate Books, Ward One, Church Street, Kensington Central Library, Local Studies Department, 1876, 1881 and 1886.

13 Trial of Jeffries, op. cit. – Jeffries sold 121, 111 and 105 Church Street between 1881 and 1886. See Chelsea Rate Books, op. cit.

14 Charles Terrot, *The Maiden Tribute* (London: Frederick Muller, 1959), pp. 90–91.

15 Fraxi, op. cit., p. xliii.

16 Ibid.

17 Ibid., p. xl.

18 Trial of Jeffries, op. cit.

19 Ibid.

20 John Tosh, *Masculinity and the Middle-Class Home in Victorian England* (London and New Haven: Yale University Press, 1999), pp. 170–95; George Sala, *Twice Around the Clock, or The Hours of Day and Night in London* (London: Richard Marsh, 1862), p. 213.

21 Elizabeth Lynn Linton, *Modern Women and What is Said of Them:*

Reprint of articles from the Saturday Review (London) (New York: Redfield, 1868), pp. 36–8.

22 Ibid.

23 Tosh, op. cit., pp. 157–8 and p. 172.

24 Ibid., p. 172.

25 Ibid., p. 182.

26 Judith R. Walkowitz, *City of Dreadful Delight: Narratives of Sexual Danger in Late-Victorian London* (Chicago: University of Chicago Press, 1992), p. 21.

27 Edward Carpenter, *Loves Coming of Age* (South Carolina: Forgotten Books, 2010), p. 18.

28 Mary Lyndon Shanley, *Feminism, Marriage and the Law in Victorian England 1850–1895* (New Jersey: Princeton University Press, 1989), p. 160.

29 John Stuart Mill, *The Subjection of Women* (London: Longmans, Green, Reader and Dyer, 1870), p. 64.

30 Shanley, op. cit., p. 160.

31 Harriet Devine Jump, ed., *Women's writing of the Victorian period, 1837–1901* (Edinburgh: Edinburgh University Press, 1999), pp. 224–5.

32 Ibid.

33 London Census, St Luke's Parish Chelsea, 1881.

34 Mackintosh vs Mackintosh divorce petition, 1883 & 1884 (TNA: PRO copy), J77/292/8656 and J77/315/9396.

35 Ibid.

36 Ibid.

37 Ibid.

38 Ibid.

39 Trial of Jeffries, op. cit.

40 Ibid.

41 Ibid.

42 Adam Hochschild, *King Leopold's Ghost: a story of greed, terror and heroism in Colonial Africa* (London: Macmillan, 2006), p. 88.

43 Alain Corbin, *Women for Hire: prostitution and sexuality in France after 1850*, trans. Alan Sheridan (Cambridge, Mass.: Harvard University Press, 1996), pp. 2–10.

44 Ibid.; pamphlet, *Brussels, Antwerp and Paris by Night: The Gay Women Or Cocottes, Paris*, n.d. 1870? (publisher and author unknown).

45 *The Lancet*, London, 1837, vol. 2, p. 16; 'Prostitution', *Encyclopædia Britannica* (11th edn., 1911).

46 Nickie Roberts, *Whores in History* (London: HarperCollins, 1993), p. 234.

47 Ibid., p. 199.
48 Ibid., p. 236.
49 'The Maiden Tribute of Modern Babylon', *Pall Mall Gazette*, London, Friday 10 July 1885.
50 Thomas William Snagge, 5 July 1881, Report from the Select Committee of the House of Lords on the Law Relating to the Protection of Young Girls (HCPP), HC 448 (1881), ix. 355, p. 20.
51 Interview with Mr J. B. Wookey, *The Christian Commonwealth*, London, 28 May 1885; unnamed French police officer quoted in Terrot, op. cit., p. 25.
52 John Shoveller, Superintendent of the Record Department, 12 July 1881, Report from the Select Committee of the House of Lords on the Law Relating to the Protection of Young Girls, op. cit., p. 46.
53 Ibid., testimony of Thomas William Snagge, 5 July 1881, p. 16
54 Pamphlet, William Stead, *The Armstrong Case: Mr Stead's Defence in Full*, 1885 (CC), Papers of William Stead, GBR/0014/STED 4/2, p. 6.
55 The Earl of Dalhousie, 'Motion for a Select Committee', Hansard, HL Deb, 30 May 1881, vol 261 cc1603–13, hansard.millbanksystems.com.
56 Ibid.
57 *Pall Mall Gazette*, London, Thursday 26 December 1878.
58 Dyer, op. cit., p. 16; Correspondence Respecting Immoral Traffic in English Girls to Belgium (TNA: PRO copy), HO 45/9546/59343.
59 Correspondence Respecting Immoral Traffic, op. cit.
60 Death Certificate, Edwin Tanner, 21 February 1877, General Register Office, DYC 829825.
61 Correspondence Respecting Immoral Traffic, op. cit.
62 Ibid.
63 Claudia Nelson, *Family Ties in Victorian England* (Santa Barbara: Greenwood Publishing, 2007), pp. 81–4.
64 Henry James, *Portrait of a Lady* (London: Penguin Classics, 2003), p. 537.
65 Ibid., p. 366.
66 Correspondence Respecting Immoral Traffic, op. cit.
67 Ibid.
68 Ibid.
69 Ibid.
70 Ibid.; 'Maiden Tribute of Modern Babylon', *Pall Mall Gazette*, London, 6–10 July 1885.
71 Correspondence Respecting Immoral Traffic, op. cit.
72 Edward Francis Rimbault, *Soho and its Associations: Historical, Literary and Artistic* (London: Dulau, 1895), p. 201; George Sala,

Gaslight and Daylight (London: Chapman and Hall, 1859), pp. 88–92 and pp. 166–70.
73 Correspondence Respecting Immoral Traffic, op. cit.
74 *Sentinel*, London, January 1886.
75 Correspondence Respecting Immoral Traffic, op. cit.
76 Emma Liggins, *George Gissing, the working woman and urban culture* (Farnham: Ashgate, 2006), pp. 118–19.
77 Correspondence Respecting Immoral Traffic, op. cit.; Dalhousie, op. cit.
78 Correspondence Respecting Immoral Traffic, op. cit.
79 T. W. Snagge, 'Report on the Alleged Traffic in English Girls for Immoral Purposes in Foreign Towns' (Women's Library, London Metropolitan University) (WL), Archives: 3AMS/B/05/21, 1881.
80 Dyer, op. cit., p. 22.
81 Ibid.
82 Correspondence Respecting Immoral Traffic, op. cit., p. 166.
83 Dyer, op. cit., p. 22.
84 'The Maiden Tribute of Modern Babylon', *Pall Mall Gazette*, London, Friday 10 July 1885.
85 Correspondence Respecting Immoral Traffic, op. cit.
86 Snagge, op. cit.
87 Correspondence Respecting Immoral Traffic, op. cit.
88 Ibid.
89 Richard Mullen, *The Smell of the Continent: the British discover Europe 1814–1914* (London: Macmillan, 2011), p. 147.
90 J. R. Scott, *The Family Guide to Brussels* (London: Edward Stanford, 1883), pp. 140–42.
91 Correspondence Respecting Immoral Traffic, op. cit.
92 Scott, op. cit., p. 16.
93 'The Maiden Tribute of Modern Babylon', *Pall Mall Gazette*, London, Friday 10 July 1885.
94 Letter, Josephine Butler to William Vernon Harcourt, Home Secretary, 8 November 1880 (TNA: PRO copy), HO 45/9599/98018; Correspondence Respecting Immoral Traffic, op. cit.
95 *Brussels, Antwerp and Paris by Night*, op. cit.
96 Correspondence Respecting Immoral Traffic, op. cit.; Michael Pearson, *The Age of Consent: Victorian Prostitution and its Enemies* (Newton Abbot: David and Charles, 1972), p. 50.
97 Correspondence Respecting Immoral Traffic, op. cit.; Jane Jordan, ed., *Josephine Butler and the Prostitution Campaigns: Diseases of the Body Politic*, vol. IV, *Child Prostitution and the Age of Consent* (Oxon: Routledge, 2003), pp. 58–79.
98 Correspondence Respecting Immoral Traffic, op. cit.

99 Dyer, op. cit., pp. 4–5.
100 *Sentinel*, London, January 1886; Census Report, Toxteth Park, Lancs., 1881. In this Census Ellen Newland is listed as residing with Josephine Butler; the *Sentinel* reports that a scoundrel, Schultz, had 'seduced and then conveyed abroad two girls, who had been rescued and were then [1881] in Mrs Butler's charge'.
101 Dyer, op. cit., pp. 9–26.
102 Correspondence Respecting Immoral Traffic, op. cit.
103 Ibid.
104 Henry Lee, 'Lectures Delivered at the Lock Hospital, London', *Association Medical Journal*, London, Friday 2 June 1854, p. 478; Franz Eder, *Sexual Cultures in Europe: themes in sexuality* (Manchester: Manchester University Press, 1999), pp. 39–44, and for Dr Thiry specifically see p. 54 n52 and p. 55 n68.
105 Correspondence Respecting Immoral Traffic, op. cit. There was some debate at the time as to whether Adelene's experiences at the hospital were credible. Thomas Jeffes, British Vice Consul to Brussels, disputed her claims when interviewed by the Lords Select Committee in July 1881. The barrister T. W. Snagge, however, a more neutral outsider employed by the Home Office to investigate the traffic, stated before the same Committee that 'the facts of Adelene Tanner's case were all proved in evidence [and] her declarations were substantially true'. See Report from the Select Committee of the House of Lords on the Law Relating to the Protection of Young Girls (HCPP), HC 448 (1881), ix. 355, 5 and 12 July 1881.
106 Correspondence Respecting Immoral Traffic, op. cit.
107 Ibid.
108 Ann Stafford, *The Age of Consent* (London: Hodder and Stoughton, 1964), p. 93.
109 Dyer, op. cit., p. 18.
110 Snagge, op. cit.
111 Ibid.
112 Correspondence Respecting Immoral Traffic, op. cit.
113 Snagge, op. cit.
114 Ibid.; Jordan, op. cit., pp. 58–79.
115 *The Christian*, London, Thursday 23 July 1885.
116 Pamphlet, Helen S. Dyer, 'The Perils of Girls Away from Home' (Library of the Religious Society of Friends), Tracts 443/6, n.d.
117 *Lloyd's Weekly*, London, Sunday 9 July 1882.
118 Trial of Jeffries, op. cit.
119 Ibid.
120 Ibid.

Chapter Five: They Called Me a Fool

1 Trial of Jeffries (TNA: PRO copy), HO 144/468/X124.
2 Jeremiah Minahan, Pamphlet, *How an Inspector of the Metropolitan Police was punished for faithfully performing his duty to the public*, 1884, Printed: 350 420941 JOS.
3 Ibid.
4 Ibid.
5 Ibid.
6 Ibid.
7 Ibid.
8 Ibid.
9 Steven Fielding, *Class and Ethnicity: Irish Catholics in England 1880–1939* (Buckingham and Philadelphia: Open University Press, 1993), p. 86.
10 The permanent under-secretary was named Thomas Henry Burke.
11 Michael Burleigh, *Blood and Rage: A Cultural History of Terrorism* (London: Harper Perennial, 2009), pp. 1–18.
12 Ibid.
13 *The Irish World and American Industrial Liberator*, New York, Saturday 19 January 1884.
14 Burleigh, op. cit., pp. 1–18.
15 Letter, Robert Charles Clipperton, Her Majesty's US Consul, to the Home Secretary, Sir William Harcourt, 15 January 1884, Bodleian Libraries, University of Oxford, Harcourt Papers (HP), MS. 98, ff. 37–44.
16 Ibid.
17 Burleigh, op. cit., pp. 1–18.
18 Ibid.; *North Eastern Daily Gazette*, Middlesbrough, Friday 16 March 1883.
19 *North Eastern Daily Gazette*, Middlesbrough, Friday 16 March 1883.
20 *The Times*, London, Friday 16 March 1883.
21 Roger Swift, *The Irish in the Victorian City* (Abingdon: Taylor & Francis, 1985), pp. 3–4.
22 Ibid.
23 *Lancet*, London, 5 January 1861, vol. 1, p. 17.
24 Minahan, op. cit.
25 T. C. Barker and Michael Robbins, *A History of London Transport*, vol. 1, *The Nineteenth Century* (London: George Allen & Unwin, 1963), pp. 246–8.
26 Ibid.
27 London Census, Stanley Ward, Chelsea, 1871.

28 Minahan, op. cit.
29 Ibid.
30 *The Times*, London, Saturday 3 May 1890.
31 Photograph of Captain Douglas William Parish Labalmondiere by Camile Silvy (London: National Portrait Gallery), 27 March 1861, NPG Ax52137; George Sala, *Breakfast in Bed, Or Philosophy Between the Sheets* (New York: John Bradburn, 1863), p. 151.
32 www.labalmondiere.co.uk; British War Office, *A List of the Officers of the Army and the Corps of the Royal Marines* (London: Pinkney, 1839), p. 262.
33 *Pall Mall Gazette*, London, Monday 3 August 1885.
34 Minahan, op. cit.
35 Ibid.
36 Ibid.
37 Ibid.
38 Ibid.
39 Ibid.
40 *Pall Mall Gazette*, London, Monday 3 August 1885.
41 Trial of Jeffries, op. cit.
42 Ibid.
43 Ibid.
44 Ingrid Sharp, ed., *Josephine Butler and the Prostitution Campaigns: Diseases of the Body Politic, The Moral Reclaimability of Prostitutes*, vol. I (London: Routledge, 2003), pp. 131–9.
45 Chris Williams, *A Companion to Nineteenth Century Britain* (Oxford: Wiley-Blackwell, 2004), p. 436.
46 Sharp, op. cit., pp. 131–9.
47 Ibid., p. 135.
48 Judith R. Walkowitz, *Prostitution and Victorian Society: Women, Class and the State* (Cambridge University Press, 1980), pp. 108–10.
49 Ibid.
50 Ibid.
51 Ibid., p. 109.
52 Ibid., p. 110.
53 Ibid., p. 247.
54 Josephine Butler, *Personal Reminiscences of a Great Crusade* (Tennessee: General Books, 2010), p. 9.
55 Ibid.
56 John Tosh, *A Man's Place: Masculinity and the Middle-Class Home in Victorian England* (London and New Haven: Yale University Press, 1999), p. 181; Harold Perkin, *The Rise of Professional Society: England since 1880* (London: Routledge, 1990), pp. 95–100.

57 Sally Mitchell, *Daily Life in Victorian England* (Oxford: Greenwood Publishing, 1996), p. 21.
58 Tosh, op. cit., pp. 180–83.
59 Ibid., p. 180.
60 A. G. Gardiner, *The Life of Sir William Harcourt*, vol. I, *1827–1886* (London: Constable, 1923), p. 607.
61 Frank Mort, *Dangerous Sexualities: medico-moral politics in England since 1830* (Oxon: Routledge, 2000), p. 103.
62 Hansard, HC Deb, 20 April 1883, vol 278 cc749–858, hansard.millbanksystems.com.
63 Transcript of baptisms, St Martin in the Fields Westminster (London: Metropolitan Archives), 1851 DL/T Item, 093/073, www.ancestry.co.uk.
64 Though formally a police officer was obliged to treat all members of society the same, irrespective of their social position, in reality it was the lower classes who suffered the most constant supervision. When it came to the middle and upper classes, as little police interference as possible was preferred. See Haia Shpayer-Makov, *The Making of a Policeman: a social history of a labour force in metropolitan London, 1829–1914* (Aldershot: Ashgate, 2002), pp. 146–8.
65 Minahan, op. cit.
66 Charles Clarkson and Richardson J. Hall, *Police!* (New York: Garland, 1984), pp. 100-101.
67 Minahan, op. cit.
68 Quoted in Shpayer-Makov, op. cit., p. 145.
69 Karen Chase, *The Victorians and Old Age* (Oxford: Oxford University Press, 2009), p. 26.
70 Minahan, op. cit.
71 Ibid.
72 Ronald Charles Sopenoff, *The Police of London: the early history of the Metropolitan Police*, Ph.D., 1978 (Pennsylvania: Temple University), pp. 196–7.
73 Minahan, op. cit.
74 Ibid.
75 Ibid.
76 Gardiner, op. cit., p. 370.
77 Patrick Jackson, *Harcourt and Son: A political biography of Sir William Harcourt, 1827–1904* (Madison: Fairleigh Dickinson University Press, 2004), p. 81.
78 Ibid.
79 Ibid., p. 83.
80 Ibid., p. 22.

81 Gardiner, op. cit., p. 20.
82 Ibid. p. 370.
83 Ibid.; Jackson, op. cit., p. 31.
84 Jackson, op. cit., pp. 86–92.
85 Jill Pellow, *The Home Office 1848–1914: from Clerks to Bureaucrats* (London: Heinemann Educational Books, 1982), pp. 36–8; Jackson, op. cit., p. 39; Gardiner, op. cit., p. 477.
86 Michael P. Roth, *Historical Dictionary of Law Enforcement* (Connecticut: Greenwood Publishing, 2001), p. 333.
87 *Lloyd's Weekly*, London, 4 November 1883.
88 Minahan, op. cit.
89 Ibid.
90 Ibid.

Chapter Six: How Do You Do Ducky?

1 Elizabeth Gaskell, *Mary Barton: a tale of Manchester Life* (London: Chapman and Hall, 1848), vol. 1, p. 34.
2 Walter Thornbury, 'Paternoster Row', *Old and New London:* vol. 1 (1878), pp. 274–81. http://www.british-history.ac.uk.
3 Ibid.
4 *Derby Daily Telegraph*, Tuesday 20 October 1885; *Illustrated Police News*, London, Saturday 13 April 1895; Laura Ugolini, *Men and Menswear: sartorial consumption in Britain 1880–1939* (Hants: Ashgate, 2007), pp. 29–31.
5 Trial of Jeffries (TNA: PRO copy), HO 144/468/X124.
6 Ibid.
7 Jeremiah Minahan, Pamphlet, *How an Inspector of the Metropolitan Police was punished for faithfully performing his duty to the public*, 1884, printed: 350 420941 JOS.
8 *Daily Telegraph*, London, Friday 17 December 1880; Minahan, op. cit.
9 Personal notes by William Vernon Harcourt, n.d. c. 1885, Bodleian Libraries, University of Oxford, (HP), MS. 99, ff. 46–57.
10 Minahan, op. cit.
11 Letter from Josephine Butler to William Vernon Harcourt, Home Secretary, 8 November 1880 (TNA: PRO copy), HO 45/9599/98018; Correspondence Respecting Immoral Traffic (TNA: PRO copy), HO 45/9546/59343.
12 Contagious Diseases Acts: Conduct of Police at Dover, March–May 1881 (TNA: PRO copy), HO 144/78/A4010. The two constables were named Carley and Griffiths.
13 Ibid.

14 Ibid.
15 Ibid.
16 *Daily News*, London, Friday 6 May 1881.
17 *Daily News*, London, Monday 9 May 1881; *Bristol Mercury and Daily Post*, Tuesday 10 May 1881; *Derby Mercury*, Wednesday 11 May 1881; *Reynolds's Weekly*, London, Sunday 15 May 1881.
18 Conduct of Police at Dover, op. cit.
19 *Reynolds's Weekly*, London, Sunday 15 May 1881.
20 *Daily News*, London, Monday 9 May 1881.
21 Benjamin Scott, *Six Years' Labour and Sorrow* (London: Dyer Bros., 1885), p. 49. Scott does not name Dr Elizabeth Blackwell, referring instead to 'a lady well known in philanthropic circles, residing on the South Coast'. But Blackwell is the only woman fitting this description at the time and she was to become one of Jeremiah Minahan's most generous benefactors. See Chapter Ten.
22 George Dodd, *Chambers Handy Guide to the Kent and Sussex Coast* (Edinburgh: Chambers, 1863), pp. 112–13.
23 Ibid.
24 Ibid.
25 Ishbel Ross, *Child of Destiny: the life story of the first woman doctor* (London: Victor Gollancz, 1950), pp. 267–72.
26 Ibid., p. 271.
27 Scott, op. cit., p. 49.
28 Ibid.
29 The full title of the Committee was the London Committee for the Suppression of the Foreign Traffic in British Girls for the Purposes of Continental Prostitution.
30 Scott, op. cit., p. 50.
31 *Pall Mall Gazette*, London, Monday 3 August 1885.
32 Scott, op. cit., p. 49.
33 Denys P. Leighton, *The Greenian Moment: T.H. Green, Religion and Political Argument in Victorian Britain* (Exeter: Imprint Academic, 2004), p. 192.
34 The Nonconformist ethic directly inspired the philosophy of T. H. Green. See ibid., p. 187.
35 Ibid., p. 200.
36 Kathryn Gleadle, *The Early Feminists: Radical Unitarians and the Emergence of the Women's Rights Movement, 1831–51* (New York: St Martin's Press, 1995), pp. 9–10.
37 Ibid., pp. 102–3.
38 Ibid.
39 Trial of Jeffries, op. cit.
40 Catherine Hall, *Defining the Victorian Nation: race, class, gender*

and the British Reform Act of 1867 (Cambridge: Cambridge University Press, 2000), p. 123.

41 Leighton, op. cit., p. 199.

42 Daniel Born, *The Birth of Liberal Guilt in the English Novel: Charles Dickens to H.G. Wells* (North Carolina: University of North Carolina Press, 1995), pp. 10–13; Brian Harrison, *Drink and the Victorians: the Temperance Question in England,* (London: Faber & Faber, 1971), pp. 380–81.

43 Robert John Morris, *Class, sect and party: the making of the British middle class: Leeds 1820–1850* (Manchester: Manchester University Press, 1990), pp. 330–81.

44 Paul McHugh, *Prostitution and Social Reform* (London: Croom Helm, 1980), p. 187.

45 Scott, op. cit., p. 1.

46 Trial of Jeffries, op. cit.

47 Ibid.

48 Max Schlesinger, *Saunterings in and about London* (London: Nathaniel Cook, 1853), p. 51.

49 Trial of Jeffries, op. cit.

50 *Pall Mall Gazette*, London, Wednesday 4 November 1885.

51 Ibid.

52 *Illustrated Police News*, London, Saturday 20 June 1885.

53 Ibid.

54 Scott, op. cit., p. 51.

55 Letter, Josephine Butler to W. V. Harcourt, 3 May 1881, Correspondence Respecting Immoral Traffic, op. cit.

56 *Sentinel*, London, January 1886.

57 Ibid.

58 Scott, op. cit., p. 25.

59 Trial of Jeffries, op. cit.; Scott, op. cit., pp. 50–52; *Sentinel*, London, May 1885.

60 Scott, op. cit., p. 51; Sheldon Amos, *A Comparative Survey of Laws in Force for the Prohibition, Regulation and Licensing of Vice in England and Other Countries* (London: Stephens and Sons, 1877), pp. 524–5.

61 Scott, op. cit., p. 52; Census Report, 1881, Chelsea.

62 Trial of Jeffries. op. cit.

Chapter Seven: I Will Have It My Way

1 Trial of Jeffries (TNA: PRO copy), HO 144/468/X124.

2 Ibid.; Charles Terrot, *The Maiden Tribute* (London: Frederick Muller, 1959), p. 95.

3 *Sentinel*, London, May 1885.
4 *Builder*, London, Saturday 17 January 1846.
5 *Reynolds's Newspaper*, London, Sunday 31 May 1885.
6 *Builder*, op. cit.
7 Ibid.
8 Ibid.
9 Montagu Williams, *Leaves of a Life* (London: Macmillan, 1890).
10 Stanley Jackson, *The Life and Cases of Mr. Justice Humphreys* (London: Macmillan, 1952), p. 19.
11 Ibid.
12 Cyril Arthur Gull, *The Great Acceptance: The life story of F.N. Charrington* (London: Hodder and Stoughton, 1913), p. 181.
13 Trial of Jeffries, op. cit.
14 *Sentinel*, London, May 1885.
15 Paul Belien, *A Throne in Brussels: Britain, the Saxe-Coburgs and the Belgianisation of Europe* (Exeter: Imprint Academic, 2005), p. 102.
16 Trial of Jeffries, op. cit.
17 *Echo*, London, Thursday 16 April 1885.
18 Belien, op. cit., p. 102.
19 The Trial of Richard Risley, London Central Criminal Court, 25 October 1869, t18691025-903, www.oldbaileyonline.org.
20 Henry Hales, 'Street Ruffians', *Daily News*, Friday 20 August 1869.
21 Stuart Thayer, *American Circus Anthology: Essays of the Early Years*, © Stuart Thayer and William L. Slout, 2005, www.circushistory.org; The Trial of Richard Risley, op. cit.
22 Thayer, op. cit.; *Era*, London, Sunday 24 February 1867; Fred S. Kleiner, *Gardner's Art through the Ages* (Boston: Cengage Learning, 2008), p. 829.
23 *Era*, London, Sunday 3 May 1868.
24 Ibid.
25 Hales, op. cit.
26 Trial of Richard Risley, op. cit.
27 Ibid.
28 Hales, op. cit.
29 Trial of Richard Risley, op. cit.
30 Hales, op. cit.
31 Trial of Richard Risley, op. cit.
32 Robert Louis Stevenson, *Strange Case of Dr Jekyll and Mr Hyde* (Oxford: World's Classics, 2008), p. 52.
33 Ibid., p. 9.
34 Claire Harman, *Robert Louis Stevenson: A biography* (London: Harper Perennial, 2005), pp. 52–4.

35 Ibid.
36 Ibid., p. 58.
37 J. A. Smith, *Henry James and Robert Louis Stevenson: a record of friendship and criticism* (London: Rupert Hart-Davis, 1948), p. 155. Richard Risley, with his secret shame, was a natural fit alongside the respected Edinburgh businessman/armed robber William Brodie and the lauded surgeon/shady anatomist John Hunter, whose legendary duplicity also fascinated and inspired the author. See: Harry M. Geduld, ed., *The Definitive Dr. Jekyll and Mr. Hyde Companion* (New York: Garland, 1983), pp. 3–6; Jenni Calder, *RLS: a life study* (Glasgow: Richard Drew, 1990), pp. 221–3; Wendy Moore, *The Knife-Man* (London: Bantam, 2005), pp. 321–2.
38 Harman, op. cit., pp. 63–4.
39 Stevenson, op. cit., p. 10.
40 Ibid., p. 5.
41 Ibid., p. 6.
42 Ibid., p. 7.
43 Ibid.
44 Hales, op. cit.; trial of Richard Risley, op. cit.
45 Hales, op. cit.
46 Ibid.
47 Stevenson, op. cit., p. 7.
48 Ibid.
49 Ibid.
50 Ibid.
51 Hales, op. cit.; trial of Richard Risley, op. cit.
52 Stevenson, op. cit., p. 7.
53 Alexander Welsh, *George Eliot and Blackmail* (Cambridge, Mass.: Harvard University Press, 1985), pp. 3–4.
54 Ian Bell, *Robert Louis Stevenson: dreams of exile* (London: Headline, 1992), p. 76.
55 Stephen Kern, *A Cultural History of Causality: science, murder novels and systems of thought* (Princeton: Princeton University Press, 2006), p. 277.
56 *Daily News*, London, Wednesday 27 October 1869.
57 *Era*, London, Sunday 21 June 1874.
58 Harman, op. cit., pp. 307–8.
59 George W. Johnson, ed., *Josephine Butler: an autobiographical memoir* (Bristol: J. W. Arrowsmith, 1911), p. 183.
60 Heather Scott Morton, *Victorian Authors on Trial* (University of Virginia, 2008), Ph.D. thesis, pp. 34–5.
61 Ibid.

62 David Cannadine, *The Decline and Fall of the British Aristocracy* (London: Picador, 1991), pp. 326–7.
63 *Reynolds's Newspaper*, London, Sunday 31 May 1885.
64 Trial of Jeffries, op. cit.
65 Ibid.
66 *Pall Mall Gazette*, London, Saturday 11 April 1885.
67 Trial of Jeffries, op. cit.
68 Ibid.
69 *Reynolds's Newspaper*, London, Sunday 19 April 1885.
70 *Sentinel*, May 1885; Hansard, HC Deb, 12 August 1885, vol 300 cc1870–1 and 13 August 1885, vol 301 c29, hansard.millbanksystems.com.
71 Ibid.
72 *Daily News*, London, Friday 17 April 1885; Hansard, HC Deb, 16 April 1885, vol 296 cc1852–3, hansard.millbanksystems.com.
73 Henry William Lucy, *Later Peeps at Parliament taken from Behind the Speaker's Chair* (London: George Newnes, 1905), p. 328.
74 Hansard, 16 April 1885, op. cit.
75 Ibid.; Lucy, op. cit., p. 321.
76 Horace Gordon Hutchinson, *Portraits of the Eighties* (London: T. Fisher Unwin, 1920), p. 66.
77 *Pall Mall Gazette*, London, Tuesday 27 October 1885.
78 *West London Press*, Saturday 9 May 1885.
79 Benjamin Scott, *Six Years' Labour and Sorrow* (London: Dyer Bros., 1885), p. 53.
80 *Christian*, London, Thursday 14 May 1885.
81 *Sentinel*, London, June 1885.
82 *Echo*, London, Wednesday 6 May 1885.
83 *West London Press*, Saturday 9 May 1885.
84 Graham, *Ordering the Law: The Architectural and Social History of the English Law Court to 1914* (Hants: Ashgate, 2003), pp. 89–90.
85 George Railton, ed., *The Truth About the Armstrong Case and the Salvation Army: Mr Stead's Defence* (London: Salvation Army, 1885), p. 8.
86 *West London Press*, Saturday 9 May 1885.
87 *Christian Commonwealth*, quoted in *Christian*, Thursday 14 May 1885.
88 Scott, op. cit., p. 52.
89 *Christian*, Thursday 14 May 1885.
90 *West London Press*, Saturday 9 May 1885.
91 Trial of Jeffries, op. cit.
92 Letter, Benjamin Scott to Richard Cross MP, Friday 13 November 1885 (TNA: PRO copy), HO 144/468/X124.

93 *West London Press*, Saturday 9 May 1885.
94 Licences of Parole for Female Convicts (UK), 1853–1871 and 1883–1887, www.ancestry.com.

Chapter Eight: I Want One Younger Than You

1 Pamphlet, William Stead, *The Armstrong Case: Mr Stead's Defence in Full*, 1885 (CC), Papers of William Stead, GBR/0014/STED 4/2, p. 6.
2 Trial of Rebecca Jarrett et al., t18851019-1031, www.oldbaileyonline.org.
3 J. W. R. Scott, *Life and Death of a Newspaper* (London: Camelot Press, 1952), p. 59.
4 Raymond L. Schults, *Crusader in Babylon: W.T. Stead and the Pall Mall Gazette* (Lincoln: University of Nebraska Press, 1972), pp. 43–4.
5 W. T. Stead, Draft Autobiography, 15 April 1893 (CC), Papers of William Stead, GBR/0014/STED.
6 *North Eastern News*, Friday 17 July 1885, www.attackingthedevil.co.uk; Grant Richards, *Memories of a Misspent Youth 1872–1896* (London: Heinemann, 1932), p. 307; Frederick Whyte, *The Life of W.T. Stead*, vol. II (London: Jonathan Cape, 1925), pp. 341–2.
7 *Pall Mall Gazette*, London, Monday 6 July 1885.
8 Ibid.
9 *Christian*, London, Thursday 14 May 1885.
10 Ibid.
11 Ibid.
12 *Pall Mall Gazette*, London, Tuesday 27 October 1885.
13 Hansard, HC Deb, 21 May 1885, vol 298 cc1022–5, hansard.millbanksystems.com.
14 Horace Gordon Hutchinson, *Portraits of the Eighties* (New Hampshire: Ayer Publishing, 1920), p. 66.
15 Hansard, op. cit.
16 Ibid.
17 *Reynolds's Newspaper*, London, Sunday 24 May 1885.
18 Letter, W. V. Harcourt to Arnold White, 31 May 1885, Bodleian Libraries, University of Oxford (HP), MS. 214, ff. 74–5.
19 Pamphlet, Henry Varley, 'To the Men and Women of Derby!', 19 October 1885, Bodleian Libraries, University of Oxford (HP), MS. 214, ff. 119–20.
20 Glen Petrie, *A Singular Iniquity: The Campaigns of Josephine Butler* (London: Macmillan, 1971), p. 207.
21 Trial of Jeffries, op. cit.

22 Ibid.
23 Charles Dickens, *Bleak House* (London: Penguin Classics, 1996), p. 249.
24 *Christian Commonwealth*, London, Thursday 11 June 1885.
25 Ibid.
26 A. G. Gardiner, *The Life of Sir William Harcourt*, vol. 1, *1827–1886* (London: Constable, 1923), pp. 520–23.
27 Ibid., p. 527.
28 'Rebecca Jarrett', early 20th century, Salvation Army International Heritage Centre (SAC), London, Papers of Rebecca Jarrett, RJ/2/4, p.1.
29 Jane Jordan, ed., *Josephine Butler and the Prostitution Campaigns*, vol. IV, *Child Prostitution and the Age of Consent* (Oxon: Routledge, 2003), pp. 237–65; Pamela J. Walker, 'The Conversion of Rebecca Jarrett', *History Workshop Journal*, issue 58, 2004.
30 Pamela J. Walker, *Pulling the Devil's Kingdom Down: the Salvation Army in Victorian Britain* (Berkeley: University of California Press, 2001), p. 168.
31 Rebecca Jarrett, *Rebecca Jarrett: her experiences written by herself* (handwritten autobiography), early 20th century, Salvation Army International Heritage Centre (SAC), London, Papers of Rebecca Jarrett, RJ/2/1, p. 2.
32 *Lloyd's Weekly*, London, Sunday 6 September 1885.
33 Jarrett, op. cit., RJ/2/1, p. 2.
34 Rebecca Jarrett, *Rebecca Jarrett: written by own self* (typescript account of Rebecca Jarrett's life written in the first person), early 20th century, Salvation Army International Heritage Centre (SAC), London, Papers of Rebecca Jarrett, RJ/2/2, p. 1.
35 Ibid.
36 Ibid.
37 Jarrett, op. cit., RJ/2/2, p. 3; Walker, op. cit., pp. 170–71.
38 Trial of Rebecca Jarrett et al., op. cit.
39 Ibid.
40 Ibid.
41 Walker, op. cit., p. 169.
42 Trial of Rebecca Jarrett et al., op. cit.
43 Gustave Doré and Blanchard Jerrold, *London: A Pilgrimage, 1872* (London: Anthem Press, 2005), p. 166.
44 Ibid.
45 Montagu Williams, *Round London: Down East and Up West* (London: Macmillan, 1893), p. 4.
46 Trial of Rebecca Jarrett et al., op. cit.

47 Doré and Jerrold, op. cit., p. 171.
48 Trial of Rebecca Jarrett et al., op. cit.
49 Ibid.
50 Ibid.
51 *Lloyd's Weekly*, London, Sunday 12 July 1885.
52 Trial of Rebecca Jarrett et al., op. cit.
53 Ibid.
54 Ibid.; *Penny Illustrated Newspaper*, Saturday 12 September 1885.
55 Trial of Rebecca Jarrett et al., op. cit.
56 *Spectator*, London, Saturday 4 June 1870.
57 Trial of Rebecca Jarrett et al., op. cit.
58 *Lloyd's Weekly*, London, Sunday 12 July 1885.
59 Trial of Rebecca Jarrett et al., op. cit.
60 Ibid.
61 Ibid.
62 *Lloyd's Weekly*, London, Sunday 13 September 1885.
63 Chris White, *Nineteenth Century Writings on Homosexuality: a source book* (London: Routledge, 1999), p. 327.
64 Henry Mayhew, *London Labour and the London Poor*, vol. IV (London: Griffin, Bohn, 1862), p. 235.
65 Trial of Rebecca Jarrett et al., op. cit.
66 *Lloyd's Weekly*, London, Sunday 13 September 1885.
67 Trial of Rebecca Jarrett et al., op. cit.
68 Ibid.
69 Now Upper Montague Street in Marylebone.
70 *Lloyd's Weekly*, London, Sunday 16 August 1885.
71 Ibid.
72 Ibid.
73 Ibid.
74 Ibid.
75 Ibid.
76 Trial of Rebecca Jarrett et al., op. cit.
77 Ibid.
78 Ibid.

Chapter Nine: Oh! What Horrors We Have Seen!

1 Estelle W. Stead, *My Father: Personal and Spiritual Reminiscences* (London: Heinemann, 1913), pp. 123–5.
2 Ibid.
3 Ibid.
4 Ibid.; J. W. R. Scott, *The Life and Death of a Newspaper* (London: Camelot, 1952), p. 126.

5 Judith Walkowitz, *City of Dreadful Delight: Narratives of Sexual Danger in Late-Victorian London* (Chicago: University of Chicago Press, 1992), p. 95.
6 Frederick Whyte, *The Life of W.T. Stead* (London: Jonathan Cape, 1925), vol. I, pp. 304–6.
7 Ibid.
8 Ibid.; Walkowitz, op. cit., p. 95.
9 Scott, op. cit., p. 114.
10 Ibid., p. 116.
11 George Railton, ed., *The Truth about the Armstrong Case and the Salvation Army* (London: Salvation Army Books, 1885), p. 9.
12 Letter, Howard Vincent to W. V. Harcourt, 25 June 1884, Bodleian Libraries, University of Oxford (HP), MS. 123, ff. 63–5.
13 Ibid.
14 *Pall Mall Gazette*, London, Monday 6 July 1885.
15 Ibid.
16 *Pall Mall Gazette*, London, Thursday 9 July 1885.
17 Pamphlet, *Speech Delivered by Mr W.T. Stead at the Central Criminal Court on Wednesday, November 4 1885* (London: Moral Reform Union, 1885), p. 37.
18 Matthew Arnold, *Complete Prose Works* (Ann Arbor: University of Michigan Press, 1977), p. 202.
19 *Pall Mall Gazette*, London, 6–10 July 1885.
20 *Speech Delivered by Mr W.T. Stead*, op. cit., p. 22.
21 *Christian Commonwealth*, London, Thursday 30 April 1885.
22 Ibid.
23 *Reynolds's Newspaper*, London, Sunday 31 May 1885.
24 Hansard, HC Deb, 20 July 1870, vol 203 cc587–8, hansard.millbanksystems.com.
25 Christopher Hibbert, *Edward VII: The Last Victorian King* (Basingstoke: Palgrave Macmillan, 2007), p. 140.
26 Émile Zola, *Nana* (London: Penguin Classics, 1972), p. 157.
27 Keith Middlemas, *The Life and Times of Edward VII* (London: Weidenfeld and Nicolson, 1972), pp. 68–80.
28 Angus McLaren, *Sexual Blackmail: A Modern History* (Cambridge, Mass.: Harvard University Press, 2002), p. 40.
29 *Albany Law Journal*, vol. 2 (London: Weed, Parsons, 1870), p. 436.
30 *Pall Mall Gazette*, London, Monday 6 July 1885.
31 Letter, Josephine Butler to Anna Maria Priestman, 5 June 1885, Women's Library (WL), London Metropolitan University, Archives JBL/24/01-31.
32 *Pall Mall Gazette*, London, 6–10 July 1885.

33 Michael Pearson, *The Age of Consent: Victorian Prostitution and its Enemies* (Newton Abbot: David and Charles, 1972), p. 143.
34 *Pall Mall Gazette*, London, 6–10 July 1885.
35 Ibid.
36 Ibid.
37 Ibid.
38 Ibid.
39 A. G. Gardiner, *The Life of Sir William Harcourt*, vol. I, *1827–1886* (London: Constable, 1923), p. 528.
40 *Speech Delivered by Mr W.T. Stead*, op. cit., p. 26.
41 Ibid.
42 Pearson, op. cit., p. 142.
43 Ibid.
44 Metropolitan Police Statements, 24–28 September 1885 (TNA: PRO copy), HO 144/154/A40202F.
45 Ibid.
46 Ibid.
47 Ibid.
48 Charles Dickens Jnr., *Dickens' Dictionary of London 1888: An Unconventional Handbook* (Moretonhampstead: Old House Books, 1993), p. 67; *The Electrical Review*, vol. 13, 1883, London, p. 12
49 *Pall Mall Gazette*, Friday 10 July 1885.
50 Ibid.
51 Ibid.
52 Estelle Stead, op. cit., p. 126.
53 *Pall Mall Gazette*, London, Monday 6 July 1885.
54 Walkowitz, op. cit., p. 82.
55 *Pall Mall Gazette*, London, Thursday 9 July 1885.
56 *Pall Mall Gazette*, London, Monday 13 July 1885.
57 Quoted in *Western Mail*, Cardiff, Wednesday 8 July 1885.
58 *Pall Mall Gazette*, London, Monday 6 July 1885.
59 Ibid.
60 Ibid.
61 Raymond L. Schults, *Crusader in Babylon: W.T. Stead and the Pall Mall Gazette* (Lincoln: University of Nebraska Press, 1972), pp. 158–9.
62 Ibid.; *Christian Commonwealth*, London, Thursday 28 May 1885.
63 Lord Snell, *Men, Movements and Myself* (London: J. M. Dent, 1936), p. 178.
64 Hansard, HC Deb, 9 July 1885, vol 299 cc197–211, hansard.millbanksystems.com.

Chapter Ten: It is Excellent to Have a Giant's Strength but Tyrannous to Use it

1 Letter, Josephine Butler to Anna Maria Priestman, 5 June 1885 (WL) Archives, JBL/24/01-31.
2 Mrs Archibald Little, www.readaroundasia.co.uk.
3 Letters of Josephine Butler, May to June 1886, Women's Library, London Metropolitan University, Archives 3JBL/25/22-26; *Sentinel*, London, August 1885.
4 *Christian*, London, Thursday 30 July 1885.
5 Ibid.
6 *Pall Mall Gazette*, London, Thursday 23 July 1885.
7 Lewis Harcourt, Journals, 21 May 1885, Bodleian Libraries, University of Oxford (HP), MS. 369; M. C. Rintoul, *Dictionary of Real People and Places in Fiction* (London: Routledge, 1993), p. 281.
8 Hansard, George Cavendish-Bentinck, HC Deb, 27 July 1885, vol 300 cc62–3, hansard.millbanksystems.com.
9 Ibid.
10 Ibid.
11 A. G. Gardiner, *The Life of Sir William Harcourt*, vol. I, *1827–1886* (London: Constable, 1923), pp. 536–45.
12 Horace Gordon Hutchinson, *Portraits of the Eighties* (London: T. Fisher Unwin, 1920), pp. 28–32.
13 Stephen Gwynn, *The Life of the Rt. Hon. Charles W. Dilke, Bart*, vol. 1 (London: John Murray, 1917), pp. 365–6.
14 Ibid.
15 Ibid.
16 Patrick Jackson, *Harcourt and Son: A Political Biography of Sir William Harcourt 1827–1904* (Madison: Fairleigh Dickinson University Press, 2004), p. 194.
17 Ibid.
18 Ibid.
19 Hansard, HC Deb, 31 July 1885, vol 300 cc794–808, hansard.millbanksystems.com.
20 Ibid.
21 *Leeds Mercury*, Monday 3 August 1885; *Freeman's Journal*, Dublin, Tuesday 4 August 1885.
22 *Pall Mall Gazette*, London, 3 August 1885.
23 F. Hugh O'Donnell, *A History of the Irish Parliamentary Party*, vol .1 (London: Longmans, Green, 1910), pp. 315–16.
24 Hansard, HC Deb, Monday 3 August 1885, vol 300 cc843–5, hansard.millbanksystems.com.

25 Ibid.
26 Ibid.
27 *Liverpool Mercury*, Tuesday 4 August 1885.
28 Ibid.

Chapter Eleven: A Special Correspondent

1 Trial of Rebecca Jarrett et al., t18851019-1031, www.oldbaileyonline.org.
2 *Sunday School Teacher's Magazine*, London, 1851, vol. 2, pp. 76–9.
3 Trial of Rebecca Jarrett et al., op. cit.
4 Ibid.
5 Ibid.
6 Ibid.
7 Michael Pearson, *The Age of Consent: Victorian Prostitution and its Enemies* (Newton Abbot: David and Charles, 1972), p. 171.
8 *Penny Illustrated Newspaper*, Saturday 12 September 1885; trial of Rebecca Jarrett et al., op. cit.
9 Ibid.
10 H. J. Dyos, *The Victorian City* (Oxon: Routledge, 1999), p. 169.
11 Trial of Rebecca Jarrett et al., op. cit.
12 Ibid.
13 Anne B. Rodrick, *Self-Help and Civic Culture: Citizenship in Victorian Birmingham* (Hants: Ashgate, 2004), p. 17.
14 Ibid., p. 20.
15 Asa Briggs, *History of Birmingham*, vol. II (Oxford: Oxford University Press, 1952), pp. 1–5.
16 Ibid., p. 6.
17 Justin McCarthy, *British Political Portraits* (New York: Outlook Company, 1903), p. 77.
18 Census Reports 1841 and 1851, Birmingham, www.ancestry.co.uk.
19 Census 1851, op. cit.
20 Charles Dickens, 'Speech: Birmingham, 6 January 1853', *Speeches Literary and Social* (Adelaide: ebooks@adelaide), 2005.
21 *Liverpool Mercury*, Thursday 15 April 1875; *Daily News*, London, Friday 16 April 1875.
22 *Lloyd's Weekly*, London, Sunday 12 July 1885.
23 Ibid.
24 Trial of Rebecca Jarrett et al., op. cit.
25 Ibid.
26 Ibid.

27 Charles Booth, *Life and Labour of the People in London*, vol. I (London: Macmillan, 1892), pp. 124–6.
28 Ibid.
29 Ibid.
30 Ibid.
31 Edward Harold Begbie, *Painted Windows; a Study in Religious Personality, by a Gentleman with a Duster* (New York: G. P. Putnam's Sons, 1922), pp. 139–55.
32 Ibid.
33 Trial of Rebecca Jarrett et al., op. cit.
34 Ibid.
35 *Lloyd's Weekly*, London, Sunday 19 July 1885.
36 Ibid.
37 Begbie, op. cit.
38 Trial of Rebecca Jarrett et al., op. cit.
39 Ibid.
40 Ibid.
41 *Lloyd's Weekly*, London, Sunday 9 August 1885.
42 Ibid.
43 Ibid.
44 Ibid.
45 Ibid.
46 Ibid.
47 Ibid. Hales' italics.
48 *Lloyd's Weekly*, London, Sunday 16 August 1885.
49 Raymond L. Schults, *Crusader in Babylon: W.T. Stead and the Pall Mall Gazette* (Lincoln: University of Nebraska Press, 1972), p. 176.
50 Home Office File, August 1885 (TNA: PRO copy), HO 44/156/A40661.
51 *Lloyd's Weekly*, London, Sunday 16 August 1885.
52 Thomas Catling, *My Life's Pilgrimage* (London: John Murray, 1911), pp. 181–2.
53 *Lloyd's Weekly*, London, Sunday 16 August 1885.
54 Ibid.
55 Catling, op. cit., p. 180.
56 Ibid.
57 Ibid.
58 *Lloyd's Weekly*, London, Sunday 16 August 1885.

Chapter Twelve: It Will Be A Fearful Business If All This Appears

1 T. Wemyss Reid, *Life, Letters and Friendships of Richard Monckton Milnes*, vol. 2 (New York: Cassell, 1890), p. 492.

2 Lewis Harcourt, Journals, 5 August 1885, Bodleian Libraries, University of Oxford (HP), MS. 371.
3 *New York Times*, n.d. 1905, New York, www.nytimes.com; Mrs. Annie Brassey, *Voyage in the Sunbeam* (Chicago: Belford Clarke, 1881), p. 2.
4 Harcourt, op. cit., 6 August 1885.
5 Ibid.
6 Patrick Jackson, *Loulou: Selected extracts from the Journals of Lewis Harcourt (1880–1895)* (Madison: Fairleigh Dickinson University Press, 2006), p. 10.
7 Patrick Jackson, *Harcourt and Son: A Political Biography of Sir William Harcourt 1827–1904* (Madison: Fairleigh Dickinson University Press, 2004), p. 65.
8 Print, 'Lady (Maria) Theresa Lewis when Mrs Lister' by Samuel Cousins (London: National Portrait Gallery), DP3563, n.d.
9 A. G. Gardiner, *The Life of Sir William Harcourt*, vol. I, *1827–1886* (London: Constable, 1923), p. 112.
10 Letter, R. Monckton Milnes to W. V. Harcourt, 29 August 1859, Bodleian Libraries, University of Oxford (HP), MS. 726, ff. 126–7.
11 Ibid.
12 *Graphic*, London, Saturday 5 February 1898.
13 Osbert Wyndham Hewett, *Strawberry Fair: A Biography of Frances, Countess Waldegrave 1821–1879* (London: John Murray, 1956), p. xii; Kathleen Carroll, *Lady Frances Waldegrave Political Hostess at Strawberry Hill 1856–1879*, Borough of Twickenham Local History Society Paper no. 66, April 1998.
14 Ibid.
15 Clarissa Campbell Orr, *Wollstonecraft's Daughters: womanhood in England and France, 1780–1920* (Manchester: Manchester University Press, 1996), pp. 98–101.
16 Hewett, op. cit., p. xii.
17 Ibid., p. 125.
18 Ibid., p. 144.
19 *Oxford Dictionary of National Biography* (Oxford: Oxford University Press, 2004–2011), www.oxforddnb.com.
20 Jackson, op. cit., p. 20.
21 Letters, Lady Elizabeth Bulteel (née Grey) to Henry George Grey, 3rd Earl Grey, March 1856, Durham University Library, Earl Grey Papers, GRE/B79/13/39–55.
22 Jackson, op. cit., p. 20.
23 Ibid.
24 Lady Elizabeth Bulteel, op. cit.
25 Hewett, op. cit., p. 144.

26 Ibid., p. 120; Gardiner, op. cit., p. 53.
27 Gardiner, op. cit., p. 115.
28 Ibid.
29 Bodleian Libraries, University of Oxford (HP), MS. 726, f. 137.
30 *Liverpool Mercury*, Weather Report, Monday 2 February 1863.
31 Patricia Jalland, *Death in the Victorian Family* (Oxford: Oxford University Press, 2000), p. 258.
32 Jackson, op. cit., p. 24.
33 Gardiner, op. cit., p. 118.
34 Letter, W. V. Harcourt to Lady Minto, 9 January 1864, Bodleian Libraries, University of Oxford (HP), MS. 726, f. 190.
35 Jackson, op. cit., p. 31.
36 Robert Lytton, *Julian Fane: A Memoir* (London: John Murray, 1871), p. 265; Gardiner, op. cit., p. 53.
37 William C. Lubenow, *The Cambridge Apostles, 1820–1914: Liberalism, imagination and friendship* (Cambridge: Cambridge University Press, 1998), p. 31.
38 Ibid., p. 38.
39 Ibid., pp. 39–40.
40 Richard Dellamora, *Masculine Desire: the sexual politics of Victorian aestheticism* (University of North Carolina Press, 1990), pp. 18–20.
41 Lubenow, op. cit., p. 240.
42 Gert Hekma et al., *Gay Men and the sexual history of the political left*, Part 1 (London: Routledge, 1995), p. 274.
43 Henry Adams, *The Education of Henry Adams: an autobiography* (Boston: Houghton Mifflin, 1918), p. 124.
44 Florence Nightingale, *Ever Yours: selected letters* (Cambridge, Mass: Harvard University Press, 1990), p. 40.
45 Florence Nightingale, *Florence Nightingale on Society and Politics, Philosophy, Science, Education and Literature*, vol. 5 (Ontario: Wilfrid Laurier University Press, 2003), p. 490.
46 Dellamora, op. cit., p. 20; Donald Thomas, *Swinburne: the poet and his world* (London: Allison & Busby, 1999), p. 64.
47 Harford Montgomery Hyde, *A History of Pornography* (London: Four Square, 1964), p. 22.
48 James Pope-Hennessy, *Monckton Milnes: The flight of youth, 1851–1885* (London: Constable, 1951), pp. 115–16.
49 Mario Praz, *The Romantic Agony* (London: Oxford University Press, 1951), pp. 215–16 and p. 278 n41; Ian Gibson, *The Erotomaniac: The Secret Life of Henry Spencer Ashbee* (London: Faber, 2001), p. xii; Goncourts, *Journal*, vol. ii, Lundi 7 Avril 1862, p. 27.

50 Thomas, op. cit., pp. 98–9.
51 Praz, op. cit., p. 215.
52 Harcourt, op. cit., 6 August 1885.
53 Ibid.
54 Ibid.

Chapter Thirteen: I And I Alone Am Responsible

1 Henry James, *The Reverberator* (Los Angeles: Aegypan Press, 2010), p. 39.
2 Quoted in *Aberdeen Weekly Journal*, Tuesday 25 August 1885.
3 *Northern Echo*, Darlington, Monday 24 August 1885.
4 Ibid.
5 *Aberdeen Weekly Journal*, Tuesday 25 August 1885.
6 Ibid.
7 Thomas Catling, *My Life's Pilgrimage* (London: John Murray, 1911), pp. 179–83.
8 *Lloyd's Weekly*, London, Sunday 16 August 1885.
9 *Lloyd's Weekly*, London, Sunday 30 August 1885. On Sunday 23 August 1885, *Lloyd's Weekly* published its sensational findings on the Armstrong case in a 'Special Edition', which was reprinted in full the following Sunday, 30 August 1885. I have used the latter version as my reference.
10 *Pall Mall Gazette*, London, Saturday 22 August 1885.
11 Ibid.
12 *Lloyd's Weekly*, Sunday 30 August 1885.
13 Trial of Rebecca Jarrett et al., op. cit.
14 Ibid.
15 William Booth, *Twenty One Years Salvation Army* (London: Salvation Army, 1887), p. 120.
16 Trial of Rebecca Jarrett et al., op. cit.
17 George Railton, ed., *The Truth About the Armstrong Case and the Salvation Army: Mr Stead's Defence* (London: Salvation Army Books, 1885), p. 16.
18 This is not strictly true. Mrs Armstrong had previously visited the Salvation Army Headquarters with Inspector Borner to request her daughter's whereabouts. She and Charles Armstrong then sent William Booth a letter formally demanding their daughter's return. Unfortunately Booth did not receive the letter, which was filed by a Salvation Army clerk, until it was too late.
19 Trial of Rebecca Jarrett et al., op. cit.
20 Ibid.
21 Ibid.

22 *Daily News*, London, Monday 24 August 1885; *Northern Echo*, Darlington, Monday 24 August 1885; *Western Mail*, Cardiff, Monday 24 August 1885; *Leeds Mercury*, Monday 24 August 1885.
23 *Northern Echo*, Darlington, Monday 24 August 1885.
24 *Western Mail*, Cardiff, Monday 24 August 1885.
25 Ibid.
26 Circular Letter to Josephine Butler from Isabel Cooper-Oakley and Alicia Bewicke, Women's Library, London Metropolitan University, Archives: 3JBL/24, August 1885.
27 *Daily News*, London, Monday 24 August 1885.
28 Quoted in *Pall Mall Gazette*, London, Tuesday 25 August 1885.
29 Raymond L. Schults, *Crusader in Babylon: W.T. Stead and the Pall Mall Gazette* (Lincoln: University of Nebraska Press, 1972), p. 174; *Western Mail*, Cardiff, Monday 24 August 1885; quoted in *Pall Mall Gazette*, 25 August 1885.
30 *Northern Echo*, Darlington, Monday 24 August 1885.
31 David Cannadine, *The Decline and Fall of the British Aristocracy* (London: Picador, 1991), pp. 25–31.
32 Michael Pearson, *The Age of Consent: Victorian Prostitution and its Enemies* (Newton Abbot: David and Charles, 1972), p. 164.
33 Schults, op. cit., pp. 191–2.
34 Kennedy Jones, *Fleet Street and Downing Street* (London: Hutchinson, 1920), p. 115.
35 Claire Harman, *Robert Louis Stevenson: A biography* (London: Harper Perennial, 2005), p. 281.
36 Robert Louis Stevenson, *Strange Case of Dr Jekyll and Mr Hyde* (Oxford: World's Classics, 2008), p. xxiv.
37 Henry James, *The Notebooks of Henry James*, ed. F. O. Matthiessen and Kenneth B. Murdock (Chicago: University of Chicago Press, 1981), p. 82.
38 Ibid.
39 James, *The Reverberator*, op. cit., p. 39.
40 *Pall Mall Gazette*, London, Saturday 8 August 1885.
41 David Nicholls, *A Lost Prime Minister: a life of Sir Charles Dilke* (London: Hambledon Press, 1995), p. 178.
42 Cannadine, op. cit., pp. 326–8.
43 Ibid., p. 28.
44 Jane L. Chapman, *Journalism Today: A Themed History* (Chichester: John Wiley & Sons, 2011), p. 123.
45 Cannadine, op. cit., pp. 326–8.
46 Ibid., pp. 28–31.
47 *Northern Echo*, Darlington, Monday 24 August 1885.

48 *Lloyd's Weekly*, Sunday 30 August 1885.
49 Ibid.
50 Ibid.
51 Pamela J. Walker, *Pulling the Devil's Kingdom Down: the Salvation Army in Victorian Britain* (Berkeley: University of California Press, 2001), pp. 168–9.
52 Trial of Rebecca Jarrett et al., op. cit.
53 Walker, op. cit., p. 169.
54 Trial of Rebecca Jarrett et al., op. cit.
55 Ibid.; letter, Rebecca Jarrett to Florence Booth, c. July 1885 (SAC), Papers of Rebecca Jarrett, RJ/1/18.
56 Trial of Rebecca Jarrett et al., op. cit.
57 Walker, op. cit., pp. 170–71.
58 Trial of Rebecca Jarrett et al., op. cit.
59 Ibid.
60 Letter, William Bramwell Booth to William Stead (CC), Papers of William Stead, STED 1/9 Correspondence B, Part 7, n.d.
61 Trial of Rebecca Jarrett et al., op. cit.
62 *Lloyd's Weekly*, Sunday 30 August 1885, op. cit.
63 *Northern Echo*, Darlington, Monday 24 August 1885.
64 Ibid.

Chapter Fourteen: Men of Derby! The Time Has Come!

1 Patrick Jackson, *Harcourt and Son: A political biography of Sir William Harcourt, 1827–1904* (Madison: Fairleigh Dickinson University Press, 2004), p. 20.
2 *Derby and Chesterfield Reporter*, Friday 30 October 1885.
3 Hansard, HC Deb, 6 August 1885, vol. 300 cc1386–428, hansard.millbanksystems.com.
4 Ibid.
5 W. V. Harcourt notes on 'Minahan', n.d. Bodleian Libraries, University of Oxford (HP), MS. 99, ff. 46–57.
6 Ibid.
7 Hansard, op. cit.
8 Ibid.
9 Harcourt, op. cit.
10 Hansard, op. cit. Author's italics.
11 Gerard Moran, 'The Rise and Fall of an Irish Nationalist MP, 1868–1885', *Journal of the County Louth Archaeological and Historical Society*, vol. 22, no. 4 (1992), pp. 395–411.
12 Hansard, op. cit.
13 Moran, op. cit.

14 Hansard, op. cit.
15 Ibid.
16 Raymond L. Schults, *Crusader in Babylon: W.T. Stead and the Pall Mall Gazette* (Lincoln: University of Nebraska Press, 1972), pp. 177–8.
17 *Sentinel*, London, November 1885.
18 Richard Collier, *The General Next to God: the story of William Booth and the Salvation Army* (London: Collins, 1968), p. 125.
19 Michael Pearson, *The Age of Consent: Victorian Prostitution and its Enemies* (Newton Abbot: David and Charles, 1972), p. 187.
20 Before the Representation of the People Act 1918 limited them to a single day, general elections in England could last between one and three weeks; see Homer Lawrence Morris, *Parliamentary Franchise Reform in England from 1885–1918* (New York: Columbia University Press, 1921), pp. 167–8.
21 Jackson, op. cit., pp. 139–40.
22 *Derby and Chesterfield Reporter*, Friday 23 October 1885.
23 D. M. Lewis, 'Varley, Henry 1835–1912', *Oxford Dictionary of National Biography* (Oxford: Oxford University Press, 2004).
24 *Pall Mall Gazette*, London, Friday 21 August 1885.
25 Ibid.
26 Ibid.; Henry Varley (Jnr.), *Henry Varley's Life Story: by his son* (London: Alfred Holness, 1916), pp. 132–3.
27 *Derby Daily Telegraph*, Tuesday 20 October 1885.
28 Henry Varley pamphlet, October 1885, Bodleian Libraries, University of Oxford (HP), MS. 214, f. 136.
29 Ibid.
30 Ibid.
31 Ibid.
32 Ibid.
33 *Derby Daily Telegraph*, Tuesday 20 October 1885.
34 Ibid.
35 Ibid.
36 Ibid.
37 Ibid.
38 Ibid.
39 Ibid.
40 Ibid.
41 Ibid.
42 *Derby Daily Telegraph*, Wednesday 21 October 1885.
43 *Sentinel*, London, November 1885.
44 *Derby Daily Telegraph*, Thursday 22 October 1885.
45 Ibid.

46 *Derby Daily Telegraph*, Friday 23 October 1885.
47 Letter, Mr Moody to W. V. Harcourt, Monday 19 October 1885, Bodleian Libraries, University of Oxford (HP), MS. 214, f. 133.
48 Ibid.
49 Patrick Jackson, *Loulou: Selected extracts from the Journals of Lewis Harcourt (1880–1895)* (Madison: Fairleigh Dickinson University Press, 2006), p. 110.
50 Varley (Jnr.), op. cit., p. 133.
51 A. G. Gardiner, *The Life of Sir William Harcourt*, vol. I, *1827–1886* (London: Constable, 1923), p. vii.
52 James Lees-Milne, *The Enigmatic Edwardian* (London: Sidgwick & Jackson, 1986), p. 338.
53 Ibid., p. 24.
54 Ibid., pp. 21–2.
55 Peter Fraser, *Lord Esher: A Political Biography* (London: Hart-Davis, MacGibbon, 1973), p. 9.
56 Ibid.; Lees-Milne, op. cit., p. 24.
57 Letter, Sir William Harcourt to Lady Brett, 27 December 1877, Bodleian Libraries, University of Oxford (HP), MS. 727, ff. 213–14.
58 Fraser, op. cit., p. 12.
59 Jackson, *Loulou*, op. cit., p. 17.
60 Lees-Milne, op. cit., p. 338.
61 Ibid., p. 110.
62 Ibid., p. 111.
63 Ibid., p. 112.
64 Ibid., p. 137.
65 Ibid., p. 337.
66 Sean Hignett, *Brett: from Bloomsbury to New Mexico, a biography* (London: Hodder and Stoughton, 1984), pp. 30–31.
67 Lees-Milne, op. cit., p. 176.
68 Dr R. V. Krafft-Ebing, *Psychopathia Sexualis: A medico forensic study* (Pioneer Publications: New York, 1947), pp. 552–60.
69 John E. B. Myers, *Evidence in Child Abuse and Neglect Cases*, vol. 1 (Aspen Publishers Online, 1997), p. 164.
70 Edward James, *Swans Reflecting Elephants: my early years* (Weidenfeld and Nicolson, 1982), pp. 26–7.
71 Ibid.
72 Ibid.; Matthew Parris, *Great Parliamentary Scandals* (London: Robson Books, 1997), pp. 83–5.
73 Ibid., Parris, pp. 83–5.
74 James, op. cit., p. 28.
75 Parris, op. cit., p. 85.
76 Lees-Milne, op. cit., p. 338.

77 Parris, op. cit., p. 85. A fire at Milne's Fryston Hall destroyed much of his vast library. It is not known exactly how much of his collection survived.
78 Krafft-Ebing, op. cit., p. 556.
79 Havelock Ellis, *Studies in the Psychology of Sex: sexual inversion* (Google Books: The Minerva Group Inc., 2001), p. 153.
80 Gardiner, op. cit., p. viii; Jackson, *Harcourt and Son*, p. 31.
81 Jackson, *Harcourt and Son*, p. 20; see also fragment of a note by William Harcourt, n.d. c. 1855, Somerset Heritage Centre, Strachie Family Papers: DD/SH/59/261.
82 Letter, Harcourt to Robert Lytton, 7 January 1881, Bodleian Libraries, University of Oxford (HP), MS. 728, f. 1.
83 Jeremiah Minahan, Pamphlet, *How an Inspector of the Metropolitan Police was punished for faithfully performing his duty to the public*, 1884, Printed: 350 420941 JOS.
84 *Reynolds's Newspaper*, London, Sunday 31 May 1885.

Chapter Fifteen: Tell Him Not to Grieve

1 Oscar Wilde, *An Ideal Husband* (Boston: John W. Luce, 1906), p. 23.
2 Katie Graham, *The Former Drill Hall, York Road, Great Yarmouth: Historic Building Report*, English Heritage Research Department Report Series no 95-2009, November 2008–January 2009, p. 9.
3 www.picturethepast.co.uk.
4 *Derbyshire Advertiser and Journal*, Friday 30 October 1885.
5 *Derby Daily Telegraph*, Saturday 24 October 1885.
6 *Derbyshire Advertiser and Journal*, Friday 30 October 1885.
7 *Derby Daily Telegraph*; *Derby Express*, Saturday 24 October 1885.
8 *Pall Mall Gazette*, London, Monday 27 October 1885.
9 *Derby Daily Telegraph*, Saturday 24 October 1885.
10 Ibid.
11 Ibid.; *Derby Express*, Saturday 24 October 1885.
12 *Derbyshire Advertiser and Journal*, Friday 30 October 1885.
13 Lewis Harcourt's Journals, 23 November 1885, Bodleian Libraries, University of Oxford (HP), MS. 373.
14 *Sentinel*, London, November 1885.
15 Charles Knight, *Knight's Cyclopaedia of London* (London: Charles Knight, 1851), pp. 679–81.
16 *Pall Mall Gazette*, London, Friday 23 October 1885.
17 Pamphlet by W. T. Stead, *Why I went to Prison* (London: Stead's Publishing House, c. 1912).
18 Ibid.

19 *Pall Mall Gazette*, London, Monday 6 July 1885 and Tuesday 27 October 1885.
20 *Penny Illustrated*, London, Saturday 12 September 1885.
21 Ibid.
22 Ann Stafford, *The Age of Consent* (London: Hodder and Stoughton, 1964), p. 204.
23 Ibid., p. 205.
24 *Penny Illustrated Newspaper*, London, Saturday 12 September 1885.
25 *Lloyd's Weekly*, London, Sunday 13 September 1885.
26 Trial of Rebecca Jarrett et al., t18851019-1031, www.oldbaileyonline.org.
27 Ibid.
28 Richard Tames, *The Victorian Public House* (Osprey Publishing: London, 2008), p. 8.
29 In the past Mrs Armstrong had also been charged with assault and with disorderly conduct in the streets. See *Lloyd's Weekly*, London, Sunday 13 September 1885.
30 Trial of Rebecca Jarrett et al., op. cit.
31 *Daily News*, London, 26 October 1885.
32 Ibid.
33 Ibid.
34 Ibid.
35 Trial of Rebecca Jarrett et al., op. cit.
36 Ibid.
37 (Biography of) *Rebecca Jarrett*, typed biography, early 20th century (SAC), Papers of Rebecca Jarrett, RJ/2/4, p. 11.
38 Rebecca Jarrett, *Rebecca Jarrett: written by her own self*, early 20th century (SAC), Papers of Rebecca Jarrett, RJ/2/2, pp. 15-16.
39 *Daily News*, London, Saturday 31 October 1885.
40 Ibid.
41 Letter, Rebecca Jarrett to Mrs Booth, 9 July 1885 (SAC), Papers of Rebecca Jarrett, RJ/1/19.
42 Letter, Rebecca Jarrett to Mrs Booth, 3 August 1885 (SAC), Papers of Rebecca Jarrett, RJ/1/20.
43 Rebecca Jarrett, *Rebecca Jarrett: written by her own self*, op. cit., p. 17.
44 *Daily News*, London, Saturday 31 October 1885.
45 Ibid.
46 Ibid.
47 Ibid.
48 Trial of Rebecca Jarrett et al., op. cit.
49 Ibid.

50 *Daily News*, London, Tuesday 3 November 1885.
51 Stafford, op. cit., pp. 227–8; trial of Rebecca Jarrett, op. cit.
52 *Daily News*, London, Saturday 31 October 1885.
53 Ibid.
54 Alison Plowdon, *The Case of Eliza Armstrong: A Child of 13 Bought for £5* (London: BBC Books, 1974), p. 109.
55 Ibid.
56 *Lloyd's Weekly*, London, Sunday 8 November 1885.
57 Letter, Arnold White to W. V. Harcourt, 31 October 1885, Bodleian Libraries, University of Oxford (HP), MS. 214, f. 147.
58 Official Subpoena, Bodleian Libraries, University of Oxford (HP), MS. 214, f. 118.
59 Letter, W. V. Harcourt to Charles Russell, 30 October 1885, Bodleian Libraries, University of Oxford (HP), MS. 728, f. 361.
60 *Bristol Mercury and Daily Post*, Thursday 5 November 1885.
61 *Pall Mall Gazette*, London, Wednesday 4 November 1885.
62 *Lloyd's Weekly*, London, Sunday 8 November 1885.
63 J. W. R. Scott, *Life and Death of a Newspaper* (London: Camelot Press, 1952), pp. 130–32.
64 *Lloyd's Weekly*, London, Sunday 8 November 1885.
65 Ibid.
66 Ibid.
67 Ibid.
68 Stafford, op. cit., p. 235.
69 Scott, op. cit., p. 132.
70 *Lloyd's Weekly*, London, Sunday 8 November 1885.
71 Ibid.
72 Raymond L. Schults, *Crusader in Babylon: W.T. Stead and the Pall Mall Gazette* (Lincoln: University of Nebraska Press, 1972), p. 181.
73 Quoted in *Pall Mall Gazette*, London, Monday 9 November 1885.
74 Quoted in *Pall Mall Gazette*, London, Saturday 14 November 1885.
75 Judith R. Walkowitz, *Prostitution and Victorian Society: Women, Class and the State* (Cambridge: Cambridge University Press, 1980), pp. 251–2.
76 Ibid.
77 Ibid.
78 Lawrence James, *The Middle-class: A History* (London: Little, Brown, 2006), p. 324.
79 Celia Marshik, *British Modernism and Censorship* (Cambridge: Cambridge University Press, 2006), pp. 46–72.
80 Ibid., p. 72.
81 George Bernard Shaw, *Unpublished Shaw* (Pennsylvania: Penn

State Press, 1996), p. 214; Joel H. Kaplan, *Theatre and Fashion: Oscar Wilde to the Suffragettes* (Cambridge: Cambridge University Press, 1995), p. 71.

82 George Bernard Shaw, *Pygmalion* (London: Penguin Books, 2003), p. 33.
83 Ibid., p. 30.
84 Ibid., p. 65.
85 Ibid., p. 78.
86 Gareth Stedman Jones, 'Working-class Culture and Working-class Politics in London, 1870–1890: notes on the remaking of a Working-class', *Journal of Social History*, vol. 7, summer 1974, www.jstor.org.
87 Shaw, op. cit., p. 3.
88 Robert Louis Stevenson, *Strange Case of Dr Jekyll and Mr Hyde* (Oxford: World's Classics, 2008), p. 56.
89 *Derby and Derbyshire Gazette*, Friday 30 October 1885; *Daily News*, London, Monday 9 November 1885.
90 Lewis Harcourt, Journals, 25 November 1885, op. cit.
91 Bexhill-on-Sea Street Directory, 1886. p. 92, *UK, City and County Directories*, www.ancestry.co.uk.
92 Robert Buchanan, *The Poetical Works of Robert Buchanan* (London: Chatto and Windus, 1884), p. 115.

Epilogue: Shocking Affair at Haywards Heath

1 *Sussex Evening Times*, Brighton, Friday 5 April 1895.
2 *Mid-Sussex Times*, Haywards Heath, Tuesday 9 April 1895.
3 Wyn K. Ford and A. C. Gabe, *The Metropolis of Mid Sussex: A History of Haywards Heath* (Haywards Heath: Clarke, 1981); Haywards Heath 1896, *Old Ordnance Survey Map*, Gateshead, Alan Godfrey Maps, n.d.; Judy Middleton, *Around Haywards Heath in Old Photographs* (Gloucester: Sutton, 1989); Wyn K. Ford and Lillian Rogers, *The Story of Haywards Heath* (East Sussex: S. B. Publications, 1998); Anon., *Souvenir Guide and History of Haywards Heath and District* (Haywards Heath, 1911).
4 *Mid-Sussex Times*, Haywards Heath, Tuesday 9 April 1895.
5 Census Report, Keymer, Sussex, 1891; England and Wales FreeBMD Death Index: 1837–1915, Matilda Field (Oct–Nov–Dec), 1893, www.ancestry.co.uk.
6 *Mid-Sussex Times*, Haywards Heath, Tuesday 9 April 1895.
7 Ibid.
8 Ibid.
9 Ibid.

10 Ibid.
11 'Register of Admissions: East Sussex County Lunatic Asylum', 27 June 1894, East Sussex Records Office (ESRO), HC 32/8.
12 *Journal of Mental Science*, London, January 1888.
13 Census Report, Brighton, 1891.
14 Interview conducted by author with Sister Eileen Austin, great-niece to Margaret Hayes, October 2009.
15 Census Report, Devonport, 1891.
16 Bexhill-on-Sea Street Directory, 1886, p. 92, *UK, City and County Directories*, www.ancestry.co.uk.
17 James Gardner, *Sweet Bells Jangled Out of Tune: A History of the Sussex Lunatic Asylum, Haywards Heath* (Brighton: James Gardner, 1999), pp. 4–11.
18 C. Lockhart Robertson, 'A Descriptive Notice of the Sussex Lunatic Asylum Haywards Heath', *Journal of Mental Science*, London, vol. IV, no. 6, April 1860.
19 Ibid.
20 Ibid.
21 Gardner, op. cit., pp. 98–9.
22 Ibid.
23 Sussex County Lunatic Asylum Case Books 1896–1897 (ESRO), HC 33/1.
24 Ibid.
25 Register of Removals, Discharges and Deaths, Pauper Cases, 28 November 1894 (ESRO) HC 32/15; *Mid-Sussex Times*, Haywards Heath, Tuesday 9 April 1895.
26 *Mid-Sussex Times*, Haywards Heath, Tuesday 9 April 1895.
27 Ibid.
28 Ibid.
29 Ibid.
30 Ibid.
31 Ibid.
32 Ibid.
33 Ibid.
34 Haywards Heath 1896, *Old Ordnance Survey Map*, Gateshead, Alan Godfrey Maps, n.d.
35 *Mid-Sussex Times*, Haywards Heath, Tuesday 9 April 1895.
36 Ibid.
37 Ibid.
38 Ibid.
39 Ibid.
40 Deborah Hayden, *Pox: Genius, Madness and the Mysteries of Syphilis* (New York: Basic Books, 2003), pp. 34–5 and 44.

41 Ibid., p. 58.
42 Register of Admissions, East Sussex County Lunatic Asylum, 27 June 1894 (ESRO), HC 32/8.
43 *Popular Science Monthly*, New York, vol. 31, no. 41, October 1878, pp. 707–8.
44 *Mid-Sussex Times*, Haywards Heath, Tuesday 9 April 1895.
45 Metropolitan Police Statements, 24–28 September 1885 (TNA: PRO copy), HO 144/154/A40202F.
46 Dr Henry Maudsley, *Body and Mind: an inquiry into their connection and mutual influence specially in reference to mental disorders* (New York: D. Appleton, 1890), p. 43.
47 Ibid., pp. 93–4.
48 Owen Davies, *Murder, magic and madness: the Victorian trials of Dove and Wizard* (Essex: Pearson Education, 2005), p. 84.
49 *Mid-Sussex Times*, Haywards Heath, Tuesday 9 April 1895.
50 Ibid.
51 Ibid.
52 Ibid.
53 Ibid. In March 2012 the author asked Professor Derrick J. Pounder, Head of Forensic Medicine at the University of Dundee, to consider the 1895 findings of Dr Newth. Professor Pounder found some of Newth's findings 'suspicious' reporting that: 'the "swollen tongue" suggests tongue protrusion, [Barbara's] face was congested and there was foam at the lips; all of this raises the possibility of a mechanical asphyxiation. [However] the brain was described as pale rather than congested which would not be expected in an asphyxial death . . . On the other hand, a sudden cardiac death is a real possibility. The state of medical knowledge at the time would not have recognised that coronary artery disease could cause such a sudden death. [Considering all the evidence] it would be fair to accept this as a sudden cardiac death, of a type well recognised and quite common in our society 100 years later'.
54 *East Sussex News*, Lewes, Friday 12 April 1895.
55 Ibid.
56 Ibid.
57 Ibid.
58 Quoted in Neil McKenna, *The Secret Life of Oscar Wilde* (London: Arrow Books, 2004), p. 340.
59 Jeremiah Minahan, Death Certificate 26 August 1897, General Register Office, DYC 284445.
60 Sussex County Lunatic Asylum Register of Burials, 26 August 1997

(ERSO), HC 11/2; Burnand, Sir Francis Cowley, *The Catholic Who's Who and Year Book* (London: Burnes and Oates, 1939).
61 Robertson, op. cit.

Afterword

1 *Pall Mall Gazette*, London, Friday 14 May 1886.
2 Melissa Hope Ditmore, *Encyclopedia of Prostitution and Sex Work*, vol. 1 (Santa Barbara: Greenwood Publishing, 2006), p. 323.
3 *The Times*, London, Monday 7 October 1912.
4 Louise A. Jackson, *Child Sexual Abuse in Victorian England* (London: Routledge, 2000), pp. 1–27.
5 J. W. R. Scott, *The Life and Death of a Newspaper* (London: Camelot Press, 1952), p. 82.
6 Celia Marshik, *British Modernism and Censorship* (Cambridge: Cambridge University Press, 2006), p. 68.
7 Roy Hattersley, *Blood and Fire: William and Catherine Booth and their Salvation Army* (London: Little, Brown, 1999), p. 324.
8 *Pall Mall Gazette*, London, Thursday 25 February 1886.
9 Thomas Catling, *My Life's Pilgrimage* (London: John Murray, 1911), p. 183.
10 Death Certificate, Adelene Tanner, 18 November 1890 (General Register Office) DYC 890416.
11 *Pall Mall Gazette*, London, Thursday 29 September 1887; *Reynolds's Newspaper*, London, Sunday 2 October 1887.
12 *Leeds Mercury*, Saturday 26 November 1887.
13 Last Will and Testament of Mary Frances Jeffries, 20 November 1891, London Probate Registry.
14 *War Cry*, London, Saturday 10 March 1928.

Acknowledgements

For permission to consult archives and reproduce key texts I would like to thank Stephen Spencer, assistant archivist at the Salvation Army International Heritage Centre, Laure Bukh at the Churchill Archives Centre, Churchill College, Cambridge and the staff of the Special Collections at the Bodleian Library. The letters and note by Sir William Harcourt, extract from the journals of the 1st Viscount Harcourt and further correspondence received by Sir William are reproduced with permission of the copyright's owner, and the Bodleian Library, Oxford. While every effort has been made to trace any other copyright holders, I am happy to correct any omissions in future editions.

I am also grateful to Mrs Jane Fawcett, for her insight, kindness and her time in answering my many questions about her ancestors, and also for her advice about the McKenny Hughes papers she donated to the Manuscripts Department of Cambridge University Library and to the Sedgwick Museum, Cambridge. Having visited both these archives I am also grateful for the assistance of Frank Bowles at the Cambridge University Library and Sandra Marsh at the Sedgwick Museum. Amidst Jeremiah Minahan's distant kin, I am indebted to the knowledge and genealogical detective work of Maresa McNamara in County Limerick, who spent an entire day helping me get to grips with the Minahan clans of Pubblebrien, before taking me on a whistle-stop tour of local Minahan landmarks. I would also like to thank Maresa's daughters, Caoimhe and Aoibhinn, for their interest in my research and particularly Caoimhe, who patiently accompanied Maresa and me as we travelled around the beautiful county. My Limerick tour was topped off by the many invaluable tales about the Minahan family and its character, recounted by Sean O'Casey and his wife Sheila who also provided a wonderful Irish farmhouse tea. Letters, photographs and memories of Jeremiah Minahan's relations in England were generously lent by James Austin and by Sister Eileen, of the Carmelite Monastery in Dolgellau, Snowdonia.

Needless to say, despite all these assistances, any remaining mistakes are my own.

More generally I am indebted to the staff of the National Archives, the British Library and the British Newspaper Library, the Metropolitan Police Historical Collection, Trinity College Archives, Dublin, the East Sussex Records Office, Birmingham City Archives, the Religious Society of Friends Archive, the Somerset Heritage Centre, the Limerick Local Studies library, Kensington Central Library and Durham University Library.

For their professional expertise, I am grateful to Professor Derrick Pounder, head of the Department of Forensic Medicine at the University of Dundee, who advised me on the inquest notes of Barbara Minahan. Thanks also to Keith Arrowsmith for his legal assistance and to Eleanor Rowley, for her translation skills and her friendship.

Inspector Minahan Makes a Stand began as part of an MA in Creative Non-fiction Writing at City University, and I would like to thank all the tutors and literary mentors on the course for their early input into my book, as well as their inspiring teaching and writing advice, particularly Julie Wheelwright, Sarah Bakewell, Neil McKenna, Carole Seymour-Jones and Kate Summerscale.

I am of course, hugely indebted to my agent, Andrew Gordon at David Higham. His counsel, support and sagacity have been constant since we first met two years ago. I would also like to thank Nicky Lund for her enthusiasm and feedback.

At Picador I was fortunate enough to fall in with a really exceptional team, particularly my lovely editor, Kate Harvey, my copy editor, Nicholas Blake, also Sophie Jonathan and Alison Menzies.

I would also like to thank those who supported my writing endeavours at their earliest and most fumbling beginnings: Sasha

Regan at the Union Theatre, James Brown, Kath Viner, Decca Aitkenhead, Polly Vernon, Nicola Jeal and Mike Herd. And finally, of course, thank you to Jes, to my friends and family for their positivity and support and most importantly, thanks to my two children, Orli and Arlo, for their boundless joy.

Index

Index